William S.B. Mathews

How to Understand Music

A concise course of musical culture by object lessons and essays. Fifth Edition, Vol.

1

William S.B. Mathews

How to Understand Music
A concise course of musical culture by object lessons and essays. Fifth Edition, Vol. 1

ISBN/EAN: 9783337084806

Printed in Europe, USA, Canada, Australia, Japan

Cover: Foto ©Thomas Meinert / pixelio.de

More available books at **www.hansebooks.com**

A

CONCISE COURSE OF MUSICAL CULTURE

BY OBJECT LESSONS AND ESSAYS.

BY

W. S. B. MATHEWS.

FIFTH EDITION.

———

VOL. I.

———

PHILADELPHIA:

THEODORE PRESSER CO.,

1712 Chestnut Street.

PRESS OF WM. F. FELL & CO.,
1220-24 SANSOM STREET,
PHILADELPHIA.

PREFACE.

As a text book, the present work covers a new ground. Its prime object is to lead the student to a consciousness of music as MUSIC, and not merely as playing, singing, or theory. It begins at the foundation of the matter; namely, with the observation of musical phraseology, *the art of hearing and following coherent musical discourse.* This occupies the first two parts, and covers a wide range of topics, as will be seen by reference to the table of contents, or the chapters themselves.

From that point the studies take a different turn, and lead to the perception of the inner something which gives music its life. That inner life of music is IMAGINATION and FEELING, and almost the entire remainder of the work is taken up with the study of music in relation to these, its Content. These studies, like those in the externals of music, begin simply, at the very line where form and content touch. In their progress they take in review the principal works of the classical and modern schools, as will be seen by reference to Parts III, V, VI, VII, and VIII. The object of all this study is two-fold; first, to develop in the pupil a consciousness of the inherent relation between music and feeling; and, second, to do this by means of master-works, which, of course, form the only complete and authoritative illustrations of this relation. In this way the musical perceptions are sharpened, the student is introduced to the best parts of musical literature, and thereby his taste and musical feeling are cultivated. It is easy to see, therefore, that this book occupies a ground not previously covered by a text book.

In *form,* the chapters are object-lessons. Such and such works, or parts of works, are supposed to be played or sung to the pupils, who observe in them such and such peculiarities. This form was selected because it is the true way of communicating this instruction, which can not be taken into the mind through the reason, but must be called up within the mind through a comparison of sense-impressions with each other, and these, again, with the feelings which they awaken. Music is one thing, and ideas about music another. It is the design of this study to *bring the pupils to music*; for doing this, the book marks out a

5

plan, and furnishes along with it such ideas about music as will aid the process.

The *Illustrations*, or pieces to be played, cover a wide range, especia'ly in the higher departments, and the objection has been made that they are too difficult. To this it can only be answered that the very essence and pith of music is here in consideration, and that the points in discussion could be adequately understood only by the help of these great works, wherein they are fully illustrated. It will be found possible, generally, to omit the most difficult works in cases where there is no one to play the parts of them here wanted. In other cases, where an entire lesson turns on difficult works, it is safe to conclude that if there is no one to play any part of them, there will be no one to understand them, and the lesson may be postponed.

In Part Fourth we have, in effect, an outline of *Æsthetics*. The Author believes that the time has come when Art-appreciation, and especially Music, has much to gain by such an orientation of itself with reference to cardinal principles. These four chapters, naturally, address themselves t th mature and serious. They are not written for children, nor even for youth. A work like this addresses many adults, experienced teachers, and friends of music, on whom a discussion of this kind will not be lost. Doubtless the execution is crude, and in a subsequent edition will be improved; it is hoped that the expectation of this may serve to draw a veil of charity over any present imperfection.

The *Historical* sketches are merely sketches, and are in part reprinted by permission of Messrs. Biglow and Main, from the New York *Musical Gazette*. They m y be made the basis of lectures or schoolroom talks, in connection with their Illustrations.

The *Dictionary*, at the close, affords a mass of readily accessible information, such as is in constant demand among students and teachers, but is not elsewhere to be found except in large Encyclopedias of many volumes. The preparation of it has involved much more labor and expense than was anticipated· but its value for ready reference is unmistakable.

CONTENTS.

7

CONTENTS.

PART SIXTH.

STUDIES IN THE ROMANTIC.

PART SEVENTH.

STUDIES IN SONG.

PART EIGHTH.

BIOGRAPHICAL AND MISCELLANEOUS SKETCHES.

PART FIRST.

LESSONS IN MUSICAL PHRASEOLOGY.

LESSON FIRST.

MOTIVES, PHRASES AND PERIODS.

It is the object of this lesson to lead the pupil to observe the division of the music into periods and phrases; and subsequently to develop a perception of the different modes of period structure here distinguished as thematic and lyric. As it is the sole design of this course of lessons *to facilitate intelligent hearing*, the pupils' powers of observation are to be appealed to from the start. He is to be clearly informed of what he is expected to hear; the proper selections are then to be played over as many times as necessary until he does observe. Each stage of the lesson is to begin with a definition, or explanation of the phenomenon or peculiarity of music it is desired to observe. Inasmuch as these earliest lessons represent only the beginnings of musical discrimination, the definitions in them will possess somewhat of the character of off-hand approximations to the truth, leaving exact statements to come later, when the pupils are better prepared to appreciate them. The definitions here given represent so much of the truth as the pupil at this stage is ready to receive. As thus:

1. A passage of melody that makes complete sense is called a *Period*.

Play the first three or four of the Schubert danses twice through, and more, if necessary. Instruct the class to say "Period" aloud at the close of every period. Do not let the playing stop for them to speak, but the feeling of repose may be intensified by slightly emphasizing the cadence, and perhaps retarding a little, if found necessary. As the period forms in these danses are clearly defined, it will be found easy to observe them.

Let this be followed by No. 2 of the list of illustrations, repeating it as often as necessary, the pupils signifying every period-close by the word " Period," as before.

No. 3, treated in the same manner, will conclude this stage of the lesson.

2. A passage of melody that makes sense, but not complete sense, is called a *Phrase*.

This topic is to be treated in the same way as the previous, the pupils announcing the completion of every phrase by the word " Phrase." Begin with No. 3, for in this the phrases are clearly defined. Follow this by the next illustration, which may need to be repeated several times. Then go back to No. 2 again, for its phrases. This may be followed, if convenient, by No. 5 of the illustrations, treated separately for periods and phrases. Then take up No. 6, going over this also for both periods and phrases.

3. A fragment of melody that is reiterated over and over, or transformed and developed into a period, is called a *Motive*. (A motive is a musical *text*.)

Begin by playing several times over the first six notes of No. 6, which form a melodic figure. Then play the various transformations of this figure which occur during the piece, omitting the accompaniment. Then play the entire first part of the Novellette (preceding the slow melody), and let the pupils observe how many times the melodic figure is repeated. It will be seen that this motive is the germ of the entire movement.

Then take up No. 7, where will be found a period composed from one motive—that contained in the first four notes.

Play again No. 3, and cause it to be observed that the melody there is not developed out of a single motive, nor predominantly out of any one motive. Thus we come to recognize two different forms of period-structure. In one of them the periods are developed mainly from a single motive; in the other there is a flowing melody.

4. Music developed out of a single motive, or a small number of motives, is called *Thematic*, or motivized.

Examples of this mode are found in Nos. 6, 7, 8, 9, and 10.

5 Music not developed motivewise, but having a flowing melody, is called *Lyric*.

Examples of this kind are Nos. 1, 2, 3, 4, and the slow melodies in Nos. 5, 6, and 9.

Several lyric and thematic examples should be played one after the other in irregular order, until the pupils readily distinguish between them.

MUSICAL ILLUSTRATIONS.

1. Schubert Danses (Peters' Ed.)
2. Schubert Menuetto in B min., op. 78 (Peters' Ed. "Schubert Pieces).
3. Adagio, from Beethoven's Sonata in F min., op. 2, No. 1 (16 measures.)
4. No. 1 of Mendelssohn's "Songs Without Words" (Peters' Ed. "Kullak").
5. Allegro from Beethoven's Sonata in E♭, op. 7.
6. Schumann Novellette in E, op. 21, No. 7.
7. Thirty-two measures of Finale of Beethoven's Sonata in D min., op. 31, No. 3
8. Bach, Two-Part Inventions, No. 1, in C (Peters' Ed.)
9. Schumann Novellette in B min., op. 99.
10. First movement of Sonata in F min., op. 2, No. 1, Beethoven.

LESSON SECOND.

THEMATIC AND LYRIC.   CLOSER OBSERVATION OF MOTIVES.

This lesson pursues the same line as the first, in order to bring the point out more clearly in the pupils' minds. Begin by a recapitulation of that lesson. Play again the Schumann Novellettes and Beethoven Adagio for periods and phrases.

Then play the Novellette in E clear through, in order to call attention to the lyric middle part. Play then the *Adagio* from Sonata Pathetique, of Beethoven, first for them to determine whether it is thematic or lyric; then for phrases and periods.

The second part of the lesson is to be devoted to a Bach Prelude; the one in B min. in the second book of the Well-tempered Clavier suits well for this purpose, especially as there is a copy to be had (Root & Sons Music Co., Chicago), in which the motives are numbered. The immediate purpose is to recognize the different motives. This prelude, e. g., contains seventeen or eighteen different motives. Probably the best way of securing sharp listening will be by first playing over a single motive several times, in order to fix it securely in the minds of the listeners. Then play the entire prelude, requiring each listener to observe how many times that motive occurs in the course of the piece. When the playing is done, ask each one in turn to state how many times the motive was repeated in the course of the work. It will be found that a majority of the class will have succeeded in recognizing the motive at most of its repetitions. It will then be well to play another motive, and then go through the work again, in order to see how many times that one occurs.

Take next, *e. g.*, the Bach Two-part Invention in F, No. 8, and play it first for "Thematic or Lyric?" Then define clearly the first motive, and go through the piece, the pupils meanwhile listening to discover how many times that motive occurs *in the right hand alone;* then go through it again, to see how many times the same motive occurs in the *left hand alone.* The object of this exercise is to lead the pupils to attend to the left-hand part, as well as the treble. If there is time, it will be well to play through the Schumann Novellette in B min., for the pupils to count the number of times the leading motive occurs in it.

Play again eight measures of the *Adagio* from Sonata Pathetique, in order to show that in lyric music there is generally a flowing melody and accompaniment, and that the leading melody is not to be found in the bass or intermediate parts, as in most of the examples of thematic music thus far introduced.

6. Lyric music is founded on the people's song. It is simple, natural music. Thematic music represents a more active musical life, and was primarily derived from the dance. Excitement finds expression mainly through thematic music; repose through lyric.

MUSICAL ILLUSTRATIONS OF SECOND LESSON.

1. The Schumann Novellettes in E (op. 21, No. 1) and B min. (op. 99).
2. Adagio from Beethoven's Sonata Pathetique.
3. Bach's Prelude in B min., No. 24 in Vol. II of "Clavier."
4. Bach's Two-part Invention, No. 8.

LESSON THIRD.

ON CADENCE.

7. A cadence is a formula of chords leading to a close. Thus, *e. g.*, in the key of C:

Ex. 1.

So in the key of E*b*:

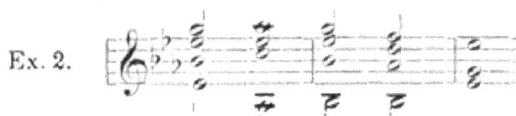

Ex. 2.

(Play also in several other keys.)

Besides this, which is called a *Complete* cadence, there are other cadences, the most common varieties of which are the Half Cadence and Plagal Cadence. The latter is the well known "Amen" cadence of church music. For example, play No. 1, above, and conclude with the following two chords, added:

Ex. 3.

This is also called the *Church* Cadence.

8. The complete cadence is used to mark the close of periods and important divisions in musical compositions.

Listen now to the *Adagio* from the first Beethoven Sonata, and when I play a cadence, say "cadence." At the end of the first phrase there is a "half-cadence." (Play it.) Those who are able may also point out the half-cadences.

Play also *Adagio* from Sonata Pathetique; also, Schubert Menuetto in B min., and, finally, the *Adagio* in E from Beethoven's Sonata in E min., op. 90.

If there is any difficulty in the pupils recognizing the cadences in these works, it will be well to introduce two or three pieces of church music, for further practice in recognizing cadences.

Point out, also, the cadences in the Bach Invention in F, No. 8, the Invention in C, No. 1, and the Fugue in G min., first volume of "Clavier."

Musical Illustrations of Third Lesson.

1. Adagios from Beethoven's Sonatas, No. 1 in F, op. 2, and op. 13 in C min.
2. Adagio from Beethoven Sonata in E, op. 90.
3. Schubert Menuetto in B, op. 78.
4. Bach's Inventions in F (No. 8), and C (No. 1).
5. Bach's Fugue in G min. (No. 16), from "Clavier," vol. 1.

LESSON FOURTH.

IMITATIVE AND FUGUE FORMS.

9. Imitation in music takes place when a second voice exactly repeats a melody or phrase already heard in another voice.

The term "voice" here means voice-part. Observe, *e. g.*, the Bach Invention presently to follow, and you will perceive that it has only two voices, a bass and soprano. It is in strict style, to the extent that each part or voice contains no chords. Each part might be sung by a single voice; and two singers, a bass and soprano, could sing the whole piece.

Listen now to the right hand alone, and point out the end of the first phrase. It is:

Ex. 4.

The first eight notes form the subject for imitation. Throughout the first period the treble leads, and the bass afterwards imitates. In the seventh measure the second period begins, and the left hand leads. (Plays.) Listen and see how many times the bass imitates the treble throughout this piece. (Seven times, viz.: in measures 1, 2, 15, 16, 17,

18, and 20.) Listen again and see how many times the treble imitates the bass. (Four times.)

Listen now to the Eighth Invention, and see how many times the treble imitates; also how many times the bass.

The subject of the Fourth Invention is this:

Ex. 5.

Listen as it is played through, and tell me how many times this subject is repeated. (Plays.)

10. A fugue is a composition in which one voice announces a subject or theme, which is taken up in turn by the other voices, each one entering after the previous has completed the subject.

In fugues the imitating voice does not enter upon the same degree as the antecedent, nor on the octave of it, as in most of the examples so far given; but replies in a different key, according to certain rules characteristic of this form of composition. The voices not performing the subject play complemental parts, called counter-subjects. As a first example, listen to the following fugue in G minor, from Bach's " Well-tempered Clavier." The subject is:

Ex. 6.

How many times is this melodic figure repeated in the course of the fugue? (Plays.)

Are fugues thematic or lyric?

Listen now to the Menuetto from Beethoven's Sonata in E♭, op. 31. Is it thematic or lyric? Observe the imitation at the beginning of the second period.

Hear also the Scherzo from Beethoven's Sonata in C, op. 2. Is this lyric or thematic? Is it imitative or not?

Hear also Schumann's Spring Song. Observe the imitation in measure 18, where the alto imitates the soprano motive in the seventeenth measure; also in measures 23 and 24, where the tenor imitates the soprano phrase of the previous two measures. (In playing, bring out these imitations by sufficient accentuation.)

MUSICAL ILLUSTRATIONS.

1. Bach's First, Fourth, and Eighth Inventions.
2. Bach's Fugue in G min., Clavier.
3. Menuetto from Beethoven Sonata in E♭. op. 31.
4. Scherzo from Beethoven's Sonata in C, op. 2, No. 3.
5. Schumann's Spring Song, from "Album for the Young." (No. 15).

———

LESSON FIFTH.

OF COUNTERPOINT AND THE CONTRAPUNTAL SPIRIT.

11. The term "counterpoint" means, in general, any new voice-part added to one already existing.

In a very rudimentary use of the term, it would be permissible to describe the bass of an ordinary people's song, like "Hold the Fort," as a counterpoint, though, to be sure, it is a very poor one. The idea of counterpoint carries with it not only the construction of an additional voice to one already existing, but of an *independent* and *individually distinct* voice, and not of a mere natural bass. Thus, e. g., observe the bass of "Hold the Fort." (Plays.) You perceive that the bass has properly no melody or movement of its own, but is all the time concerned with furnishing a proper foundation to the chords. Take now, on the other hand, Ewing's air, "Jerusalem the Golden." (Plays.) Observe the bass, how freely and independently it moves, and to what interesting harmonies it gives rise. How much more inspiring than the monotony of "Hold the Fort!" The bass of Ewing's "Jerusalem the Golden" is contrapuntally conceived.

Observe, again, this Gavotte of Bach's; it is in D (from a violin sonata). In this, properly speaking, we have little counterpoint.

Listen now to the following: It is Bach's Gavotte in D min. from one of his *suites*. Notice the bass, and you will find that it has a steady rhythmic motion of eighth notes. This bass has what is called "a contrapuntal motion," and of that variety called "two against one," that is, every melody note has two notes in the counterpoint.

Again, observe this Invention of Bach's, in E minor. In the first part there is no contrapuntal motion; but with the second period it begins. Observe. (Also referred to in the next lesson.)

Listen now to this church tune, "Dennis." Is it contrapuntal or not?

Listen to this Chorale. Is this contrapuntal or not? If contrapuntal, in which part does the counterpoint lie? (It may be proper to say that the counterpoint in this piece is of the kind called "note against note," with occasional "passing" notes; and that the principal counterpoint is the bass.)

Observe, again, the Bach Invention in E min., No. 7, in the Three-part Inventions. In the first thirteen measures there is not what is called a "contrapuntal motion." In the fourteenth measure such a "motion" begins in the bass, and from that point onwards for twenty-three measures there is a contrapuntal motion of sixteenth notes, interrupted only by the omission of a single sixteenth note at the beginning of its twelfth measure. The motive is transferred from one part to another; for four measures it runs in the bass, then for five measures it alternates between the soprano and alto; it is then transferred to the bass for four measures; the soprano retains it during the remaining ten measures. In listening to this, one should also observe that the leading motive of the piece is constantly transferred from one key to another, and one voice to another.

Counterpoint gives dignity to a music-piece. It does this because it displays *intelligence*, and that in such a way as to heighten the musical quality of the piece.

MUSICAL ILLUSTRATIONS.

1. Hold the Fort. (Any other popular song will do as well, e. g., Dr. Lowell Mason's "Work, for the Night is Coming.")
2. Ewing's "Jerusalem the Golden."
3. Gavotte in D, Bach. (Arranged by Dr. Wm. Mason.)
4. Gavotte in D min., Bach. (Pieces Favoris, Bach. Edition Peters.)
5. Bach's Three-part Invention in E min., No. 7. (Peters.)
6. Church Tune, "Dennis."
7. Chorale, "St. Paul," "Sleepers, Wake."

2

LESSON SIXTH.

VARIATIONS.

The lesson to-day begins with the following air from the Andante of Beethoven's Sonata in G, op. 14. This will be played twice in order to fix it in your memory. (Plays twenty measures.)

Observe now the following strain and see if it has any resemblance to the previous. (Plays the next ensuing twenty measures.)

In what respect is this like the air at beginning? Listen now to the harmony of the first eight measures. (Plays as before.)

Hear also this, the harmony of the first eight of the sixteen measures last played.

Ex. 7.

It will be seen that they are exactly the same, except that the melody is now in a middle voice.

Observe now the melody of the first eight measures. (Plays again eight meas. of air.) And the melody of the eight measures played afterwards. You perceive that the melody is the same, although in the latter case it is assigned to the tenor. The accompaniment, however, is considerably elaborated, and comes above the melody; the time also is cut up into half and quarter beats. We have here a *variation in the form* of the air. The melody and harmony are the same; merely the form of them is changed without imparting any essentially new meaning to the air. Observe now the second variation of the same air. (Plays.) In this you hear the melody in the soprano, but entering always on the half-beat. When it is played on the beat you at once recognize it. (Plays air in simple form.) This, also, as you see is merely a variation *in the form*. The harmony and melody are the same as before, and there is therefore no new meaning except such as is derived from or denoted by the increasing animation and complexity of rhythmic motion.

The next variation is a little more elusive in character. It begins:
Ex. 8.

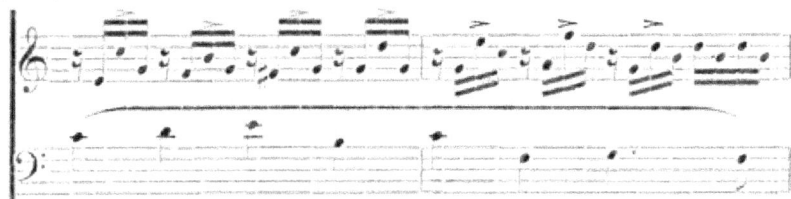

When played softly the melody is not distinctly perceived, but seems to be looking out at us through a veil. If the upper notes of the right hand part are played alone (as indicated by the accent marks,) it is at once perceived that we have here the melody in its original form. Here also the melody and harmony are unchanged, and here again, consequently, we have no essentially new meaning.

Consider now the following air from Beethoven's Sonata in A flat, op. 26. (Plays air.) Observe now the first variation. (Plays.) Here we have a more decided departure from the original. The harmony remains the same; enough of the melody remains unchanged to enable the listener to refer it to the air just heard as its source. Still it is in several respects a new air.

The second variation makes a still wider departure. (Plays.) Here you observe that the melody is cut up into repeating notes, and placed in the bass. In the third variation the key is changed to the minor of the same name, and the original harmonic figure is carried out in syncopation, producing a distortive effect, not unlike that of viewing your face in a bad mirror. In the fourth variation we have the air transformed into a *scherzo*, a playful movement, as different as possible from the repose of the original air. The fifth variation, again, brings back the original air, but much ornamented.

. In both these sets of variations is to be observed the same law of progression, namely, *from the simple towards greater variety and diversification.* The coda at the end of the last set was for the purpose of conducting the movement back again to a natural repose.

These variations in the last set (A flat, op. 26) are of a different kind from those first examined. In these not only is the form of the original air diversified, and in that way varied, but the variations are of such a nature that they have the effect of imparting or bringing out a new meaning in each variation. Beethoven was the great composer of this form of variation.

Let us examine another set of variations by Beethoven, his Eight

Variations on the theme "Une Fièbre brûlante," by Gretry, found in the volume of "Beethoven's Variations." Each one of these is to be compared with the theme until its construction is obvious, and its relation to the theme plainly understood. Another example of formal variations is to be found in the Andante and variations of Beethoven's Sonata Appassionata, op. 57. (Bülow's edition.) See also Mozart's variations in A, in one of his sonatas (No. 12, Peters' edition).

12. A variation of an air is an amplification of it, or unfolding, by means of auxiliary notes, rhythmic devices, changes of movement, etc., yet in such a way as to leave resemblance enough between the theme and variation to indicate their relation.

In order to do this and yet allow the varying to be carried to the full extent of the composer's genius, it is usual to arrange the series of variations progressively according to their elaboration, the simplest first.

13. Variations are of two kinds, *Formal* and *Character*. In the former the air or theme is elaborated without changing its original meaning or expression. Of this kind are the Beethoven variations in C and D♭ (Nos. 1 and 5, below). Character variations change the original *character* or expression of the melody, as was seen in the Beethoven variations in A♭.

LIST OF ILLUSTRATIONS.

1. Andante from Beethoven's Sonata in G, op. 14, No. 2.
2. Air and Variations in A♭. from Sonata, op. 26.
3. Variations on Gretry's " Une Fièbre brûlante," Beethoven.
4. Air and Variations in A, No. 12 of Peters' ed. of Mozart's Sonatas.
5. Andante and Variations from Beethoven's Sonata Appassionata.

LESSON SEVENTH.

RHYTHMIC PULSATION AND MEASURE

14. Rhythm means "measured flow."

Music is measured by a pulsation which goes entirely through the movement at the same rate of speed, like the human pulse. This fundamental rhythmic pulsation is commonly expressed by the accompaniment. Observe now the accompaniment of this little waltz. (Plays left-hand part of the first Schubert waltz.) Beat with your hands on the table before you, the same pulsation while I play.

Mark the pulsation in the example I now play. (Plays No. 2, in the list.)

In the same manner mark the pulsation in the example, I now play. (Plays a polka, No. 3, or any other convenient one; but not too fast. Be sure that it sounds here like four beats in the measure.)

These pulsations are grouped by means of accents into groups called *measures.*

There may be two, three, four, six, nine or twelve pulsations in a measure. Observe now the following, mark the pulsations and the accents, and tell me how many pulsations there are in a measure. (Plays No. 1, again. Be sure that every measure has a decided accent.)

Observe the following: (Plays No. 4.)

How many pulsations are there in a measure in this example? (Plays No. 5.)

Mark the pulsation in No. 6. (Plays.)

Observe now the measures in the same. (Plays again.) How many pulsations were there in a measure? (If not correctly answered, repeat the example and accent a little more.)

Observe the pulsation in this example. (Plays No. 7.) This admits of being understood in two ways: If played slowly it sounds like six pulsations in a measure. (Plays.) If played more rapidly and accented a little differently, it sounds like two triplets in the measure, and you naturally beat it as if there were two pulsations in a measure. (Plays.)

Observe the pulsation in this example. (Plays No. 8.)

Observe now the measures and tell me how many pulsations in a measure. (Plays again.)

Mark the pulsation in this example. (Plays No. 9).

How many pulsations in a measure? (Plays again if necessary.)

Observe the pulsation and the measures in this example. (Plays No. 10.)

Observe further that the same pulsation runs through an entire movement. (Plays No. 11, the class marking the pulsation by a motion of the hand for each pulse, paying no attention to the measures.)

NOTE:—There are two opinions in regard to the ultimate nature of measure, one holding it to be " a portion of time," the other "a group of pulses." The true conclusion would seem to be that measure in music is " portion of time " manifested by means of pulses and accents. Measure is the precise analogue of *foot* in poetry. Poetic quantity is also related to time. We ourselves, and every thing that we know by our senses or think of under sense-forms of thought, are related to time or space. Music is related to time, and so is meter. The time of music is in the rhythmic pulsation, measure, and rate of movement. And so measure in its ultimate nature is certainly *time;* but time is not measure until it becomes recognized as such through the rhythmic pulsation and accent; and therefore it is sufficiently correct for musical purposes to think of measure as pulse-grouping, as is here done.

LIST OF ILLUSTRATIONS.

1. The First of the Schubert Waltzes.
2. Schumann's Nachtstücke in F, op. 24, No. 4.
3. A Polka, *e.g.* Karl Merz's " Leonore Polka."
4. The Waltz from Weber's " Der Freyschütz." (Any other quick waltz will do as well.)
5. Schubert's Menuetto in B minor.
6. Two strains from the Schumann Nachtstücke in C, op. 24, No. 1.
7. " The Carnival of Venice."
8. Chopin Polonaise in A.
9. Sixteen measures of the Adagio in Sonata Pathetique.
10. Thirty-two measures of Rondo in same sonata.
11. Allegro from Sonata in F, op. 2, No. 1, Beethoven.

LESSON EIGHTH.

MEASURES AND RHYTHMIC MOTION.

*B*egin this lesson by recapitulating enough of the previous one to refresh the memories of the class concerning measures. Use, if convenient, other examples, only be sure to select at least two, each, in double, triple and common time.

15. A rhythmic pulsation may be called a *rhythmic motion*, and, when satisfactorily completed by an accent, is called a *Rhythm.*

(Plays here a scale in common time, like that in "table A," in Mason's Pianoforte Technics.)

The rhythmic motion may be twice as fast as the pulsation. Thus, *e.g.*, the *Adagio* in Beethoven's Sonata Pathetique is written in 2-4 time with a pulsation of sixteenth notes. The effect is as if you were to count four in a measure and each pulse had two notes. (Plays.) Counting four in a measure, the motion here is a half-pulse motion.

Example nine of the previous chapter had the same kind of motion. Observe the bass, and at the same time count the time aloud while I play. (Plays.)

Observe now the first nineteen measures of Beethoven's first sonata, example eleven of the previous chapter. Mark the pulsations and measures, and tell me whether it is a pulse-motion or a half-pulse motion. (Plays. This must be repeated until the pupils are conscious of the quarter-note motion which is unmistakable in the first nine measures, and strongly implied in the first nineteen.)

Observe again how the motion changes in the twentieth measure. (Plays again from the beginning through to the double bar.) From the twentieth to the forty-first measure there is what sort of a motion? ("Half-pulse." But play it until they observe it.) What kind of a motion begins at the forty-first measure? (Quarter-pulse. Plays it.)

Observe now example five, especially in regard to the change of motion. What sort of a motion has it at beginning? (Plays, "Pulse-motion.") Where the motion changes, raise your hands. (Plays again. "Half-pulse" motion begins in tenth measure of the second period.)

Observe the trio of the same. What sort of a motion has it?
(Plays.)

LIST OF ILLUSTRATIONS.

1. Scale of C or G in 4s (rhythm completed).
2. Adagio from Sonata Pathetique.
3. Rondo of same Sonata.
4. Allegro from first Sonata.
5. Menuetto from Beethoven's Sonata in F min. (op. 2, No. 1).

LESSON NINTH.

MEASURES, RHYTHMIC MOTION AND MOTIVIZATION.

In the examples of the previous lessons we have observed in
every piece a rhythmic pulsation carried through the piece at a uniform
rate; and in connection with this a full-pulse, half-pulse or other rhythmic motion, which changes several times in the course of a piece, being
generally quicker towards the last.

Thus, e. g. observe the first eight measures of Pauer's "Cascade."
What is the pulsation? What the motion? (Observe the half-pulse
motion in the bass.) (Plays.)

Observe now that the melody has a certain definite motivization
of its own. Its rhythm is

Ex. 9.

This rhythmic figure is repeated over and over. Observe now the
rapid motion that begins after the theme is completed. Here we have
an eighth-pulse motion in the fine work, a half-pulse motion in the
bass, and a full-pulse motion in the melody. (Plays.)

Observe the combination of measure-pulses, rhythmic motions and
motivization in the Bach Invention in E min. In the first thirteen
measures there is a half-pulse motion, except the fifth measure, which
has a quarter-pulse motion. (Plays, the pupils marking the measure-
pulses by motions of the hand.)

Along with this is the melodic subject which runs through the
piece. Its rhythm is

Ex. 10.

At the fourteenth measure a quarter-pulse motion begins in the
counterpoint and continues for twenty-three measures. (Plays.)

Again, take the Allegro of the sonata (No. 3, on the list of this chapter). This is in 6-8 time and has the effect of two pulses in a measure. Throughout the first twenty-four measures there is a triplet (or "third-pulse") motion transferred from bass to treble, and back again, but not interrupted. (Plays twenty-five measures.) From there to the thirty-ninth measure there is no uniform motion, but two different rhythms alternately appear. (Plays.) From the thirty-ninth to the fifty-ninth the triplet motion appears again. At this point the triplets disappear and we have a full-pulse motion for eight measures.

Observe, again, the rhythm of this polonaise. (Plays the Chopin Polonaise in A, No. 4, of the list.) Here we have a three-pulse measure, with half and quarter-pulse motion.

Ex. 11.

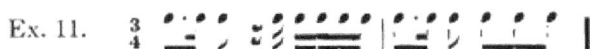

At the entrance of the second subject (in D maj.), the rhythm of the melody changes to this figure.

Ex. 12.

Rhythm is the primary element in a motive, and is in fact that to which it owes its name of motive, or mover.

A conspicuous example of rhythmic uniformity carried through almost an entire long movement is afforded by Beethoven's *Allegretto* in the Seventh Symphony, which moves in this figure.

Ex. 13.

It will also be useful to study the manner in which rhythmic characterization of subjects is managed in long movements generally; as *e. g.* in any of the binary and ternary forms analyzed in the second part of this work. (See Lessons Thirteenth and Fourteenth.)

LIST OF ILLUSTRATIONS.

1. Pauer's Cascade.
2. Bach's Invention in E min. (Three-part, No. 7.)
3. Allegro of Sonata in E flat op. 7, Beethoven.
4. Chopin's Polonaise in A.

PART SECOND.

LESSONS IN MUSICAL FORM.

LESSON TENTH.

THE ELEMENTARY FORMS. CLOSED FORMS. VAGUE. PERIOD-GROUPS.

16. A Form in music is a period, or group of periods belonging together; or possibly belonging together only to the extent of being connected with each other, and more or less contrasted with a following homogenous and well-closed period group.

By "well-closed" is meant "fully and decidedly closed." Thus for example, observe the following three waltzes of Schubert. (Plays the first three numbers in Schubert's Danses.) The first has for its leading motive this:

Ex. 14.

This motive occurs six times in the first two periods. The second has for leading motive this:

Ex. 15.

This occurs five times in two periods. Analyze the third in the same way.

Observe, again, that the first waltz begins and ends in the key of A flat. So also the second and third. The cadences are complete and satisfactory. This will be better observed by playing the accompaniment alone.

26

Observe, further, that the first two periods are intimately connected by reason of the predominance of the same leading motive in both. So also are the two periods of the second waltz. Two of these periods together, make "a form." The two periods in each form are homogenous, because in the same key and having the same ruling motive. Each form is a "closed form" because it concludes in its own principal key and is shut off from the following periods by the entrance of new motives and a new movement.

Again, listen to the first twenty measures of Beethoven's first sonata, in F min. op. 2. (Plays.) Mention the periods. There are two of them. The first ends in the dominant of the principal key, in the eighth measure. The second begins with the same leading motive, but immediately forsakes it, and builds with the second motive of the first period. The first period begins in F minor, and ends with the dominant of it. This is a half-cadence, and denotes incompleteness. The second begins in C minor, and finally ends in E flat, as the dominant of A flat, the key of the next-following period. The first period is the principal subject of this sonata, and is not a "closed form." The second period is modulatory or transitional, and is designed to lead across to the introduction of the second principal subject, which enters at the last beat of the twentieth measure.

Take, again, the Adagio of this same sonata. Observe the periods of the first sixteen measures. (Plays.) Here, again, we have two periods. They are homogenous, because the second period concludes with the principal motive of the first, and in the same key. Both periods begin and end in F major. They are sharply cut off from the next following periods, because these latter begin in a new key and with new motives. These first sixteen measures, therefore, form a homogenous period-group of two periods, which unite to make "a closed form." The next following fifteen measures also contain two periods. The first one has eleven measures. It begins in D minor. It ends in C major. It is followed by an abridged period of four measures, or perhaps better, an independent section of a transitional character. These two periods are not homogenous, their modulatory structure is vague, and therefore they do not unite to make a form.

Observe now the Menuetto of the same sonata. (Plays.) How many Periods have we? (Plays.) The first subject has this motive. (Plays motive of Menuetto.) When the form is complete and a new one enters, say "Form." (Plays.) Class listens and says "form" as the forty-first or forty-second measure is begun. The three periods in these forty-one measures should then be examined again in order to discover whether they unite to make a homogenous period-group, and a closed form. The *trio* may then be examined in the same way.

Examine in the same way the first sixteen measures of the *Adagio* of Sonata Pathetique. Then the next following twelve measures. Then the eight measures following this (the repetition of the theme.) And the fourteen measures following this. All these are period-groups, more or less homogenous.

Take next the first seventeen measures of the Finale of the same sonata. This also is a closed form.

It would be well to introduce also a *salon* piece, as, *e. g.*, Wollenhaupt's Whispering Winds, the pupils watching for new subjects, and pointing out the ends of the closed forms. Mason's Danse Rustique is another good example.

MUSICAL ILLUSTRATIONS.

1. The first three of Schubert's Danses   (Peters' Ed., No. 150.)
2. Part of first movement of Beethoven Sonata, op. 2, No. 1.
3. Part of the Adagio of the same.
4. Menuetto of the same.
5. Part of the Adagio of Sonata Pathetique.
6. Part of Finale of the same.
7. Salon Pieces, such as Wollenhaupt's " Whispering Winds," and Mason's " Danse Rustique."

LESSON ELEVENTH.

FURTHER EXAMINATION OF OPEN AND CLOSED FORMS.

In the previous lesson Closed Forms were the subject of our examination. In opposition to the term "closed," we might apply to imperfectly closed period-groups the term "open," although the expression "open form" is to a certain extent a solecism. If, now, we listen attentively to the period-group immediately following the double-bar in the principal movement of a sonata, we shall find it to consist of from two to four or five imperfectly closed periods, freely modulating. (Plays fifty-seven measures in E minor, *Allegro molto e con brio*, of first movement of Sonata Pathetique.) Now observe the first part of the same movement. (Plays.) We see that this contains two distinctly marked forms; and that the part following the double-bar is in reality a free-fantasy on certain leading motives out of the first part.

Again, observe the Impromptu in A flat, (op. 29,) of Chopin. (Plays.) Of how many closed forms does this consist? Analyze the first form into its periods. (Plays again, and again until successfully analyzed.)

Observe the Schumann Novellette in E, No. 7, op. 21. (Plays.) Of how many closed forms does this consist? (Plays again.)

Note.—It may be well to remark that this work consists of three forms, the melody in the middle (in A maj.) being the second, and standing between the other two.

Examine now the Bach Gavotte in D minor, No. 3 in Bach's "Pieces Favoris." (Plays.) Listen again and point out the periods. (Plays.) Does this consist of one form or more than one? (One, since the same motive prevails throughout the movement.)

Observe now the Gavotte in D, immediately following the previous. (Plays.)

This, as you perceive, is composed on the same motive as the previous, but in a major key, whereas that was in minor. This also constitutes a single " closed form."

Observe now the first Mendelssohn Song without Words. (Plays.) Define the periods as I play. (Plays again.) How many forms have we in this? (Ans. One form, of three periods.)

We have thus discovered that a long piece of music may consist of several shorter forms.

17. A piece consisting of a single form is said to be in " Unitary Form," whether of one, two, three, or four periods.

Generally a unitary form will contain not more than three periods, the first and last of which at least must be homogenous with each other.

Examples of unitary forms are numerous and owing to their brevity easily recognized.

Single church-tunes are one-period unitary forms.

Examine Schumann's "Traumerei; Also the " Entrance " and "Wayside Inn" of the Forest Scenes, op. 82, Nos. 1 and 4. Also Mendelssohn's " Hunting Song." Test them separately and repeatedly for (1) periods, (2) homogeneity of periods, and (3) for close of forms.

MUSICAL ILLUSTRATIONS.

1. Extract from Allegro of Sonata Pathetique.
2. Impromptu in A flat, op. 29, Chopin.
3. Schumann Novellette in E, No. 7, op. 21.
4. Gavotte in D min. from Bach's " Pieces Favoris." (Peters' Edit., No. 221.)
5. First Song without Words. Mendelssohn.
6. " Traumerei " Schumann.
7. " Hunting Song." Mendelssohn.

LESSON TWELFTH.*

IRREGULAR PERIOD-FORMS AND PERIOD GROUPS.

The natural length of the simple period is eight measures in slow or moderate time, and sixteen in quick time. But in good writing these lengths are constantly varied by shortening, extending, etc., to such a degree that period-lengths of forty or fifty measures are sometimes found.

The true way to distinguish periods from each other is by their *motives* and the relation of Antecedent and Consequent.

The simple period consists of two similar sections (or halves) standing in the relation of antecedent and consequent.

Each of these sections, again, consists in general of two phrases, making four phrases in the period. As a rule two of these phrases are entirely or very nearly alike, and the other two correspond or answer to each other, having a similar rhythm, but different harmony and melody.

Thus, (Beethoven),

Ex. 16.

In the same manner analyze the first eight measures of the *Adagio* in the Beethoven sonata in F, op. 2, No. 1. Also the first eight measures of the Adagio of Sonata Pathetique. This is the simplest form of period. The first eight measures of the Beethoven sonata in G, op. 14, No. 2, afford an example of a period in which the antecedent contains the same phrase twice repeated; and a consequent entirely different.

*This Lesson may be omitted at the dictation of the teacher.

The *Antecedent* in the period is the part that asks a question; it presents the subject in an incomplete form. The *Consequent* completes the form, answers the question, and so forms an equipoise to the antecedent. It does this by (1) completing the rhythm (*i. e.*, by filling up the natural number of eight or sixteen measures,) and (2) by returning to the tonic. Thus in the example above, No. 16, the first section leads to the dominant; the second returns to the tonic.

Sometimes the period does not return to the tonic, but leads off to some foreign key. In that case the period is incomplete, and is either of a transitional or a modulating character, or else is intended to be properly finished at some subsequent appearance of the same subject. An example of this kind is found in the first eight measures of Schumann's *Aufschwung*, where the antecedent is in F minor, and the consequent concludes in A flat.

Periods are extended to nine, ten or twelve measures, by prolonging the cadence, or by inserting matter just before the point where the cadence was expected.

A complex period is one in which the antecedent is repeated, usually in a higher pitch, thus intensifying the feeling of expectation and making the consequent more satisfactory when it does come. An example of this is found in Schubert's Sonata in C. Thus:

Ex. 17.

One of the most remarkable examples of this kind is a period in Chopin's Scherzo in B flat minor, op. 31, (beginning with the sixty-fourth measure) which extends to fifty-three measures, the antecedent being repeated four times: viz., in G flat, A flat, D flat, and in D flat in octaves. It may be proper to add, however, that many would regard this passage as in reality consisting of two periods, the first ending with the first consequent. It is a question of names merely, the last antecedent and consequent having precisely the same content as the first, additionally emphasized by means of the octaves.

A period-group is a succession of periods on the same motives (as in unitary forms) or on different motives, as in transitional periods and the "elaboration" of sonatas. (See Chap. VI.) These parts of composition may be easily studied by the student privately, using the Ditson reprint of the Bülow (Stuttgart) edition of the Beethoven Sonatas.

For our present purposes it is enough to be able to recognize the principal subjects in extended movements. Ability to follow the treatment of transitional passages and elaborations is a more mature accomplishment.

LESSON THIRTEENTH.

BINARY FORMS.

18. A Binary Form is a form composed of two unitary forms, which may or may not be connected by means of intervening passages or transitional periods. The two forms uniting to compose a binary form, stand in the relation of Principal and Second. The Principal stands at the beginning, and is repeated after the Second. Thus the Principal occurs twice; the Second once. This is for the sake of unity.

This is the form, e. g., of the Menuetto of the Beethoven Sonata in F min., op. 2, No. 1. (Plays until the class clearly perceive the construction.)

In the older forms of this kind we sometimes find the Second composed from the same motives as the Principal, but changed from minor to major, or vice versa. Bach's Gavotte in D minor is an example of this kind. (Plays as many times as necessary.)

Observe also the Menuetto by Schubert, in B minor, op. 78. (Plays, as before.)

In both these cases the Second comes in what is sometimes called a milder form than the Principal, and is of a softer and less pronounced character. In this form it is called a *trio*, probably because in the olden time these parts were performed by a smaller number of instru-' ments.

Observe also, the Chopin Polonaise, in A, op. 40. (Plays until the class perceive this form.)

In other cases, again, the Second is of a more animated character. Observe the Adagio from Beethoven's first sonata. (Plays.)

Sometimes the Second is not so distinctly a unit as the Principal. This is the case, *e. g.*, in the Largo of Beethoven's second sonata. (Sonata in A, op. 2, No. 2.) (Plays.)

Binary forms are frequently extended by a Coda composed of new material, put in after the repetition of the Principal in order to lead more satisfactorily to a close. Such an example we have already in the Largo last played. Observe again, the Scherzo from Beethoven's Sonata in C, op. 2. No. 3. (Plays, and repeats, until the class success-fully analyzes it.)

Very many popular pieces are in this form. For example, Wollen-haupt's "Whispering Winds." (Plays.) The first page is introduction. The next four constitute the first form, the Principal. The part in six flats is the Second. Then the Principal occurs again, but in an abridged form. This is followed by a new strain serving as Coda, or conclusion.

Observe also Chopin's little waltz in D flat, op. 64. (Plays.)

Also the Chopin Impromptu in A flat, op. 29. (Plays.)

The Chopin Scherzo in B flat min., op. 31, is another example of this form.

LIST OF ILLUSTRATIONS.

3

LESSON FOURTEENTH.

TERNARY FORMS.

19. Any musical form consisting of three distinct unitary forms, is called *Ternary*.

Observe, *e. g.*, the following: (Plays Adagio of Sonata Pathetique.) The first subject is this: (Plays eight measures.) The second is this: (Begins in seventeenth measure and plays seven measures.) The third subject is this: (Plays fourteen measures in A flat minor, beginning after the repetition of the Principal, which ends in the thirty-sixth measure.)

These subjects we will designate as Principal, Second and Third. Observe now when I play the movement through, and as I begin each subject, say "Principal," "Second" or "Third," as the case may be. (Plays.) Observe again the character of the different movements. The Principal is a pure lyric; the Second is much less reposeful; the Third, again, is lyric, but the triplet motion in the accompaniment evinces an excitement such as we do not find in the Principal. Observe again while the movement is played through from beginning to end, and see how many times each subject occurs. (Plays. The Principal occurs three times, the Second and Third once each.)

This movement is type of a rare class, namely, of a slow movement in ternary order.

Another example of ternary form is to be found in No. 2 of Schumann's Kreisleriana. This work consists of a Principal, the first thirty-seven measures. First Intermezzo, or "Second," twenty-six measures; Principal, thirty-seven measures. Second Intermezzo, or "Third," fifty-four measures; Transitional matter bringing back the Principal, and the conclusion of the whole, forty-seven measures.

20. The most common form of this order is the Rondo, or round, a form deriving its name from its returning to the same theme, circularwise, after every digression.

Observe, *e. g.*, the following. (Plays two periods, seventeen measures of the Beethoven Rondo in C, op. 51.) This is the Principal.

Then follows a transition of seven measures, leading to the key of G. (Plays.) Then the Second in G, ten measures. (Plays.)

This is followed by the "return," a series of passages leading back to the Principal. (Plays nine measures.) Then follows the Principal shortened to eight measures. (Plays.) Here enters the Third subject in C minor. It consists of three periods: First, eight measures; Second, seven, and Third, six. Twenty-one in all. (Plays.)

This is followed by a transition of three measures, the Principal in A flat, thirteen meas., and passage of three meas. leading back to the Principal in C, shortened to thirteen measures, followed by the conclusion, thirty-one measures. (Plays.)

Thus we see that the primary elements of this Rondo are three. The Principal, (Plays eight meas.,) the Second, (Plays ten meas.,) and the Third, (Plays eight meas.) Everything else in the Rondo is subordinate to these three leading ideas. These, again, are subjected to the Principal, which by its four recurrences impresses itself upon the attention as the principal idea of the work.

Observe again these three ideas. (Plays them again.) Now let us see if you know them when you hear them. (Plays the first three or four measures of each several times in various orders until the class easily recognize them.)

Observe now while I play the entire work through and designate the leading ideas as "Principal," "Second" and "Third" as they appear. (Plays, the class responding.)

Still further exercise in this form may be had by treating other pieces in the same way. In order to save space, the work is not given here entire, but only the analysis.

Thus, another example is the Rondo from Beethoven's sonata in C, op. 2, No. 3. Its plan is: Principal and transition twenty-nine measures; Second and transition thirty-eight; Principal and transition thirty-four; Third, in F, much elaborated, seventy-eight; Principal thirty-seven; Second and transition thirty-five; Conclusion sixty.

(NOTE.—In treating a work so large as this, it is better to begin by playing separately the three principal ideas, and afterwards going through the entire work in the same manner as the preceding.)

The Rondo in Beethoven's sonata in A flat, op. 26, is another example.

Still another is the Rondo in Beethoven's sonata in B flat, op. 22. This work consists of Principal, (two periods, 9 and 9) 18 measures; transition 4; Second 9; transition (two periods, 9 and 9) 18; Principal 18; transition 5; Third, (four periods, 6, 17, 6, 10), 39; Principal 18;

transition 6; Second abridged, and transition 29; Principal 18; Cod (12 and 5) 17.

In the Rondo of Sonata Pathetique the Principal occurs *four* times.

The Rondo is founded on the people's song, and in its essential spirit is easy and rather cheerful.

LIST OF ILLUSTRATIONS.

1. Adagio of Sonata Pathetique.
2. No. 2 of Schumann's Kreisleriana, op. 16.
3. Rondo in C, Beethoven, op. 51. (Peters' No. 207.)
4. Rondo from Sonata in C, Beethoven, op. 2, No. 2.
5. Rondo in A♭, op. 26, Beethoven.
6. Rondo in B♭, op. 22, Beethoven.

LESSON FIFTEENTH.

THE SONATA PIECE.

We begin in this lesson the examination of the most important form known to instrumental music;—so important, indeed, that many theorists designate it the " principal form," and say unqualifiedly that it is the type of all serious forms. This, as we shall see, is claiming too much for it, for there are in fact two primitive types, the people's song the type of the *lyric*, and the ancient binary form the type of the *thematic*.

The form we now take up is called the " Sonata-Piece," or simply the Sonata-form, because it is this form which gives name to the three or four separate forms combined in the sonata.

Observe now this piece. It consists of three large divisions. The first part contains several distinct ideas, as thus: (Plays the following motives:)

Ex. 18.

(Plays then the first page of Beethoven's Sonata in F. op. 2, as far as the double bar.)

Observe again this entire page. (Plays again.)

Now listen to the following while I play, and tell me if your hear any motives you have heard before. (Plays fifty-two measures beginning at the double bar.)

Let us familiarize ourselves with the original motives. (Plays the motives Nos. 1, 2 and 3 in different orders until the class is able to name each one as heard "one" "two" or "three.") Now listen to these fifty-two measures again, and when either of these original motives occurs, name it "one," "two" or "three," according to which it is. (Plays then the part again, and very clearly, the class naming each motive as it occurs.)

Observe now the continuation of this movement. (Plays the remainder of the movement, from the re-entrance of the theme.) Does this resemble either of the two parts previously played? (Play again until the class discover that it is precisely similar to the first part.)

21. Thus we find our sonata-piece to consist of three parts, the third of which is like the first, and the second is a fantasia on the leading motives of the first. The fantasia is called the "Elaboration."

The first subject is called *Principal;* the next the *Second* (or by the Germans the *Song-group* or "lyric period"); the third, the *Close.*

Again observe this. (Plays the first part of Beethoven's Sonata in C minor, op. 10 No. 1, as far as the double bar.)

Listen again and designate the Principal, Second and Close (This will prove a matter of some difficulty. The Principal ends in the thirty-first measure. The Second begins in measure fifty-six. The melodious passage beginning in measure thirty-two is really of a transitional nature. This will become plain by hearing several times the two passages; the transition, measure thirty-two to forty-eight, and the Second, fifty-six to eighty-six; it will then appear that the latter is a completely organized period, a consistent melody, whereas the former is merely a series of melodic and harmonic sequences. The part from forty-eight to fifty-five inclusive is a pedal-point. Measures seventy-six to ninety-four a continuation of the cadence of the Second. In measures eighty-six, etc., the motives of the Principal are recalled

The Elaboration should then be studied until its motives can be referred to their origin in the first part of the work. The Elaboration ends at the fifty-third measure after the double bar; at that place a pedal point begins, lasting until the re-entrance of the theme in the sixty-third measure.

The Sonata-piece is of so important a character, including, as it does, the genius of all seriously composed music, that it will be well to return to the subject several times, at considerable intervals. On these occasions new examples should be taken up, for which purpose the following analyses are appended. The early sonatas in the Stuttgart edition (Ditson's reprint) as far as op. 53, are analyzed in respect to their form, and will be found very convenient for studies of this character.

The first movement in Beethoven's sonata in G, op. 31, has this plan: Principal in G, thirty measures; Passage fifteen; Transition proper twenty; Second, in B maj. and B min. (twenty-three and ten) thirty-three; partial conclusion thirteen. The Elaboration begins at the double bar, and for twenty measures handles the second motive of the Principal. It then takes up the " passage " figure out of the first part and carries that through to the forty-eighth measure, where the harmony remains stationary on the dominant seventh of the principal key. This is continued as a sort of pedal-point to the seventy-ninth measure, where the Principal is resumed.

The first movement of Beethoven's Sonata Appassionata contains four important ideas. The analysis of the whole movement is as follows:

Principal, F min. (sixteen and eight), twenty-four measures; Transition eleven; Second, and passage, in Ab, fifteen; partial conclusion (ten and five) fifteen. The Elaboration contains six periods. The first from the Principal, little changed, in E min., thirteen measures; then, the same motive capriciously handled, passing through E min., C min., Ab to Db, fifteen measures; third, transition, as before, little changed, sixteen measures; fourth, leading idea of the Second, capriciously evading a cadence and passing through Db, Bb min., Gb, B min., G, F min., fourteen measures; fifth, passage work on diminished seventh of E, seven measures; sixth, pedal-point on C, dominant of F min., the principal key of the work, thus leading back to the Principal which then follows, five measures. The Recapitulation closes with the conclusion very much extended. For whereas in the first part the partial conclusion had only two periods, fifteen measures in all, the full conclusion has no less than nine periods, and seventy-four measures, as thus: I. Same as in partial conclusion, ten. II. Partial conclusion extended, eleven. III. Motives from Second, seven. IV. Cadence work,

nine. V. Passage, nine. VI. From transition in first part, four.
VII. From Second, nine. VIII. New matter, eight. IX. Pedal point
to close, seven measures.

The Sonata-piece is sometimes used for slow movements, in which
case the elaboration is less extended. An example of this is furnished
by the *Adagio* of the sprightly Sonata in B flat, op. 22 of Beethoven.
Its plan is this. FIRST DIVISION, not repeated: Principal, E flat, twelve
meas.; transition, six; Second, B flat, nine; partial conclusion, three.
ELABORATION: I, motive from principal, nine; II, seven. REPETITION:
Principal, E flat, eleven; transition, eight; Second nine; conclusion,
three.

Quite a number of the last movements in the Beethoven Sonatas
are designated *Finale*. These are generally not Rondos, but precisely
like the Sonata-piece, except that directly after the double bar there
follows a third melody, called a Middle-piece *(Mittelsatz)* which takes
the place of the Elaboration. An example of this is furnished by the
Finale of the first Sonata of Beethoven, F min., op. 2. These movements may be distinguished from Rondos even by inexperienced students, by means of the double bar, which does not occur in Rondos.

The Sonata-piece is derived from the "Ancient Binary Form,"
which is the form of the Bach gavottes, courantes, etc. It consists of
two parts, the first of which is repeated. In Courantes the first part is
generally about three periods long, on the same or very slightly different
motives. In the Sonata-piece these three periods have been expanded
into separate subjects. After the double bar the original motives were
worked up in the dominant of the principal key. This part has become the elaboration. A return to the subject in the principal key
completed the movement, as in the Sonata-piece.

ILLUSTRATIONS.

1. First movement of Sonata in F, op. 2. No. 1. Beethoven.
2. First movement of Sonata in C minor, op. 10, No. 1. Beethoven.
3. First movement Sonata in G, op. 31. No. 1. Beethoven.
4. First movement Sonata Appassionata, op. 57, Beethoven.
5. *Adagio* from Sonata in B flat, op. 22. Beethoven.

LESSON SIXTEENTH.

THE SONATA AS A WHOLE.

The name " Sonata," as we have already seen, properly belongs to a certain form, or single movement; but in process of time it has come to be applied to an entire work, consisting of three or four movements, only one of which is properly a sonata. In this larger sense all trios, quartetts and chamber music generally, as well as all symphonies are sonatas, having the same form as pianoforte sonatas, only somewhat longer.

The sonata as a whole consists of three or four movements, or forms, of which at least one is a sonata-piece. In general the sonata-piece is the first form. The second is an *Adagio* or other slow movement. The third either a Rondo or a Finale.

When the sonata has four movements, a Minuet, Allegretto, or Scherzo, intervenes between the slow movement and the Rondo. In a few cases this short movement precedes the slow movement. The general plan of the sonata, therefore, is this:

SONATA-PIECE; SLOW MOVEMENT; RONDO (OR FINALE).

Or this:

SONATA-PIECE; SLOW MOVEMENT; SCHERZO; FINALE.

Let us begin with an easy example. Observe the Beethoven Sonata in F, op. 2, No. 1. (Plays the entire sonata.) You recognize the separate movements, having already heard three of them in the previous lessons. What we wish to observe now is that the movements thus associated into a single work have no motives in common, are in different keys, and generally contrasted with each other; yet that they go together to make up a sort of story, a musical cycle, which seems more and more satisfactory as we become better acquainted with it. Listen again to the whole work. (Plays again.)

Sonata Pathetique is an example of a sonata in three movements, unless we count the *Grave* introduction for an independent form. In this work the contrasts are extremely strong, not only between the leading ideas of each movement but between the different movements.

The Introduction opens as follows: (Plays eight measures.) This very slow movement is followed by a very tumultuous one. (Plays the first period of *Allegro*.) And this, again, by a wonderfully deep and reposeful Adagio. (Plays eight measures.) After this comes the Rondo, a cheerful yet plaintive movement. (Plays first period.)

These different movements are not without certain bonds of union. These are, first, the *Sequence of Keys*. The Introduction and Allegro are in C minor; the Adagio in A flat, a nearly related key; and the Rondo, again, in C minor. Besides this there is a certain *Rhythmic Pulsation* common to all the movements. Thus a sixteenth-note in the *Grave* is nearly of the same length as the half-note in the Allegro, a sixteenth in the Adagio, and a half-note in the Rondo.

NOTE.—The contrasts in this sonata are intensified by the usual, and probably correct, tempos, which make the half-note of the Allegro considerably quicker than the sixteenth in the Introduction, recovering the movement again in the Adagio where the sixteenth corresponds to the sixteenth in the Introduction. The Rondo goes slightly faster, but not quite so fast as the Allegro, (the half-note of the Allegro being at the metronome rate of 144, and of the Rondo about 126.)

The principal point to observe in hearing a sonata is the progress of the emotion, the cycle of feeling. In the first movement we have generally the trouble, the conflict; in the second repose; and in the closing movement the return to the world again.

In the same manner should be examined Mozart's Sonata in F, (No. 6, Peters' edition,) Beethoven's Pastoral Sonata, op. 28, the Sonata in G, op. 31, that in C minor, op. 10, etc.

This exercise should be distributed over a considerable lapse of time; it occurs again in a later chapter. (Lesson XXIX.)

PART THIRD.

THE CONTENT OF MUSIC.

LESSON SEVENTEENTH.

CONTENT DEFINED.

We have here three small pieces of music, all well made, and in fact works of genius.

The first is the Bach Invention in F, (No. 8 of the two-part Invention) already known to us. The second is the first two strains of the *Andante* in Beethoven's Sonata in F minor, op. 57. The third, the Schubert Menuetto in B minor, op. 78. Observe them. (Plays.)

Let us consider the impression they leave upon our consciousness. The first has the spirit of a bright, rather talkative, but decidedly talented person, who is not wanting in a certain mild self-conceit. The second is full of repose and deep feeling. As we hear it over again a seriousness comes over us, as when one enters a forest in an autumn day. The third has a spice of the heroic in it, as well as a vein of tenderness; the latter especially in the second part (the trio).

2. Or take, again, two other pieces. The first is the Adagio of Sonata Pathetique; the second Chopin's Polonaise in A. (Plays.) The first has a deeply tender spirit, sad yet comforted. In the second we have the soul of a hero and patriot who hears his country's call.

3. Or take again two pieces by a single author, and for our first trial let them be by Bach. They are the Inventions in F, (No. 8, as before,) and the three-part Invention in E minor, No. 14. (Plays.) The first has the character already assigned to it. The second is full of repose and quiet meditation.

4. Or take, again, two pieces by Chopin. Let them be the Nocturne in E flat, op. 9, and the Polonaise in A, already heard. (Plays.)

42

In the nocturne we have a soft and tender musing, as when at twilight one sinks into a tender day-dream.

From these and multitudes of other examples that might be adduced it will be seen that there is in music something beyond a pleasant turning of words and phrases, something more than a symmetrical succession of well-contrasted periods. Every piece leaves a greater or less effect upon the feelings. It has its own spirit of grave or gay, heroic or tender. This inner something, this *soul of the music* we call Content.

22. The whole Content of a piece is the total impression it leaves upon the most congenial hearer. Or, as another has said, "The whole Content of a piece is all that the author put into it, technical knowledge and skill, imagination and feeling." *

The Content is to be found out by hearing the piece a sufficient number of times for its meaning to be ascertained. The Content is not some peculiarity of the piece that can be pointed out, but the final impression it leaves after repeated hearings. It is for that reason that the examples thus far referred to have been such as were already familiar through previous citation.

Pieces lacking Content are merely empty forms—bodies without souls. There are many such to be met with.

A piece may be of considerable length and elegantly written and yet contain but a small Content. Compare, *e. g.* these two pieces. The first is Fields' nocturne in B flat, one of his cleverest works. The second, Schumann's Romance in F sharp, op. 28. (Plays.) The first is an elegant piece of verse, but it says very little. The second is extremely earnest and heartfelt; yet even this is not of such deep meaning as, *e. g.*, the Largo of Beethoven's second sonata. (Plays.)

(These works should be repeated until the pupils or the greater part of them perceive the differences of which mention is made. It is a mistake to tell them beforehand the qualities they are to find. Let them learn to *feel them* for themselves.)

As music is a much more complete emotional expression than speech, it will be found impossible to fitly describe in words the general impression musical master-works make upon the feelings of congenial listeners. "*Congenial* listeners," is said, because when one lacks a musical soul, or is out of the mood for it, a piece makes no impression upon him.

The principal difference between the creations of genius and those of an inferior order is one of Content.   Any student who will study the best models, and follow the directions of competent teachers, may master the technical art of the musical composer, so as to satisfy a technical criticism in all respects.   But unless he happens also to have musical feeling of a high order, his works will be nearly or quite wanting in Content.   Even among the greatest composers there are some (Francis Joseph Haydn, e. g.,) whose works are masterly in form and taste, but as a rule elegant rather than deep.

In general every piece falls into one of two categories.   Either it is *stimulative* or *restful*.   All well-written thematic works belong to the former category; lyric movements to the latter.

The stimulative effect resides in the quick movement, and a vigorous harmonic and melodic movement.   The restful, in a quiet movement, generally slow or at least moderate, and a lyric structure.

LIST OF ILLUSTRATIONS.

1. Bach Invention in F. (No. 8.)
2. Andante from Beethoven's Sonata in F min., op. 57. (sixteen meas.)
3. Schubert Menuetto in B min.
4. Adagio of Sonata Pathetique. (sixteen meas.)
5. Chopin's Polonaise Militaire in A.
6. Bach's three-part Invention in E min. No. 14.
7. Chopin Nocturne in E flat, op. 9.
8. Field's Nocturne in B flat.
9. Schumann's Romance in F sharp.
10. Largo of Beethoven's Sonata in A, op. 2, No. 2.

LESSON EIGHTEENTH.

THE INTELLECTUAL AND EMOTIONAL.

Let us observe again two of the pieces out of the last lesson. They are the Bach Invention in F, No. 8, and the theme of the Andante in the Beethoven Sonata appassionata, op. 57. (Plays.)

Which of these seems to mean the most? Which one has the more feeling in it? (This point must be dwelt upon and the pieces played repeatedly until the pupils perceive that there is more feeling in the Andante.) Let us analyze' the phraseology of the Andante. Its interest is chiefly harmonic. Its peculiarly serious expression is due to the alternation of the tonic and subdominan* chords, thus:

Ex. 19.

The effect of gravity is also partly due to the low position of the chords in absolute pitch, especially of the seventh-chord which opens the second period. To the same impression the slow movement conduces. The passage presents nothing of outward sensuous melody for the ear to seize upon.

On the other hand, observe again the phraseology of the Bach Invention. (See Chap. IV, where it is analyzed.) It consists almost wholly of two motives which are repeated many times in different keys and in both voices. The first is the bold arpeggio figure, the first six notes of the treble. The last tone of this motive is also the first of the second figure, the descending run in sixteenths. These two motives together make a phrase and form the principal idea of the piece.

This phrase occurs entire ten times in the Invention; besides these the first motive occurs six times, and an inverted imitation of it (see measure 21, in the bass) several times more.

Thus it would hardly be too much to say that the entire Invention consists of nothing more than this single idea, and that the two speakers, or rather singers (the treble and bass) arrive at nothing new after all their prolonged discussion.

In the harmonic structure of this piece we find a decided plan. It begins in F major. At the seventh measure it goes into C major, and makes a cadence in this key in the eleventh measure, closing with the accent of the twelfth measure. Then ensues the middle part which begins in C, passes into G minor, D minor, B flat and so back to F. The climax occurs in the nineteenth or twenty-first measures.

The construction of so elaborate a piece from so few materials is an evidence of intellectual activity on the part of the composer.

2. Another example of a similar mode of construction is afforded by the Bach Invention in C, No. 1, analyzed in Chap. IV. This work also consists of a single phrase imitated, transformed, transposed, carried through C, G, D minor, A minor, F, and so back to C, and all this within a compass of twenty-two measures.

3. Yet another example of this mode of construction is afforded by the Bach Fugue in C minor. (Clavier, No. 2, Plays.)

In all these a leading subject is taken as a text, not to come back to and repeat entire as in the Rondo and other binary and ternary forms, but to *work with*, to transpose and transform, to elaborate by means of harmonic treatment until an entire movement is built up out of it. This is the type of musical composition as it existed in Bach's time. Some pieces are more emotional than others, but all of them are built up on this plan. They contain *Musical Thought.* These transformations of motive are equivalent to reasoning in language. To appreciate them properly one needs to follow the idea through all its modifications and modulations.

The opposite of this mode of structure, as we have long ago seen, is the lyric, the natural type of the emotional. Observe now, for the sake of the contrast, the first sixteen measures of the Beethoven Adagio from the Sonata in F, op. 2, No. 1. (Plays.)

In general the following may be advanced as a sound doctrine regarding the Intellectual in Music.

All thematic music is of an intellectual character. In order to fully appreciate it, the hearer needs to firmly seize the leading motive, so as to be able to follow it through its various transformations. Such a following out and participating in the author's musical thought, implies an unconscious comparison of the motive with its various transformations. All thematic music is characterized by more varied modulations and a more artificially contrived, or at least a freer, harmonic structure than is found in lyric. Here, again, in this elaborate harmonic setting, we have the trace of mastership on the part of the composer; a token of his musical *thinking*, as distinguished from merely meditating.

Yet this kind of music is not unemotional. On the contrary, it is sometimes intensely exciting. When this is the case the effect is due to a fitly chosen harmonic progression by means of which a climax is attained, and the intensification of the effect through the reiteration of the leading motives.

The leading motive is repeated many times in all music, for in this way only can unity be attained in a music-piece. There is this difference, however, between the repetitions in thematic and lyric pieces, viz., that in lyric pieces the motive is repeated unchanged, but in thematic pieces with manifold changes.

Thematic music is at first unattractive to hearers in general, because they do not know how to hear it properly. When they hear the same piece many times they become reconciled to it, and in the end enjoy it and even prefer it to lyric pieces they at first thought more beautiful.

One of the most decided examples of the intellectual in music is afforded by counterpoint. (See Lesson V.) The simplest theme treated contrapuntally acquires a dignity which was before wanting. In double counterpoint the intellectual is even more strongly marked.

The strictest type of musical composition is the Fugue. In this a single subject forms the substance of it. This subject can not be transformed with absolute freedom, but each imitation must take place on a particular degree of the scale. Thus, e. g., if the antecedent is in the tonic, the imitation or answer ("consequent.") must be on the dominant, and *vice versa*. When a modulation takes place and the subject appears in a foreign key, the imitation takes place in the dominant of that.

Besides these restrictions there is also the "counter-subject" which every voice must take up immediately after finishing the subject. Thus the counter-subject forms almost an invariable accompaniment to the subject throughout the Fugue. In spite of these limitations Bach was able to use this form with such freedom as to leave us a very great number of Fugues which are not only masterly in their construction but emotional and thoroughly free and musical, and among the most cherished treasures of the musician's repertory.

NOTE.—Students desiring to study Fugue analytically can do so in Mr. James Higgs' "Fugue" (in Novello's "Music Primers," price one dollar.) Those able to read German will find a very interesting treatment of the subject in the third vol. of J. C. Lobe's *Kompositionslehre*, in which he bases his theories on Bach's remarkable work "*Die Kunst der Fuge*" (Peters' Ed.) a series of twenty-four Fugues on a single subject.

The subject of this lesson may be continued through another one, in which case the "list of additional illustrations" will be found useful.

LIST OF ILLUSTRATIONS.

1. Bach's Invention in F.
2. Andante from Beethoven's op. 57. (sixteen meas.)
3. Bach's Invention in C, No. 1.
4. Allegro from Beethoven's Sonata in F, op. 2 No. 1.

ADDITIONAL ILLUSTRATIONS, NOT ANALYZED ABOVE.

1. Bach's Fugue in C minor, Clavier, No. 2.
2. Schubert Impromptu in C minor, op. 90, No. 1.
3. Bach's Fugue in G minor, Clavier, No. 16.
4. Schubert Impromptu in E flat, op. 90, No. 2.
5. Lefebre-Wely's "Titania."
6. First movement of piano solo in Chopin's Concerto in E minor, op. 11.
7. Handel Chaconne and variations in G. No. 3 of Köhler's Handel's "Lessons, Pieces, and Fugues." (Peters' Ed. No. 40.)
8. Handel's Capriccio in G minor, No. 2 of "Seven Pieces" in same volume.

LESSON NINETEENTH.

PASSAGES, CADENZAS AND EFFECTS.

Sequence is the general name given to the immediate repetition of a phrase or motive whether in unchanged or modified form.

In thematically composed periods the motive is followed by several repetitions of it in a somewhat changed form. The Sequence thus formed proceeds no farther than compatible with a graceful return to the key in which the period is intended to conclude. A Sequence not thus returning and completing itself into a period, becomes either an independent section, or a *passage*, which is the general name given to such parts of a music-piece as do not fall into periods. The following, *e. g.*, is a very simple passage.

Ex. 20.

Here is one slightly more complex.

Ex. 21.

Observe the following two passages from Cramer's First study. (Plays as far as the middle of the eighth measure.) Observe also the passage descending from the second beat of the tenth measure to the first note of the thirteenth. (Plays.) Also the ascending and descending passages following. (Plays the whole study.) Explain the construction of these passages. Thus, e. g., the right hand ascends in the thirteenth measure and three measures after by sequencing on the figure at a Ex. 22.

Later it descends by sequencing on figure b, Ex. 22.

Ex. 22.

Such passages as these differ from regularly constructed phrases in this, that being composed of a merely artificial sequencing on a single motive, whatever sensible or definite may come of it must be owing to the harmonic treatment and progressions.

Passages in musical composition serve the purpose of gracefully connecting one part of a work with another, and of relieving the attention from the strain of the thoughtful or deeply expressive periods between which they intervene. In this use we find them in Bach, Handel, Haydn, Mozart, Beethoven, and in fact all good composers. In modern writers, however, they have been very much developed and have been made the vehicle for the display of bravoura effect, especially on the pianoforte. The effectiveness of a passage is in proportion to its apparent difficulty, which impression, again, is derived either from the visible labor of the player, or from the inability of the hearer to understand the construction of it. Any such Sequence as those in Exs. 20 and 21 is easily comprehended by even an inexperienced ear. But we find in various modern works passages not susceptible of ready analysis by the ear, especially when played rapidly. Thus, e. g., observe this cadenza from Liszt's Rigoletto. (Plays Chromatic Cadenza on p. 4 of that piece.) When played rapidly it produces an immense effect. It is derived from the chromatic scale. Let us build it. Suppose we take a descending chromatic scale of one octave.

Ex. 23.

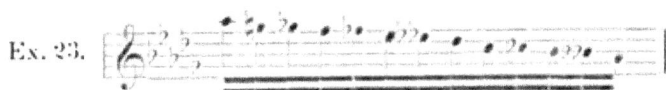

Instead of descending simply, in this way, let us go down by

4

sequences of a motive ascending one degree, played with both hands.

Ex. 24.   etc.

Now let the little finger play a chromatic scale a sixth above the treble and a sixth below the alto. Then the right hand will play this:

Ex. 25.   etc.

And the left hand this:

Ex. 26.   etc.

And both hands this:

Ex. 27.   etc.

In Chopin's works we find a great variety of passages consisting generally of a combination of sequences of diminished sevenths resolved chromatically. Of such a kind are, e. g., the following from the Concerto in E minor. Here (p. 165 of the Augener edition of Klindworth's Chopin) are two ascending sequences of diminished chords, differently treated (second and third lines).*

On p. 168 of the same edition we have a different passage constructed on the same general plan. (See in general, the chain of passages following the soft melody in C, middle part of the first movement of the Chopin Concerto.)

Reference may also be made if convenient to the Cadenza in the Rivé-King edition of Liszt's Second Rhapsody.

*Reference is here made to the sequences immediately preceding the close of the solo part in E major, first movement of Concerto in E minor.

LIST OF ILLUSTRATIONS.

1. Cramer's First Study.
2. Cadenza from Liszt's "Rigoletto."
3. Passages from Chopin Concerto in E minor.

LESSON TWENTIETH.

THE SENSUOUS AND THE IDEALIZED.

In dance music all its good harmony and melody, and graceful treatment generally, are made subservient to the sense of physical motion. Thus, e. g., observe the following. (Plays a part of Strauss' "Blue Danube Waltzes.") This music unquestionably is genuine and valid, but it appeals mainly to the dancing instinct. As played by the the orchestra it is much more voluptuous than it appears on the pianoforte.

Observe now another waltz. (Plays Karl Merz's "Pearl of the Sea.") In this we have the dance-instinct also addressed, but not in so enticing and voluptuous forms as in the Strauss music. This belongs to the class of "drawing-room waltzes," and partakes of the naïveté of the People's Song.

Again, take a still less pronounced type. (Plays the Chopin Waltz in E flat, op. 18.) Here we have also a waltz; the same rhythm and the same form. Yet in this piece the sensuous element has retired. It is not now an actual flesh-and-blood dance to which the composer invites us, but to a poetically conceived meditation upon a waltz. Here the fancy runs wild. This we see in the extremely rapid tempo, which is more than three times as rapid as a waltz could be danced.

The Strauss "Blue Danube" reminds us of the whirling ballroom, the thickly perfumed air, the blazing lights, and all the sensuous intoxication that goes with it. The Merz waltz is still a dance, a flesh-and-blood dance, but no longer so exciting. It is a nice, hearty family dance under the trees in open sky. The Chopin waltz leaves the physical scene entirely. This is the idealized dance.

Observe again the following. (Plays the waltz from Gounod's "Faust.") And then this. (Plays the Chopin Waltz in A flat, op. 42.)

Here again we have the same contrast. One of the pieces invites us to a real waltz; the other to an idealized revery. Which is the material? And which the poetic?

If convenient it will be well to show here how the physical " Faust " waltz is itself idealized, although in a sensational direction, in Liszt's arrangement of Gounod's " Faust." Here we have the dreamy melody in the middle of the waltz dwelt upon and idealized, and the slow movement interposed, recalling the first meeting of Faust and Marguerita.

The same distinction between dance music proper, and parlor music in dance forms, prevails throughout all the movements originally designed to control the physical motions, such as the March, Waltz, Polka, Mazurka, Minuet, etc. It will be felt by the observant that those pieces which most strongly suggest and invite to physical motions (as the Strauss waltzes, for example) stop there, and do not possess a poetic Content.

LIST OF ILLUSTRATIONS.

1. Strauss' Blue Danube Waltz. (Any other *superior* dancing waltz will do.)
2. Karl Merz's " Pearl of the Sea."
3. Chopin Waltz in E flat, op. 18.
4. Waltz from Gounod's " Faust." (Sydney Smith, perhaps.)
5. Chopin Waltz in A flat, op. 42.
6. Liszt's Gounod's " Faust."

LESSON TWENTY-FIRST.

DESCRIPTIVE, SUGGESTIVE AND POETIC MUSIC.

Quite in line with the previous lesson, we have here to do with music in which certain external events or objects are referred to by means of music.

Observe the following. (Plays Henry Weber's " The Storm," but without naming it.) Ask the question: " Do any of the class know this piece?" If none of them know it, ask them to tell what it means. It will prove a very amusing experiment, the accounts will be so different. If any of the class already know it, ask them to remain quiet, and allow the others to give their explanation of it. When this has been done, read aloud the author's prefatory note as follows:

"The Storm. An Imitation of Nature(!) The following is the idea conveyed by this composition. A shepherd is going home with his flock—while he is playing an air on his flute a storm approaches. The thunder, the roaring of the water, the crash of trees and the fire-bells are to be heard in succession." (Plays again.) As an "imitation of nature" this pretty little piece is scarcely successful. For although the flute and the muffled thunder are tolerably suggested, the crash of trees and roaring of the waters do not appear. The fire-bells also would scarcely be heard in a pastoral neighborhood. However, this is a point relating to the poetic conception, with which we have really nothing to do. Our question is, Do these musical figures really represent or remind us of the natural objects to which the author refers them? To this question we must return a decided negative. Even with all the resources of the modern orchestra in the hands of such a master as Wagner, a storm is very imperfectly represented.

Again, observe this. (Plays Mr. G. D. Wilson's "Shepherd Boy.") This pretty little piece has no imitation of nature as such. A name is given it which serves as a starting point. But the music gives us neither the rocks, the grass, the sheep, the sheep-bells, the boy, his crook, or the bright sky over head, but only the peaceful and monotonous spirit of such a scene. This is an Idyll and not a description.

For a still more fortunate example observe this. (Plays Schumann's "The Hobby Horse" No. 8, out of the Album for the Young, without naming it. When the piece is concluded, ask the class their impression of it, as to what it means or represents.) In such a piece as this it is not possible to infer the meaning of the author from simply hearing the piece. But when the clue is afforded, the suitability of the music becomes apparent.

Observe also "The Jolly Farmer" No. 10 in the Album for the Young. (Plays.) This piece might be called by any other name that would be sufficient to account for its simplicity, heartiness and satisfaction. Schumann's title is on the whole the easiest hypothesis by which to account for it.

Plays also "Santa Claus" No. 12 in the Album, the Spring song No. 15, the little Romance No. 19, and the Sailor's song No. 37.

It will also be advantageous to study in this connection, as time serves, Schumann's "Scenes from Childhood" op. 15. These thirteen little pieces are extremely varied and clever, and belong rather to *poetic* music, than to descriptive music proper.

The difference here implied is this:— In descriptive music it is attempted to represent the external traits of objects by means of music, in such a way that a person hearing the music will recall the object, which is practically impossible. In poetic music it is attempted *to represent the spirit* of such and such natural objects or experiences. The title serves to connect the two. Whoever hears the music without knowing the title, hears only some very animated and widely different pieces of music, interesting and fresh considered simply as music. When he knows the title he has in that a clue to the composer's intention or desire of representing something beyond the actual content of the music as such. Such pieces, therefore, form useful study for pupils not yet thoroughly musical.

Of the same class but in a lower grade are the fanciful titles so common in parlor pieces, such as "Warblings at Eve," "Monastery Bells," "Maiden's Prayer," etc., in all of which the title was an afterthought, put on to sell the piece, frequently, indeed, assigned by some other than the composer, and often with very little reference to the actual Content of the music.

Observe again this. (Plays the "Battle of Prague," without announcing title.) This, again, is an independent and fairly well made piece of music, a Sonata, indeed. That the low tones represent cannon no one would know except he knew the intention.

If convenient it will prove very interesting in this connection to observe a four-hand performance of Wagner's "Ride of the Valkyrie," one of the most singular compositions before the public.

There are also at least two of the Beethoven Sonatas which are of especial interest in this connection. They are "The Pastorale" op. 28, and "The Adieux, the Absence and the Return," op. 84.

LIST OF ILLUSTRATIONS.

1. "The Storm" by Henry Weber.
2. "The Shepherd Boy," G. D. Wilson.
3. "The Hobby Horse," etc. from Schumann's "Album for the Young," op. 68.
4. "The Battle of Prague," by Kotzwara.
5. "Scenes from Childhood" op. 15. Schumann.
6. "Sonata Pastorale," op. 28. Beethoven.
7. "The Adieux, the Absence, and the Return." Sonata op. 81. Beethoven.

PART FOURTH.

STUDIES IN ART AND THE BEAUTIFUL.

CHAPTER TWENTY-SECOND.

SECTION FIRST. THE IDEAL AND ITS PHASES.

Every thing that *is*, stone, plant, tree, landscape, building, animal and man himself, presents itself to the mind in two aspects. First as an actual appearance, an established and ordered existence, proceeding according to its own laws and expressing its own nature. Man at first accepts it in unquestioning simplicity. Presently, however, this unquestioning acceptance of whatever *is* because it *is*, gives place to a spirit of inquiry which seeks to know *why* it is. The answer to this gives the second aspect of things; namely, that every thing that is is the representation or embodiment of some particular *idea*, which existed before the appearance of it, either in the present individual or any of its predecessors.

Thus if we attentively consider a piece of crystalline rock, as of granite, we find it first a merely natural appearance, an inanimate substance, a piece of matter. But when we meditate upon it more deeply, we perceive that its particles are organized into crystals, determinate forms, in the construction of which the particles of matter have followed certain laws. Thus, beyond all we can learn of the piece of granite by mere inspection, there lies back of this its *law*, the ruling principle of its *type;* the *idea*, of which granite is the expression. So every piece of inorganic nature manifests laws, ideas, which are back of the natural appearance.

In an organized existence, as, *e. g.*, a plant, we recognize the *idea* much more clearly. For, whereas in the crystal the impelling force acted in the original formation once for all, in the plant we have before us a continual creation. With its leaves open to the sunshine

and showers, and its rootlets groping in the soil for moisture and
other elements of its being, it gathers to itself from the world about it
whatever is most necessary for its growth, and shapes and fashions it
according to the organic law of its species.   Here, then, we come upon
certain rudimental appearances of self-determination; or, as we might
otherwise say, upon a higher step in the representation of idea.

How much stronger is the expression of idea in a tree!   Take
the oak.   The acorn is a little fruit, scarcely larger than the end
of your finger.   Planted, it yields but a tender shoot.   But when a
hundred suns of summer have shone upon it, and a century's winds and
storms beat upon it, how sturdy and grand it stands!   There is in the
oak an *idea*, the law of its being; and sunshine, rain, storm and passing years, but afford it opportunity to bring this idea to expression—to
work out its own *ideal*.

Again, consider the animal, more highly organized, gifted with
self-movement, and with a certain amount of mind and intelligence;
nay, even with the more precious qualities of friendship and affection.
Yet each kind is true to its type.   Individuals differ, but there is behind all these variations the idea of the species, the type of the kind,
the *ideal*, from which no one varies in any radical degree.

Thus we come to the still higher expression of idea in man, whose
glory is his mind; his complex and wonderful intellectual and emotional
nature, the image of God.   This it is which investigates the outer
world, arranges her phenomena into orderly sequence of cause and
effect, and classifies her appearances according to their essential
character.   It is the mind of man which multiplies the wants and
capacities of life, as well as the means of gratifying them.   Still more
the mind shows itself in literature, and here in such true sense as to
make all these other achievements seem of no meaning and significance
as if they were indeed only the very "small dust of the balance."   Thus
we have in the lower department of mental effort, what we might call the
"matter-of-fact" part of literature, the newspapers and magazines through
which man learns of the doings and ideas of his fellow men throughout
the world, and the histories in which he learns of the rise and fall of
nations, and reads the lessons of the past.   How wonderful is the evidence these give of far-reaching human thought and sympathy!
But above this great practical department of literature which relates
itself to material success, we find Poetry, and Imaginative Composition
of every kind, in which the human spirit soars into higher regions of
fancy and feeling.   Here the soul is represented as unhampered by
accidents of fortune, or as triumphing over them in the exuberant

force of its own individuality. Nay! the spirit searches into the eternal principles of good and evil, and sets them in order before us. This progress goes yet further in Art. Temple, Statue, Picture, Symphony and Psalm, all unite in giving evidence of a spiritual activity in man which rises above the routine of everyday life and its necessities, into the clear and more enduring radiance of the ideal.

Thus, whether we consider the progress of creation, from the rudimental forms of the earliest geological periods to the highly organized beings which occupy the earth at the present time; or if we study one natural appearance after another and see how plainly each bears witness to the existence of a higher law, an eternal idea which determines its appearance, and then again combine these into an ascending system of excellence:—in either case we have to do with ideas and the Ideal; and so with everlasting truth, the inner nature of things, the soul, and immortal interests; for the ideal is the abiding, the eternal. As Schopenhauer says:

" For thousands of years a chemical force slumbered in matter until the touch of re-agents set it free; then it appeared, but *time* is only for the appearance not for the force itself. For thousands of years galvanism slept in copper and zinc, and they both lay resting over against silver, which as soon as all three are combined under proper conditions must burst out in flames. Even in a dry seed-corn for three thousand years the slumbering force lay hidden which in the final appearance of suitable circumstances bursts out as plant. But, as before, *time* is not for the idea itself, but only for its appearance."

Again, let us observe further that in no single individual is its own ideal fully realized. Even in the lowest types, as crystals, it is rare to find fully formed specimens, but rather they mostly appear with a corner broken here, a line or proportion distorted there, and so on. On the higher plane of plant-life the difficulty of discovering a perfect specimen is much greater. In one the branches are not symmetrical; in another the stem is distorted; even a single perfect leaf is rarely seen. A perfectly formed animal is equally rare. Whether belonging to the lowest grades of animal life or the highest, or at any intermediate place in the scale, in almost every individual we find some imperfection or other; a hard winter, a season of famine, an untimely and unsuccessful struggle for supremacy;—some one or all of these have interfered with the development of the animal, and have left their mark of imperfection upon him. In man is this much more the case. A form perfect in all its proportions we never see. It is even difficult to discover perfectly proportioned single members. In his mental disposition, likewise, the

same imperfect results are observed.   For wherever we search we discover no complete man; but on the contrary unbalanced faculties, contradictory impulses, imperfectly developed reasoning powers, undisciplined affections, and in short a general want of harmony and coherence in the manifold capacities of the soul.

Nevertheless, in all these innumerable degrees of manifestation,
the Ideal itself remains steadfast and eternal.   For although we may
not be able to discover a single individual but lacks some element of
perfection or grace, yet we have at least our idea of the *average* excellence of many individuals of the same class, and in this an imperfect
ideal.   Beyond and above this, again, is the much higher ideal arrived
at by collecting all the most eminent perfections ever known in individuals of a given class, and combining these together into the conception of a more perfect crystal, plant, animal, or character than any one
has even seen realized.

In like manner, there is no delicacy or splendor of color, nor any
sweetness and harmony of tone, no pleasant savor or odor, no symmetry
or grace of form, nor any magnificence of mental endowment or genius
of any kind, but that beyond it one immediately imagines something
more satisfactory and complete.   Thus in all these, the sensuous and
the purely spiritual as well, we have our human ideals which we form
by collecting and combining separate perfections.   These remain
steadfast, or become constantly more complete in spite of the counter-
acting influence of the discovery of imperfections in individuals.
Beyond these, again, exists the true ideal, perfectly known only to
God, but in some feeble degree imaginable to the specially gifted or
inspired; and these are the naturalists, statemen, prophets, seers,
artists and poets of the world, who all find their true distinction in
their successful divination and communication of the ideal.

Under the term *Ideal*, therefore, we properly include
every thing that is eternal and true.   Any object in nature
or art is ideal according as it manifests in outward form
the inner nature of the Ideal.

There are three great phases of the ideal which include within
themselves all possible grades of goodness and excellence; and imply
as opposites all grades of imperfection and wrong.   These all inclusive
phases are the TRUE, the BEAUTIFUL, and the GOOD.

Under the name True we include not only all truthfulness of
statement and teaching, whether relating to material objects, to history,

or to speculation, but also all genuineness and consistency, or the quality of agreement between the *appearance* and the *real nature* in any material thing or person.

The conception we call Goodness relates to the moral nature, and involves in it the idea of the exercise of benevolence and love as the habitual motive of action. This form of the ideal is that habitually appealed to in religion. In its lower applications it involves the idea of fitness, suitability, adaptation to a proposed end.

The ideal we call the Beautiful involves in it predominantly the quality of *perfection of appearance*, and is expressed in forms addressed to sense-perception, or to the inner senses. Truth is primarily addressed to the intellect; Goodness to the moral nature; Beauty to the senses.

All these, the True, the Beautiful and the Good, unite in the One Ideal, GOD.

All qualities of the ideal whether in material things, animals, or personal character, are but reflections, imperfect appearances, or intimations of the Divine.

SECTION SECOND. THE DESIGN AND SCOPE OF ART.

Art has for its object the expression of the Ideal in sense-form; or, which means the same thing, the expression of the Beautiful.

" The sole principle of Art is cognition of the ideal; its sole design the communication of this knowledge. While *Science*, tracing the restless and inconstant stream of manifold principles and sequences, in each point reached finds always something further, and never a last limit, nor yet ever can find complete satisfaction (just as little as one by running can reach the point where clouds touch the horizon); *Art*, on the other hand, is already at the limit. She arrests the object of her contemplation out of the stream of the world-course, and holds it isolated. And this Single, which in the stream was but a little vanishing part, becomes for her a *representative of the whole*, an Equivalent of the endless Many in space and time. She remains fast, therefore, by this separate. She stops the wheel of time; relations vanish for her; only the *essential*, the Idea, is the object.

" We can, therefore, straightway designate Art as *the examination of things in their eternal nature and meaning*, in contrast to the examination of things in their temporal aspects, which is the way of sense-perception and knowledge. This latter mode is an endless, like a horizontal line; the former is a perpendicular cutting the horizontal line at a chosen point. The usual mode of examining things is the reasonable one, which in practical life, as in science, is alone valid and profitable. The other is in Art the only valid and profitable. The scientific is the mode of Aristotle; the artistic, in the main, that of Plato. The first is like the furious storm, which hurries along without begining or limit, bends, moves, and carries every thing along with it; the second like the quiet sunbeam which cuts its way through the storm entirely unmoved by it. The first like the innumerable, tempestuously-moving drops of the water-fall, which, constantly changing, suffer no glance to linger upon them; the second like the rainbow resting in stillness upon this tumultuous crowd."*

The Powers of Art are thus broadly defined by Hegel: "It is the task and scope of art to bring to our perception and spiritual realization all that in our thought has a place in the human spirit. That well-known sentence, *Nihil humani a me alienum puto*, Art shall realize in us."

Its design is, therefore : To awaken and to animate the slumbering feelings, desires and passions of all kinds; to fill the heart and to permit to be conscious in man everything developed and undeveloped which human feeling can carry, experience, and bring forth, in its innermost and most secret parts; whatever the human heart in its manifold possibilities and moods desires to move and excite; and especially whatever the spirit has in its thought and in the Idea of the most Essential and High; the glory of the Honored, Eternal, and True.

"It may also express unhappiness and misery, in order thus to make wickedness and criminality conceivable, and to permit the human heart to share every thing horrible and dreadful, as well as all joy and happiness. Then fancy may at last indulge herself in vain sport of the imagination, and run riot in the ensnaring magic of sensuously entrancing contemplation."

That is to say : It is within the power of Art to portray the entire content of the human spirit; its evil no less than its good. Nevertheless the proper mission of Art, as the expression of Beauty, forbids

*Schopenhauer.

the representation of the evil except in so far as it can be used for contrast in order thereby to reveal a deeper beauty. Any use of evil in art other than in this subjection to good, makes false art.

SECTION THIRD. CONDITIONS OF ART AND OF ITS ENJOYMENT.

The effectiveness of Art rests primarily upon the fact that our knowledge of the outer world comes in through sensation and sense-perception, and thus first reaches the feelings and will. Therefore, whether it is the external reality itself which occupies the attention, or only the appearance of it (as in pictures, drawings, or representations) " by means of which a scene, or relation, or life-moment of any kind is brought to us, — it remains for our soul the same, in order to depress or rejoice us according to the nature of such an idea, to stir and excite and to thrill us with the feelings and passions of anger, hatred, and sympathy; of anxiety, fear, love, esteem, and wonder; of Honor and of Glory.

" This waking up of all sensations in us, the education of our feelings through each life-picture; to set in operation all these inner movements through a merely deceptive external presence—it is which is especially seen as the peculiar, unexcelled power of art.

" Nevertheless, Art in this manner, impresses good and bad upon the feelings and ideas; and the design should be to strengthen it to the noblest, so as to nerve it up to the most thoughtful and useful inspirations." (Hegel.)

In all art-work we have to do with two elements, " first a content, design, meaning; then the expression, representation and realization of this content; and both sides so brought together that the *outer* and material is presented only as the representation of the *inner*, and not otherwise; as that which the *covering* has received and expressed out of the *content*."*

The Fine Arts are Architecture, Sculpture, Painting, Music, and Poetry (including all imaginative composition). Each one of these

*Hegel.

seeks to express the beautiful in its own way, according to the nature and capacity of the material through which it works.

In order to thoroughly appreciate and justly estimate any master-work of art, therefore, we need to consider its conception or intention, and the technical merits of its execution. Hence, the intention of the previous parts of the present work has been to lead to an intelligent observation of the more external qualities of music as a form of art. This having been measurably accomplished, we here enter upon a consideration of the content or meaning of music, in doing which we find it most convenient and helpful to inquire also concerning the scope and meaning of all the arts, as well as the leading characteristics of the beautiful itself which they all have for their ideal.

All forms of the Beautiful as we saw in the beginning, are to be enjoyed through *contemplation* rather than *thought*. A beautiful sunset, a grand mountain view, a great moment in history, lose their charm of beauty or grandeur when we reason about them and occupy ourselves with an inquiry into the scientific principles underlying them. The drops of water in the rainbow are but ordinary examples of the substance chemically known as H_2O. It is only our own accidental position with regard to them and the sun, which enables us to perceive in them the beautiful token of God's remembrance. We look, and behold! it is there! We approach to analyze it, and lo! it is gone.

All art and all perception and enjoyment of the beautiful, come through childlike faith and openness of spirit.

And whenever for the sake of study and knowledge we analyze an art-work in order to surprise the secret of its construction, we need to re create it again, according to the simple directness of its meaning as art, in order to recover its charm and inspiration.

CHAPTER TWENTY-THIRD.

OF THE NATURE AND MEANING OF THE BEAUTIFUL.

Under the term "Beautiful" are included an innumerable manifold of meanings, so great and in their higher reaches so glorious, that language fails in power to express them, and even the mind is lost amid the bewildering splendor. For in this term we reckon together all that is pleasing in sensation, contentful and satisfactory in contemplation, or kindling and inspiring in spiritual perception. It embraces within itself every graceful and lovely existence in created things, all that artists have represented, poets dreamed, or seer and revelator made known, and every possibility of splendor, glory, and excellence, which the longest ages of eternity shall make real to the blessed.

Since, then, the Beautiful itself is not yet fully revealed, it is no wonder that a complete and satisfactory discussion of the subject has never been made, for such an achievement is in its nature impossible.

Nevertheless, every act of æsthetic judgment involves within it the determination of "beautiful" or "un-beautiful," and hence the soundness of our subsequent progress in the present studies requires of us here such preliminary consideration of this wonderful ideal as we may be able to attain to. Of all writers on this subject Ruskin is the most eloquent and suggestive, though perhaps not the most complete in scientific form. The liberty is taken, therefore, of availing ourselves of his words, to piece out the more systematic, rational, and practical classification we find ready to our hand in Lotze's work on "Æsthetics in Germany" ("*Aesthetik in Deutschland*" by Hermann Lotze, Munich, 1868).

"By the term beauty," says Ruskin,* "properly are signified two things. First, that external quality of bodies, which, whether it occurs in a stone, flower, beast, or in man, is absolutely identical, which, as I have already asserted, may be shown to be in some sort typical of the Divine attributes, and which, therefore, I shall, for distinction's sake, call typical beauty; and, secondly, the appearance of felicitous fulfilment of function in living things, more especially of the joyful and right exercise of perfect life in man. And this kind of beauty I shall call vital beauty.

*"Modern Painters," Vol. II., p. 27.

"Any application of the word beautiful to other appearances or qualities than these, is either false or metaphorical, as, for instance to the splendor of a discovery, the fitness of a proportion, the coherence of a chain of reasoning, or the power of bestowing pleasure which objects receive from association, a power confessedly great, and interfering, as we shall presently find, in a most embarrassing way with the attractiveness of real beauty."

All modes or degrees of the Beautiful may be counted in three categories. These are: (1.) The Pleasing in Sensation. (2.) The Satisfactory in Contemplation, and (3.) Beauty of Reflection.

SECTION FIRST.   THE PLEASING IN SENSATION.

All the faculties of sense-perception and sensation are susceptible of pleasurable exercise, but none of them awaken in us sensations of a distinctly elevated character save only the two ideal senses of sight and hearing.

These are the two avenues along which most of the ideas come which relate us to the kingdom of spirtual existence. In the pleasurable exercise of these senses there is not only the vision of intelligence and the voice of wisdom, but a manifold and entirely pure and proper pleasure of sensation as such.

This we have in the purity, contrasts, harmonies, and sequences of color, such as form a material foundation for our enjoyment of beauty or gorgeousness in nature or art.

So, also, in tone, we have the various grades of consonance, and especially the contrasts and agreeable combinations and gradations of tone-color as in orchestral works, and in human voices. Of this kind, also, is the pleasure derivable from chromatically modulating chords, such as we find in the works of Spohr and Gounod, and very often in Italian opera; where no idea is suggested or intended, but only the sweet, the pretty, the well-sounding.

All these are unmistakably pleasurable, and at the same time allied to the perception of the beautiful. They all have implications which suggest higher qualities of the beautiful, as one may see below in Ruskin's words on **Purity**.

"PURITY, *the Type of the Divine Energy.* — The only idea which I think can be legitimately connected with purity of matter, is this of vital and energetic connection among its particles, and that the idea of foulness is essentially connected with dissolution and death. Thus the purity of the rock, contrasted with the foulness of dust or mould, is expressed by the epithet 'living,' very singularly given in the rock, in almost all languages; singularly I say, because life is almost the last attribute one would ascribe to stone, but for this visible energy and connection of its particles; and so of water as opposed to stagnancy. And I do not think that, however pure a powder or dust may be, the idea of beauty is ever connected with it, for it is not the mere purity, but the *active* condition of the substance which is desired, so that as soon as it shoot into crystals, or gathers into efflorescence, a sensation of active or real purity is received which was not felt in the calcined *caput mortuum*.

"And again in color. I imagine that the quality of it which we term purity is dependent on the full energizing of the rays that compose it, whereof if in compound hues any are overpowered and killed by the rest, so as to be of no value nor operation, foulness is the consequence; while so long as all act together, whether side by side, or from pigments seen one through the other, so that all the coloring matter employed comes into play in the harmony desired, and none be quenched nor killed, purity results. And so in all cases I suppose that pureness is made to us desirable, because expressive of the constant presence and energizing of the Deity in matter, through which all things live and move, and have their being, and that foulness is painful as the accompaniment of disorder and decay, and always indicative of the withdrawal of Divine support. And the practical analogies of life, the invariable connection of outward foulness with mental sloth and degradation as well as with bodily lethargy and disease, together with the contrary indications of freshness and purity belonging to every healthy and active organic frame, (singularly seen in the effort of the young leaves when first their inward energy prevails over the earth, pierces its corruption, and shakes its dust away from their own white purity of life,) all these circumstances strengthen the instinct by associations countless and irresistible.

"And then, finally, with the idea of purity comes that of spirituality, for the essential characteristic of matter is its inertia, whence, by adding to it purity or energy, we may in some measure spiritualize even matter itself. Thus in the descriptions of the Apocalypse it is its purity that fits it for its place in heaven; the river of the water of life that proceeds out of the throne of the Lamb, is clear as crystal, and the pavement of the city is pure gold, like unto clear glass."

SECTION SECOND. THE SATISFACTORY IN CONTEMPLATION.

But above pleasures of mere sense-perception as such, mere ebb and flow of sensation, we must reckon the quiet pleasures one has in merely contemplating a beautiful object. One of the most obvious examples of this is the satisfaction universally experienced in looking at a beautiful face. Such is the gratification one involuntarily feels in its symmetry, its pleasantness and justice of proportion, that for a long time one overlooks whatever of emptiness or shallowness of spiritual expression it may betray. Nay, with some observers this pleasure is so strong that it suffices to overcome the strongest and best grounded elements of dissatisfaction one may have in the personal character of the owner of the face.

The foundation of this satisfaction lies in Symmetry (" the type of the Divine justice ") of which Ruskin speaks thus:

" We shall not be long detained by the consideration of this constituent of beauty, as its nature is universally felt and understood. In all perfectly beautiful objects, there is found the opposition of one part to another and a reciprocal balance obtained; in animals the balance being commonly between opposite sides, (note the disagreeableness occasioned by the exception in flat fish, having the eyes on one side of the head,) but in vegetables the opposition is less distinct, as in the boughs on opposite sides of trees, and the leaves and sprays on each side of the boughs, and in dead matter less perfect still, often amounting only to a certain tendency towards a balance, as in the opposite sides of valleys and alternate windings of streams. In things in which perfect symmetry is, from their nature, impossible or improbable, a balance must be at least in some measure expressed before they can be beheld with pleasure. Hence the necessity of what artists require as opposing lines or masses in composition, the propriety of which, as well as their value, depends chiefly on their inartificial and natural invention. Absolute equality is not required, still less absolute similarity.

"A mass of subdued color may be balanced by a point of a powerful one, and a long and latent line overpowered by a short and conspicuous one. The only error against which it is necessary to guard the reader with respect to symmetry, is the confounding it with proportion, though it seems strange that the two terms could ever have been used as synonymous. Symmetry is the *opposition* of *equal* quantities to each other. Proportion the *connection* of *unequal* quantities with each other. The property of a tree in sending out equal boughs on opposite sides is symmetrical. Its sending out shorter and smaller towards the top, proportional. In the human face its balance of opposite sides is symmetry, its division upwards, proportion.

" Whether the agreeableness of symmetry be in any way referable to its expression of the Aristotilian *Ισότης*, that is to say of abstract justice, I leave the reader to determine; I only assert respecting it, that it is necessary to the dignity of every form, and that by the removal of it we shall render the other elements of beauty comparatively ineffectual; though on the other hand, it is so to be observed that it is rather a mode of arrangement of qualities than a quality itself; and hence symmetry has little power over the mind, unless all the other constituents of beauty be found together with it."

All degrees of the satisfactory in contemplation depend chiefly upon the qualities which naturally appertain to and cluster around symmetry. They are Regularity, Moderation according to law, Harmony, and Proportion, all of which are the qualities we discover first in the beautiful things of nature.

All of these, again, show themselves equally in *space-relations*, and in *time-relations*. Those of space, or of visible forms, are already referred to in the extract from Ruskin, above.

The element of *time* properly includes every thing in music; not only its measure and rhythm, but even its harmony and melodic organization, since tone itself finds its power in regularly determined vibrations, which although physically taking place in space, enter the soul only in the forms of time. In this respect they ally themselves to a deeper department of the soul; for Schopenhauer very cleverly points out that space-relations as such are not received into abstract thought, but transformed into those of *time*, as all the equations and computations of planetary spaces are carried on in mathematical formulæ In other words, space itself is nothing more than *time made visible.* Time and Eternity are the symbols of immortality.

Now in the element of time we have in music innumerable relations and cunningly intermingled gradations of harmony, proportion, order, symmetry, and the like, as we have already seen in our studies in phraseology and form; and as we shall see yet more plainly in our studies in classical music particularly.

Moreover, these elements of beauty imply also *unity*, else there would be no *Single* in which the beauty inheres. And so it follows by implication that in *order*, *proportion*, and *harmony*, we have the " unity in variety " so often quoted and so little understood. But this element of Unity has a yet higher reach, therefore its particular discussion is reserved for the next section.

In all these together we have Formal Beauty, the outward conditions of beauty; or purely physical beauty, the *form* in which the higher spiritual beauty may inhere. And formal beauty, again, implies as its check or safe-guard yet another quality, of which Ruskin shall tell us.

MODERATION:

The Type of the Divine Government by Law.

" I have put this attribute of beauty last, because I consider it the girdle and safeguard of all the rest, and in this respect the most essential of all, for it is possible that a certain degree of beauty may be attained even in the absence of one of its other constituents, as sometimes in some measure without symmetry or without unity. But the least appearance of violence or extravagance, of the want of moderation and restraint, is, I think, destructive of all beauty whatsoever in every thing, color, form, motion, language, or thought, giving rise to that which in color we call glaring, in form inelegant, in motion ungraceful, in language coarse, in thought undisciplined, in all unchastened; which qualities are in every thing most painful, because the signs of disobedient and irregular operation.

" And therefore as that virtue in which men last, and with most difficulty attain unto, and which many attain not at all, and yet that which is essential to the conduct and almost to the being of all other virtues, since neither imagination, nor invention, nor industry, nor sensibility, nor energy, nor any other good having, is of full avail without this of self-command, whereby works truly masculine and mighty are produced, and by the signs of which they are separated from that lower host of things brilliant, magnificent and redundant, and further yet from that of the loose, the lawless, the exaggerated, the insolent, and the profane, I would have the necessity of it foremost among all our inculcating, and the name of it largest among all our inscribing, in so far that, over the doors of every school of Art, I would have this one word, relieved out in deep letters of pure gold — *Moderation.*"

SECTION THIRD.   THE BEAUTIFUL IN SPIRITUAL PERCEPTION.

We now reach the degree where the beautiful fully becomes what in the original conception it was defined to be, namely, the expression of the ideal in sense-forms (or in outward appearance). When we contemplate a gorgeous sunset, we experience much more than a merely contentful satisfaction in splendid masses of crimson and gold lying above the western horizon. It is not the magnificent and incredible purity of the colors, nor the pleasing evanescence of the silently changing cloud-masses, nor yet any sensuous gratification in the brilliant lights reflected from the mountains in the east, or the passing sails on the ocean, but rather an inspiration and kindling of spirit such as all sensitive and highly organized natures well know, and which all recognize as among the most spiritual moments of their lives. Or when one looks off from a mountain top, how grand and exhilarating the experience. So, again, as one listens to a great symphony, how it thrills and overpowers with its exquisite expression. In all these experiences, and in an endless number of similar ones left unmentioned here because so universally recognized, we have always two elements: some object or combination of objects presented to sense-perception, and as such satisfying at least the chief demands of formal beauty; and, second, a kindling of emotion in the soul, a suggestion of the unutterable and the ineffable, which for the moment makes even common natures poetic and appreciative.

This play of the imagination, this unconscious kindling of soul, ranges through all grades, from the merely pleasing to the most overpowering sense of the Infinite, as in the sublime. But it is in some degree inseparable from the highest perception of beauty, and depends more upon sensitiveness and fineness of organization in the beholder, than on any definable physical properties of the object awakening it. We call it, therefore, the beautiful in spiritual perception; or, with Kant and Lotze, the "beautiful in reflection," as if in contemplating these objects something of the radiance of the spiritual world was reflected upon the beholder, or called up from the depths of his own soul. This emotion is what Richard Wagner calls "the sense of the illimitable;" and what Ruskin eloquently describes as intimations or suggestions of Unity, Repose and Infinity:—

UNITY:—*The Type of the Divine Comprehensiveness.* "All things," says Hooker, "(God only excepted,) besides the nature which they have in themselves, receive externally some perfection from other things." Hence the appearance of separation or isolation in any thing, and of self-dependence, is an appearance of imperfection; and all appearances of connection and brotherhood are pleasant and right, both as significative of perfection in the things united, and as typical of that Unity which we attribute to God, and of which our true conception is rightly explained and limited by Dr. Brown, in his XCII lecture; that Unity which consists not in his own singleness or separation, but in the necessity of his inherence in all things that be, without which no creature of any kind could hold existence for a moment, which necessity of Divine essence I think it better to speak of as comprehensiveness, than as unity, because unity is often understood in the sense of oneness or singleness, instead of universality, whereas

the only Unity which by any means can become grateful or an object of
hope to men, and whose types therefore in material things can be
beautiful, is that on which turned the last words and prayer of Christ
before his crossing of the Kedron brook. "Neither pray I for these
alone, but for them also which shall believe on me through their word.
That they all may be one, as thou, Father, art in me, and I in thee."

"And so there is not any matter, nor any spirit, nor any creature,
but it is capable of an unity of some kind with other creatures, and in
that unity is its perfection and theirs, and a pleasure also for the be-
holding of all other creatures that can behold. So the unity of spirits
is partly in their sympathy, and partly in their giving and taking, and
always in their love; and these are their delight and their strength,
for their strength is in their co-working and army fellowship, and their
delight is in the giving and receiving of alternate and perpetual currents of good, their inseparable dependence on each other's being, and
their essential and perfect depending on their Creator; and so the
unity of earthly creatures is their power and their peace, not like the
dead and cold peace of undisturbed stones and solitary mountains, but
the living peace of trust, and the living power of support, of hands
that hold each other and are still; and so the unity of matter is, in its
noblest form, the organization of it which builds it up into temples for
the spirit, and in its lower forms, the sweet and strange affinity, which
gives to it the glory of its orderly elements, and the fair variety of
change and assimilation that turns the dust into the crystal, and sepa-
rates the waters that be above the firmament from the waters that be
beneath; and in its lowest form, it is the working and walking and
clinging together that gives their power to the winds, and its syllables
and soundings to the air, and their weight to the waves, and their
burning to the sunbeams, and their stability to the mountains, and to
every creature whatsoever operation is for its glory and for its good.

Now of that which is thus necessary to the perfection of all things,
all appearance, sign, type, or suggestion must be beautiful, in whatever matter it may appear. And so to the perfection of beauty in
lines, or colors, or forms, or masses, or multitudes, the appearance of
some species of unity is in the most determined sense of the word
essential.

But of the appearances of unity, as of unity itself, there are
several kinds which it will be found hereafter convenient to consider
separately. Thus there is the unity of different and separate things,
subjected to one and the same influence, which may be called subjec-
tional unity, and this is the unity of the clouds, as they are driven by

parallel winds, or as they are ordered by the electric currents, and this
is the unity of the sea waves, and this of the bending and undula-
tion of the forest masses, and in creatures capable of will, it is the
unity of will or of inspiration.

And there is unity of origin, which we may call original unity, which
is of things arising from one spring and source, and speaking always
of this their brotherhood, and this in matter is the unity of the branches
of the trees, and of the petals and starry rays of flowers, and of the
beams of light, and in spiritual creatures it is their filial relation to
Him from whom they have their being. And there is unity of sequence, which is that of things that form links in chains, and steps in
ascent, and stages in journeys, and this, in matter, is the unity of com-
municable forces in their continuance from one thing to another, and
it is the passing upwards and downwards of beneficent effects among
all things, and it is the melody of sounds, and the beauty of continuous
lines, and the orderly successions of motion and times. And in
spiritual creatures it is their own constant building up by true knowledge and continuous reasoning to higher perfection, and the singleness
and straight-forwardness of their tendencies to more complete com-
munion with God.

And there is the unity of membership, which we may call essential unity, which is the unity of things separately imperfect into a
perfect whole, and this is the great unity of which other unities are
but parts and means, it is in matter the harmony of sounds and consistency of bodies, and among spiritual creatures, their love and happiness and very life in God.

REPOSE:—*The Type of the Divine Permanence.* Repose, as it is
expressed in material things, is either a simple appearance of permanence and quietness, as in the massy forms of a mountain or rock,
accompanied by the lulling effect of all mighty sight and sound, which
all feel and none define, (it would be less sacred if more explicable,)
εὕδουσιν δ᾽ὀρέων κορυφαί τέ καὶ φάραγγες, or else it is repose proper,
the rest of things in which there is vitality or capability of motion
actual or imagined; and with respect to these the expression of repose
is greater in proportion to the amount and sublimity of the action
which is not taking place, as well as to the intensity of the negation
of it. Thus we speak not of repose in a stone, because the motion of
a stone has nothing in it of energy nor vitality, neither its repose of
stability. But having once seen a great rock come down a mountain
side, we have a noble sensation of its rest, now bedded immovably
among the under fern, because the power and fearfulness of its motion

were great, and its stability and negation of motion are now great in
proportion. Hence the imagination, which delights in nothing more
than the enhancing of the characters of repose, effects this usually by
either attributing to things visibly energetic an ideal stability, or to
things visibly stable an ideal activity or vitality. Hence Wordsworth,
of the cloud, which in itself having too much of changefulness for his
purpose, is spoken of as one "that heareth not the loud winds when
they call, and moveth altogether, if it move at all." And again of
children, which, that it may remove from them the child restlessness,
the imagination conceives as rooted flowers " Beneath an old gray oak,
as violets, lie." On the other hand, the scattered rocks, which have
not, as such, vitality enough for rest, are gifted with it by the living
image; they "lie crouched around us like a flock of sheep."

Thus, as we saw that unity demanded for its expression what at
first sight might have seemed its contrary (variety), so repose demands
for its expression the implied capability of its opposite, energy, and
this even in its lower manifestations, in rocks and stones and trees.
By comparing the modes in which the mind is disposed to regard the
boughs of a fair and vigorous tree, motionless in the summer air, with
the effect produced by one of these same boughs hewn square and used
for threshold or lintel, the reader will at once perceive the connection
of vitality with repose, and the part they both bear in beauty.

Hence I think that there is no desire more intense or more exalted
than that which exists in all rightly disciplined minds for the evidences
of repose in external signs, and what I cautiously said respecting
infinity, I say fearlessly respecting repose, that no work of art can be
great without it, and that all art is great in proportion to the appearance of it. It is the most unfailing test of beauty, whether of matter
or motion, nothing can be ignoble that possesses it, nothing right that
has it not, and in strict proportion to its appearance in the work is the
majesty of the mind to be inferred in the artificer. Without regard
to other qualities, we may look to this for our evidence, and by the
search for this alone we may be led to the rejection of all that is
base, and the accepting of all that is good and great, for the paths of
wisdom are all peace. We shall see by this light three colossal images
standing up side by side, looming in their great rest of spirituality above
the whole world horizon, Phidias, Michael Angelo, and Dante (and Beethoven—Ed.); and then, separated from their great religious thrones only
by less fullness and earnestness of faith, Homer, and Shakspeare; and
from those we may go down step by step among the mighty men of every
age, securely and certainly observant of diminished lustre in every

appearance of restlessness and effort, until the last trace of true inspiration vanishes in the tottering affectations or the tortured insanities of modern times.

There is no art, no pursuit, whatsoever, but its results may be classed by this test alone; every thing of evil is betrayed and winnowed away by it, glitter and confusion and glare of color, inconsistency or absence of thought, forced expression, evil choice of subject, over accumulation of materials, whether in painting or literature, the shallow and unreflecting nothingness of the English schools of art, the strained and disgusting horrors of the French, the distorted feverishness of the German;—pretence, over decoration, over divisions of parts in architecture, and again in music, in acting, in dancing, in whatsoever art, great or mean, there are yet degrees of greatness or meanness entirely dependent on this single quality of repose.

INFINITY:—*The Type of the Divine Incomprehensibility.* "Whatever beauty there may result from the dew of the grass, the flash of the cascade, the glitter of the birch trunk, or the fair daylight hues of darker things, (and joyfulness there is in all of these,) there is yet a light which the eye invariably seeks with a deeper feeling of the beautiful, the light of the declining or breaking day, and the flakes of scarlet cloud burning like watch-fires in the green sky of the horizon, a deeper feeling, I say, not perhaps more acute, but having more of spiritual hope and longing, less of animal and present life, more manifest, invariably, in those of more serious and determined mind, (I use the word serious, not as being opposed to cheerful but to trivial and volatile;) but, I think, marked and unfailing even in those of the least thoughtful dispositions. I am willing to let it rest on the determination of every reader whether the pleasure he has received from these effects of calm and luminous distance be not the most singular and memorable of which he has been conscious, whether all that is dazzling in color, perfect in form, gladdening in expression, be not of evanescent and shallow appealing, when compared with the still small voice of the level twilight behind the purple hills, or the scarlet arch of dawn over the dark troublous-edged sea." . . . . . .

" It is not then by nobler form, it is not by positiveness of hue, it is not by intensity of light (for the sun itself at noonday is effectless upon the feelings), that this strange distant space possesses its attractive power. But there is one thing it has, or suggests, which no other object of sight suggests in equal degree, and that is,—Infinity. It is of all material things the least material, the least finite, the farthest withdrawn from the earth prison-house, the most typical of the nature

of God, the most suggestive of the glory of His dwelling-place. For
the sky of night, though we may know it boundless, is dark, it is a
studded vault, a roof that seems to shut us in and down, but the bright
distance has no limit, we feel its infinity, as we rejoice in the purity
of its light."

SECTION FOURTH. THE PERCEPTION OF THE BEAUTIFUL ONE OF THE HIGHEST FACULTIES OF THE SOUL.

Thus it plainly appears that in its ultimate relations the perception
of the Beautiful is one of the highest faculties of the soul.   For as
Hegel points out, there are three kingdoms of absolutely spiritual activity, having the same content, namely knowledge of God; and differing
from each other only in the form in which they bring the ideal to consciousness.   These three kingdoms of spirit are *Art*, *Religion* and *Philosophy*.

Art communicates its content through sense-forms; Religion
through the " representing consciousness"; and Philosophy through
free thought addressed to the pure reason.   Art is most nearly related
to Religion, " because both have to do with heart and feeling" (Hegel).

Still in the very nature of the medium through which it communicates, namely *sense-forms*, Art has great temptation to remain with and
of the senses exclusively. And this we find plainly illustrated in all periods of its development.   Even in the times when there was *high* art
in the world, there has always been along with it a *low* or debased art,
appealing to the senses as such, and remaining there.   The department of Painting has been perhaps the most exposed to this debase-
ment, from which, indeed, it has never been able entirely to free itself.

Music and Poetry also have at times fallen under the same temp-
tations, as we see in the music of Strauss and Gounod, and some of the
poetry of Byron and Swinburne.   We need to be on our guard, therefore, against all forms and degrees of this low art, which may always
be known by its peculiarly sensuous charm, and its lack of higher and
deeper suggestion.

In this light also we discover the moral relations between the
practical pursuit of Art, Religion and Philosophy.   The latter, indeed,
has to do with pure reason, and is rarely found conjoined with an active condition of the artistic faculties. Between Art and Religion,
however, (as between Science and Religion,) there has long been a mis-
understanding, having its origin in the one-sidedness of their respective votaries.   The pursuit of Art in the highest sense necessarily
relates one to Religion, because it not only exercises his heart and

feelings, but calls out his highest spiritual intuitions as such. Artists in whom the religious sense is wanting, will be discovered on careful consideration to be concerned with low forms of art, either resting in the sensuous as such, or at the most not rising above the enjoyment of formal beauty. Art in the lowest stage is intoxicating in its effect upon the mind, and debilitating; in the second stage it is absorbing and contentful to those in whom the sense of formal beauty is acute, and if they yield themselves to this purely external charm, it has the effect of filling up the attention to the exclusion of the higher activities of the soul. Still, between Art in this second stage and Religion there is no contradiction nor incompatibilty. On the contrary, the influence of Art is useful provided that merely formal beauty be not made an end.

Art also exercises great influence upon Religion, and has the tendency to soften the rigor of its dogmas and practices, and encourages in it a broader humanity, as we may see plainly enough by comparing Puritanism with later forms of vital religion. Besides, Art aids Religion in a very important way by furnishing it with its revelations of beauty and truth in sense-forms, in availing itself of which Religion becomes intelligible and attractive to the common mind.

On the other hand, Religion exercises important influence upon Art, especially by elevating the thoughts of the artist, and purifying his soul, thereby permitting truth to shine into it with greater lustre. And so we may conclude on *a priori* grounds that the exercise of religion is helpful to the artist, and that we have a right to expect from him in such case a higher and more inspiring revelation of beauty, than would otherwise be possible. And this, also, experience confirms, as we see plainly in such men as Dante, Michael Angelo, Bach, Handel and Beethoven, who are of the very highest type.

CHAPTER TWENTY-FOURTH.

THE SYMBOLICAL, THE CLASSICAL, AND THE ROMANTIC IN ART.

The progress of Art has been gradual, from the imperfection and crudity of early attempts, to a well-nigh perfect beauty in the time of its full development. Thus it may be said in general that "the oldest works in all forms of art yield in themselves vague contents: in poetry, simple history, Theogenies fermenting with abstract ideas and their incomplete expression; separate saints in stone and wood, etc. The representation remains unpliant, monotonous or confused, stiff, broken. Especially in the pictorial arts is the visible expression dull; in repose not that of the spiritually deep in itself, but mere animal emptiness; or else sharply distorted and immoderate in characteristic expression.

"So likewise are the forms of the human body and their movements dead; the arms hung on the body, the bones not articulated, or else awkward, angular, sharply moved; so likewise the figure untempered, dumpy, or immoderately meagre and extended. Upon the externals, on the contrary, garments, hair, weapons and other adornments much more love and care are bestowed; but the folds of the garments, e. g., remain wooden and independent, without fitting themselves to the form of the body (as we can see often enough in the old-time pictures of the Virgin Mary, and the saints).

"Even so are the earliest poems incomplete, disconnected, monotonous, only ruled remotely by one idea or sensation; or else wild, vehement, the different ideas confusedly entangled, and the whole not yet brought together into a firm organization."*

Nevertheless these early monuments have a certain rude impressiveness and grandeur which has been felt by many generations of the human race who have appeared, admired, and passed away in the presence of these imposing memorials of the thoughts and aspirations of the earlier times.

Progress in art has arisen mainly from a clearer perception of the ideal. It may be divided into three stages, called by Hegel the Sym-

*Hegel's *Aesthetik*, II, p. 246.

bolical, the Classical, and the Romantic. These differ from each other, not only in a progressive elevation of the faculties addressed by Art, as suggested by the classification of the previous chapter, but also in the mode of conceiving the ideal itself. The complete discussion of these ideas and their illustration in the various arts would take us far beyond present limits. The barest outline will suffice.

SECTION FIRST. SYMBOLIC ART.

The Symbol is a natural object, having a plain relation to the idea it represents; thus, the lion is the symbol of courage; the fox, of cunning; the ox, of patience; the sheep of simplicity; the elephant of docility and power; etc. Besides these natural symbols derived from the animal kingdom, there are also abstract symbols, whose meaning is almost universal; such as the triangle, symbol of the trinity; the circle, of eternity; etc. Yet each one of these natural objects has in it something more than the limited meaning it affords as a symbol. Thus the lion is not only courageous, but fierce and treacherous; the ox is patient, but also slow and stupid; the fox is cunning, but in his own degree is fierce and blood-thirsty also. And in this we find a natural limitation or inherent ambiguity in symbolical art.

Symbolical art is in general the entire art of the Oriental nations. To this class belong the towers of Babel, Pyramids, Pagodas and Temples of China and India, the sculpture and temples of Assyria and Egypt; Myths, the Niebelungen lied, etc; as well as much of the poetry of the Old Testament, as, e. g., parts of Ezekiel, etc. In all these the meaning is unclear; each work of this period is a sphynx, an enigma.

The sculpture of the symbolical period is mighty and vast. One thinks of the colossal Memnon, the statues at Karnac, the figures of gods in China and India, monstrous figures outraging all principles of natural form, yet strangely impressive to so many millions of the human race, who have found in these their clearest emblem of the Divine. In all these symbolical productions the beautiful, as such, is not sought. It is the mighty, the grand, the eternal, the everlasting, the all-creating;—these are the vague forms in which the Eternal and Absolute suggests itself first to the human race.

We find that in every nation, whenever movement takes place, the symbolical in art gradually merges into the beautiful. Temples lose something of their massiveness in favor of lightness and symmetry. The gigantic structures of Egypt give place to the delicate proportions of the Parthenon and Acropolis. The many-armed gods yield precedence to the scarcely super-human forms of Jupiter, Mi-

nerva, Venus and Apollo. The eyes of Zeuxis and Apelles discover
for mankind the beauty everywhere veiled in nature. Thus Art comes
to the classical period, when beauty has become complete, in so far as
it resides in form.

SECTION SECOND.   CLASSICAL ART.

Classical art is above all unconscious of any want of harmony
between the ideal and the means by which it must be expressed. The
human form, that temple of in-dwelling spirit, is especially the chosen
type of this period, and sculpture, therefore, its distinctive expression.
Of the content and meaning of this form of utterance there will be
occasion to speak in the next chapter. For the present let it be observed that sculpture shows a progress towards the spiritual in art.
The Greek artist, in forsaking the vast masses of architecture in favor
of the comparatively insignificant bit of marble only so large as the
human form, was beginning to learn the same lesson that was taught
to one of old, hid in the cleft of the rock, that not in the lightning,
the earthquake, nor in the thunder could one find God, but in the
" still small voice." Yet here we anticipate, for the voice, as a token
of soul, was the peculiar ideal of the Romantic.

At present the artist advances only so far as to discover in the
human form the most complete expression of the beautiful. Thus
Hegel says (Bryant's translation):

" The Greek ideal has for its basis an unchangeable harmony between
spirit and sensuous form — the unalterable serenity of the immortal
gods; but this calm has about it something cold and inanimate. Classic art has not comprehended the true essence of the divine nature,
nor penetrated to the depths of the soul. It has not known how to develop its inmost powers in their opposition, and again to re-establish
their harmony. All this phase of existence, the evil, the sinful, the
unhappy, moral suffering, the revolt of the will, remorse, and the
agonies of the soul, are unknown to it. Classic art does not pass beyond the proper domain of the veritable ideal.

" As to its realization in history, it is scarcely necessary to say that
we must seek it among the Greeks. Classic beauty, with the infinite
wealth of ideas and forms which compose its domain, has been allotted
to the Greek people, and we ought to render homage to them for having raised art to its highest vitality."

This was the perfect completion of formal beauty. All the qualities of symmetry, proportion, harmony, unity, and the like that enter
into and constitute perfection of form, are here manifested in exquisite

loveliness. As Hegel says: "There neither is nor ever can be anything more beautiful."

Greek plastic art attained its highest achievements in the time of Phidias. Immediately after this Socrates, Plato and Aristotle, successively, "effected for man, once for all, the perfect distinction between idea and sensuous image — between content and form — the indissoluble union of which, it can not be too much insisted upon, constitutes the central characteristic in classic art. Thus had the human mind passed beyond the limits of the classic ideal, and henceforth the history of classic art is but a history of its decline and fall." *

SECTION THIRD.   ROMANTIC ART.

The key of romantic art is "internal beauty of spirit" as distinguished from outward beauty of form. This ideal began to appear in later sculpture. We have a token of it in the well-known Venus de Medici, where the effort is made to represent the modesty of a delicate woman appearing unclad in public. The conception is just, but untrue to the spirit of the classical ideal; for in this nothing is represented but the eternal, the enduring. This conflict between womanly delicacy and the public gaze, creates shame, an unbeautiful and temporary affection.

Collision is the principal means of the romantic. By collision is meant a conflict between opposing principles, in the out-come of which the superiority of the nobler principle is made to appear. Collision is totally foreign to architecture, and almost so to sculpture. Later sculpture, as the well-known Laocoön, introduces this element, but to the destruction of absolute formal beauty. The work of art is no longer *beautiful* out-right and in itself, but beautiful on the whole, and considering what it means.

In romantic art it is not the human form, the outward covering which furnishes the artist his ideal of beauty, but the *inner*, the soul, the disposition, the *life*. Hence sculpture which has to do mainly with form, gives place to painting, which affords perspective, places its heroes in suitable scenes, and contrasts one personage with another; painting in turn gives place to music and poetry. The meaning of these various changes will appear in the next chapter where we have to examine each art in its turn.

In all this later cycle of art the key-tone is unmistakeable; it is beauty of spirit rather than of the form.

* Bryant.

"The material of romantic art, at least with reference to the divine, is extremely limited. For, in the first place, as we have already pointed out, nature is deprived of its divine attributes; sea, mountain, and valley, streams, springs, time and night, as well as the universal process of nature, have all lost their value with respect to the representation and content of the absolute. The images of nature are no longer set forth symbolically. They are stripped of the characteristic which rendered their forms and activities appropriate as traits of a divinity. For all the great questions concerning the origin of the world — concerning the whence, the whither, the wherefore of created nature and humanity, together with all the symbolic and plastic attempts to solve and represent these problems — have vanished in consequence of the revelation of God in the spirit; and even the gay, thousand-hued earth, with all its classically-figured characters, deeds, and events, is swallowed up in spirit, condensed in the single luminous point of the absolute and its eternal process of redemption (*Erlosensgeschichte*). The entire content, therefore, is thus concentrated upon the internality of the spirit — upon the perception, the imagination, the soul — which strives after unity with the truth, and seeks and struggles to produce and to retain the divine in the individual (*Subjekt*). Thus, though the soul is still destined to pass through the world, it no longer pursues merely worldly aims and undertakings. Rather, it has for its essential purpose and endeavor the inner struggle of man within himself, and his reconciliation with God, and brings into representation only personality and its conservation, together with appliances for the accomplishment of this end. The heroism which can here make its appearance is by no means a heroism which makes its own law, establishes regulations, creates and transforms conditions, but a heroism of submission, for which everything is settled and determined beforehand, and to which there thenceforth remains only the task of regulating temporal affairs according to it, of applying to the existing world that higher principle which has validity in and for itself, and, finally, of rendering it practically valuable in the affairs of every-day life. We may now comprise in a single word this relation between content and form as it appears in the romantic — for here it is that this relation attains to its complete characterization. It is this: just because the ever-increasing universality and restless working depth of the soul constitute the fundamental principle of the romantic, the key-note thereof is *musical*, and, in connection with the particularized content of the imagination, *lyrical*. For romantic art the lyrical is, as it were, the elementary characteristic — a tone which the epic and the drama also strike, and which breathes about the works of the arts of visible representation themselves, like a universal, fragrant odor of the soul; for here spirit and soul will speak to spirit and soul through all their images."*

CHAPTER TWENTY-FIFTH.

THE IDEAL AS MANIFESTED IN THE DIFFERENT FORMS OF ART.

In each one of the different arts we are able to trace the progress of the human mind through the various stages of art-conception described in the previous chapters, although the complete progress is not fully illustrated in any one of them.

SECTION FIRST.   ARCHITECTURE.

The oldest of the arts is architecture. Hegel enumerates three general classes of structure which are essentially symbolical in character. These are: (1) Works built for a union of people; such were the great works of the Assyrians, Egyptians, etc., all of which were in effect religious works. So Goethe says, "What is holy? That which binds many souls together."

(2) Works intermediate between buildings and sculpture. Such are the Indian Pagodas, the Obelisks, the Memnon, Sphynx, and Labyrinth, expressive of vague ideas or mystical conceptions.

(3) The transition to the classical, as in the Egyptian tombs, Pyramids, etc.

Classical architecture we find in the Greek temples. Romantic architecture finds its expression in the Gothic Cathedrals of the middle ages.

Architecture in general is related to the Ideal as the expression of the symmetrical, the regular, the united, the grand; — the utterance of spirit which has seized the material from without and formed it, but which is neither represented nor conceived as residing in it. So, *e. g.*, the Memnon had no voice of its own, but was played on from without by the rising sun.

*Hegel, Bryant's translation.

6

SECTION SECOND.   SCULPTURE.

Sculpture has for its central idea "the wonder that soul should dwell in body."* Again: "Sculpture, in general, perceives the wonder that spirit imagines itself in the wholly material, and so forms this externality that it becomes actually present in it, and acknowledges therein the suitable look of itself."

"Sculpture is the peculiar art of the classical ideal as such."† Thus it belongs properly to the classical epoch, and the few works of the symbolic period are to be regarded rather as apprentice works in which the artist is acquiring the plastic control over his material, than as independent and significant expressions of the ideal.

Hegel speaks of three styles in classical sculpture: 1. The *Hard, Austere, Strong*, characterized by great masses and simple content.

2. *The Purely Beautiful*, characterized by a more living beauty, and represented in the works of Phidias.

3. The *Pleasing* style, where beauty gives up something of its eternal repose for the sake of gaining a greater appearance of human interest. The Apollo Belvidere if not properly to be reckoned in this category, is at least transitional between the style next preceding and this.

The Content and meaning of this form of art is already fully expressed in the previous chapter on "Classic Art," to which reference is again made. The pith of it all is in the following sentence in the third volume of the *Aesthetik:* "Sculpture has for its principle and content, *Spiritual Individuality* as the classical ideal, so that the Inner and Spiritual finds expression to the spirit in the immediate bodily appearance, which art has here to represent in actual art-existence." Or, again, as Bénard phrases it, "The Content of sculpture is the essence, the substantial, true, invariable part of character," as distinguished from what is accidental and transient.

So, also, Mr. Wm. M. Bryant: "Sculpture constitutes the first step in advance beyond Architecture, and it *pauses with this first step.* It takes as its object the simple form of the human body, and by this form it expresses spirit, because spirit does not yet know itself apart from this form."

Doubtless the artist turned himself to the human form as the most suitable expression of the ideal in consequence of living in Greece, a land so mild of climate and so simple in mode of life as to afford on every side attractive examples of fully developed, healthful, beautiful

* Hegel.   † Bryant's Hegel's Philosophy of Art, " Introductory Essay."

men and women. This outer manifestation of vital beauty was encouraged by the influence of the games and gymnastic training, so that taking one reason with another it may be doubted whether any part of the world at any period of its history ever afforded a sculptor so satisfactory a surrounding as Greece in its prime. At the same time intellectual life had become more vigorous. The imagination had long been kindled by the Homeric poems, recited universally by the strolling minstrels. The constant wars between the different States, and the varying fortunes of defense against the Persians did much to stimulate the mind and bring out the force of individual character. Thus it happened that the works of Phidias were produced soon after the times of Pythagorus, and shortly before the days of Socrates. This was the moment when the classical idea reached an equilibrium between form and content.

As already pointed out, Socrates, and after him Plato and Aristotle, accomplished once for all the separation between *form* and *content* in art. The human spirit went forward to a higher development; it turned inward to deeper and more immortal thoughts. It was then that Romantic Art became inevitable, and therein a revelation of the idea, in living, self-determined beauty, for which sculpture was inadequate.

SECTION THIRD. PAINTING.

When we think seriously upon the art of painting and remember its list of triumphs from the days of Appelles and Praxiteles to Raphael, Correggio, and Angelo, and even to our own times, we cannot wonder that so many writers upon art have taken this as the type and complete expression of the artistic faculty.

Painting represents the dawn and progress of a deeper perception of the beauty of the visible world. Evidently it began in *color*, the effort to represent the evanescent glories of the heavens at sunrise or evening, the exquisite tints of flowers, masses of foliage, etc.

At first painting was merely decorative, and was employed to beautify the walls of the more precious shrines, the best rooms in the homes of the wealthy, etc.

Afterwards it became *imitative*. The forms and tints of flowers and fruits were its subjects. We trace this very distinctly in the well-known anecdote of the two great Greek painters who had a trial of skill. One of them painted a plate of cherries so naturally that the birds came and pecked at them; the other represented a fly on the nose of a portrait so naturally that the other artist attempted to brush it off in order to examine the picture better. Therein he acknowledged his superior; for he himself had deceived only the unreasoning birds, while the other had deceived an artist.

Painting in any large sense involves at least three arts: Drawing (the art of representing outlines as they really appear), Color and Perspective. The appearance of solid projection, that is to say, the appearance of *reality*, depends upon the latter. There is reason to suppose that color and drawing were brought to a high degree of excellence by the Greeks and Romans, as indicated by the anecdote given above, and by the Pompeian discoveries, where in some of the rooms the colors remain to the present day as clear as when first put upon the walls, nearly two thousand years ago.

The subjects of painting in that olden time, as we have said, were flowers, fruits and other natural objects not requiring difficult perspective for their intelligible representation, and the gods and goddesses of the popular mythology, episodes from Homer, and the poets, etc.

To the painters (and their brethren the poets) mankind owes its perception of the beautiful in nature. The plowman, wearily treading in the furrow the livelong day, sees not the fleecy clouds above him, nor is he inspired by the mighty pinnacles and peaks of the mountain horizon towering so grandly, as if matter herself were striving upward toward her God. Nay, he overlooks even the delicate perfection of the daisies and buttercups whose sunshine his furrow so relentlessly ends. Yet in the water he drinks to quench his thirst he might, if he would, see all these distant glories repeated; as if, out of this pure fountain of refreshing, the voice of God called to man to look upward for the secret of the beautiful and the holy. But it is only once in a thousand years that a Burns rises above the depressing influence of a plowman's environment. It is the idle painter, or his brother, the poet, lolling at ease under the shading oak to whom this deeper vision of beauty is revealed.

When we speak of painting as a form of high art, representative of the spiritual meanings of nature and life, we immediately think of that glorious company of great Italian masters of the fifteenth century, chief among whom were Raphael (1483–1520), Leonardo da Vinci (1452–1519), Titian (1477–1576), Michael Angelo (1474–1563), Tintoret (1512–1594), Paul Veronese (1532–1588). Nor can we forget their eminent successors in the next century, Claude Lorraine (1600–1682), and Rembrandt (1606–1669).

In the productions of these great artists we find the art of Painting unfolded in all its capacities except that of strict, literal *realism*—

imitation of nature as such; this was left for later masters. Every production of these old masters has its mannerisms. Natural forms are conventionalized, or at times distorted, with unhesitating boldness. Historical anachronisms are common in the historical pieces. But they show, nevertheless, a life, a meaning, an expression of spirit, such as nowhere existed in this art before.

Were we to analyze the impressions they severally produce upon us, we should find certain marked differences in the faculties to which they appeal, as pointed out in Chapter XXIII. Thus, e. g., the works of Titian and Paul Veronese are noted for their magnificent and exquisite coloring. In this quality they appeal to the "pleasing of sensation," and less decidedly to the spiritual as such. Raphael is noted for the *expression* of his works. They are characterized by a serene and matchless grace, such as one seeks in vain elsewhere. Michael Angelo, on the contrary, is neither a great colorist, nor a composer of graceful forms. But he conceives with such superhuman boldness, and pierces so deeply into the very pith and marrow of the world about him, that he stands recognized on all hands as one of the very greatest minds who have made human nature illustrious by their participation in it.

The art of Painting also shows a progress beyond sculpture, in the direction of the spiritual. The massive matter of architecture, and the solid dimensions of sculpture, have here given place to merely the *appearance* of matter. But this diminution of material is accompanied by a most important increase in power of expression, and this especially in the direction of a more complete mastery of the scale of beauty. For here at the basis of it we have the wonderful delights of color and "tone," an entire new kingdom of sense-gratification. Every facility for representing human relations and deeds, which sculpture or *basso-relievo* could furnish, here exists entire, and in the far greater perfection of natural perspective. Only in a single direction is there a loss, namely in the direction of the sublime, in which architecture certainly has greater power. Yet this concession is immeasurably atoned for by the wonderful increase in power to represent the feelings of the soul. For while Architecture gave us the mighty enigmas of Egypt, and the everlasting beauty of the Parthenon; and Sculpture revealed to man the beauty and dignity of his own form when permeated by a noble soul, and thus by images of Mercury and Jupiter led his mind toward the true God; Painting has given to mankind not only the beauties of field and flower, and preserved for him a life-like semblance of the living faces of its heroes, but has portrayed in bodily form the incarnate sufferings of his Redeemer.

SECTION FOURTH.   MUSIC.

The three forms of art previously examined have this in common, that they address the observer by means of *forms* permanently existing in *space*.   Architecture deals in matter in vast masses, only a small proportion of which in any single form comes into actual contact with spirit.   The exterior, the form, is shaped and fashioned by spirit according to its own ideal.   In a pyramid, for example, how slight a proportion of the whole is the surface.   The inner part does indeed bear the impress of spirit in the fact of its location so as to maintain the integrity of the form; yet this relation to spirit is faint at most.   In a temple the mass of matter is greatly reduced and the interior parts are, distinctly subservient to the mechanical necessities of structure.   Here therefore, soul has left its impress upon a much greater proportion by the whole mass than in the pyramid.

Sculpture again greatly reduces the quantity of matter, and is much more particular about the quality of it.   Only the finest marble will answer to the artist's demands.   But here art has to do with the *form* and with the *surface*, which practically is the form.   The inner is inert, dead. Yet sculpture conceives of this inner part as having been alive, as is indicated by the care with which muscles and joints and all particulars which indicate internal organization are represented.   The spirit does not reside even in the most speaking statue; yet one thinks it a suitable residence of soul, and scarcely wonders at the miracle of Psyche.

In painting, the quantity of matter is still further reduced, and art has to do with forms, and the *appearances of matter*, by means of which, as we saw, relations of soul are manifested.

Yet all these forms of art deal with forms permanently existing in space, outside of and entirely separate from the most appreciative observer.   As Hegel well says, " Painting, as we saw, may likewise give expression in physiognomy and shape, to the inner life and energy, the determinations and passions of the heart, the situations, conflicts and fate of the soul; but what we have always before us in painting, are objective appearances, from which the observing *I*, as inner self, remains entirely separate.   One may never so completely absorb and sink himself in the subject, the situation, the character, the form, of a statue or painting, admire the art work, gush over it, nay, may completely fill himself therewith;—it matters not, these works of art are and remain independent objects, in review of which we come not beyond the position of an observer."

Music, on the contrary, builds no permanent fabric in space. It has no *form* which can be seen. It is a voice. Out of the unseen, in cunningly modulated tones, it speaks to the heart of the hearer. Like the voice itself it no sooner utters its word than it is silent. Whenever we would recall its message we must recreate the informing word.

In this way music approaches the observer as none of the previous arts can. When it is perceived it is no longer something outside of and separate from the observer; it is within him; it has penetrated into the very center of the soul. Hence its power to absorb the observer, to carry him along with it, so that men everywhere "delight to sing with the melody, to strike with the measure, and in dance music it comes into the very bones."

This remarkable power of music lies fundamentally in the sense of hearing to which it appeals, and in *time*, which is the material of its form. For by the sense of hearing we are brought into our nearest relations to other souls. It is with the *ear* that man receives the word of reproof, the approval of his fellow, and the commandment of his God. This wonderful mechanism of hearing is particularly the sympathetic channel of feeling. Many shades of emotion may be conveyed by modulations of the speaking voice, without use of words. All this material of inflection and pitch relation, carried to an almost infinitely greater perfection of delicate organization than in speech, Music employs with such cunning mastership as to indicate very plainly that *this* was one of the ends intended in all the delicate organization of the inner ear.

But music rests its greatest power in its modulation in *time*. The beat, the measure, chimes in with the human pulse, hurries it or retards it; the motive brightens up the rhythm, modifies it, characterizes and individualizes the different moments in a piece; and measure, motivization, and rate of movement, all combine with the melodic and harmonic filling up, to complete a form of utterance in which soul speaks to soul not of its ideas and notions, but of its *feelings*, its general *states*. Thus the content of music, in general, is *Emotion*. "It extends itself in every direction for the expression of all distinct sensations and shades of joyousness, serenity, jokes, humor, shoutings and rejoicings of soul ; as well as the graduations of anguish, sorrow, grief, lamentation, distress, pain, regret, etc.; and, finally, aspiration, worship, love, etc., belong to the proper sphere of musical expression." (Hegel's *Aesthetik*, III, 144.)

Of the material of music we have already learned in the earlier

lessons of this course. Its form is a symmetrically co-ordinated succession of movements, expressive of a sequence or cycle of feelings.

Thus music in its very nature expresses spiritual relations. True
the material of hearing may lend itself to play. Mere jingle is not
without charm. Agreeable, piquant, or bizarre combinations of tone-
color may tickle or delight the sense of hearing without uttering a
message to the soul. But properly conceived all these are part of the
vocabulary of this voice ; part of its material for spiritual communication. Therefore music is in itself a romantic art. And it quite agrees
with this idea that its systematic and artistic development is the very
latest of all the arts.

Hence the terms symbolical and classical have only a modified application in it, as we shall hereafter see. The earliest attempts at music,
such as the Gregorian or Ambrosian hymns, the oldest songs of the
church, we may well enough style symbolical. They fully agree with
the peculiarities of this epoch in all the other arts. The true handling
of the material, the value of tone as tone, and the significance of time
and melodic modulation they have not yet fathomed. And yet their
quaint cadences have a strange power, and are the source of all the distinctly " ecclesiastical " conventionalities of music.

The classic in music exists in all those works which afford a conten
entirely harmonious and commensurate with their form. Such work-
are those of Bach, Haydn, Mozart, and part of those of Beethoven and
Schubert.

In many works of the latter two composers, form and content do
not coincide ; the beauty of the form as form is sacrificed to the
expressiveness and meaning of the work. Here, therefore, form is less
than content; and we have the romantic moment in art. To this category belong many of the Beethoven works, notably such as the "moonlight " sonata, and the last two or three, almost everything of Chopin's
and Schumann's, etc. The true relation of all this, we shall learn later.
(See Parts V. and VI.)

SECTION FIFTH. POETRY.

We have seen from the beginning of this discussion that the beautiful is the expression of the ideal by means of forms directly addressed
to the senses and intuitions, rather than to the reason. In architecture
the ideal merely begins to appear; in sculpture it shines out more
plainly, though even in this form the spirit is not living; in painting
are represented transition movements of human life, the very point of
spiritual defeat or triumph, and thus we go deeper than the merely

outward form, and become conscious of the inner life of spirit as represented in the appearance before us. In music we go still further in the
same direction. For here we have not a representation which stands outside of us and over against us, independent, to appreciate which requires that the beholder should at least yield himself to it; but instead of
it a finely organized and infinitely complex *voice*, which tells its story directly to the soul, and as already pointed out moves and excites the
hearer, " carries him along with it, quite otherwise than the way " in
which other arts affect him. Music represents the self-moved activity
of the soul. In no other art is the difference so great between the inspired and the merely mechanically-put-together.

Yet music also has its limitations. As already pointed out in the
passages on Romantic art, the true meaning of this stage of development is the final beauty of spirit attained through conflict and suffering.
The ideal of the romantic is none other than that of the Christian religion itself ; the attainment of complete repose, and blessedness of
spirit, in which bodily sense and appetite and all the negative or sinful
elements of the moral nature are finally subjected to the reason, itself
illumined by clear vision of the truth, and the whole spirit glorified
into the image of the Divine. This state is attainable only through
conflicts, in which one after another the evils of the nature are met and
overcome; nor yet by conflict only, but by conflict sustained in faith
and love. This is the Christian ideal. Nor is it the mission of art to
instruct or definitely or directly aid the individual in this work. Yet
in an indirect way it does do this and always will. For it is the artist
who earliest sees the beauty of every natural appearance, the deeper
meaning of the lake, and ocean; and it is the artist, the poet, who sees
deepest into the depths of the soul. Hence in art-works one finds represented the moments of this redemption conflict, through which every
individual must pass; seeing which the tempted soul takes heart again,
knowing that some one has already passed by the same path to
victory.

Now these conflicts of the spirit are not representable in architecture
or sculpture. Later sculpture tried this; but it is a work foreign to the
proper genius of that art. In painting they may come to a limited extent. But a painting is necessarily but a single moment of life; it gives
us only a position, a relation, a contrast. Whereas no account of a
soul-conflict is intelligible which does not give us the opposing principles, and also their collision and final resolution in the triumph of the
good; and this is a story too long for painting.

Music can give us a prolonged action of the soul, a life-history, and in this is its great superiority in spirituality to the other forms of art. Nevertheless we come here to its limitations. A collision is an opposition of evil and good. The good, in music, is the consonant, the well-sounding, the melodious, the pleasing; the evil is the dissonant, the discordant, the dis-united, the heterogenous. Now music itself as music has properly and chiefly to do with the consonant, or with the dissonant introduced in strict subjection to the consonant. Just as soon as the dissonant forms any considerable proportion of the musical art-work, it ceases to be music and becomes unmusical, tiresome, as we see in long passages of Wagner's later operas. The proper sphere of music is to portray the progress of the soul from grief or sadness to comfort, joy, and blessedness; it can do this with an intelligibility entirely its own. It is, so to say, the art of the ideal sphere of the soul, the sphere into which sin and its consequent suffering has never entered. Whatever is bright, tender, joyful, resolved, or noble, music expresses with peculiar power. But evil lies outside its pure province. This, then is one of its limitations.

Music suffers a second limitation in its entire want of relation to reason. It is the office of reason to receive from the senses and the understanding the apparent facts of the outer world, to compare them, discern their essential nature, and especially the deeper laws that regulate their co-ordination and succession. It is also its office to determine concerning any particular piece of conduct that in view of its real nature and its relation to other parts of the same life, it does or does not conduce to virtue; that such and such things are related to the lower parts of the nature, and such and such others to the higher. Reason is the faculty of man by means of which he generalizes and so arrives at a distinct conception of the truth. This faculty is, therefore, the ruling intelligence of the entire man with power to co-ordinate his movements and conduct as well as his thought so as to bring him more rapidly and surely along the road to goodness and God. Now music is outside of reason. Reason begins to act only when it is furnished with distinctly formulated conceptions or thoughts, and these are not found in music. Music and reason, therefore, have nothing in common with each other, but belong to different departments of the soul. Music goes in through sense-perception and addresses the feelings directly as such. Reason operates in the range of thought, and by comparisons between the information it receives from sense-perception and its own *a priori* conceptions (time, space, and causality) is able to arrive at certain forms of truth; which may or may not afterward be applied to the feelings and motives of conduct.

Thus as soon as art contemplates conflicts of soul and a blessedness of victory residing in a complete union of all the powers of the spirit, including the reason, some higher and more universal form of art becomes inevitable. Such a form we have in poetry, which expresses itself not in shapes and forms outwardly visible as such, but through words, which reason understands.

Because it finds its expression in words and through ideas and conceptions properly belonging to reason, poetry comes into near proximity to prose, to ordinary discourse. Poetry is distinguishable from prose in its *form* as well as its *content*.

The poetic form or mode of expression is imaginative and picturesque. However intensified by thought, the mode of expression must be such as to create in the inner sense *pictures of the outer world*, or of such and such living beings in such and such conflicts and relations. Thus poetry in its picturesque modes of embodying thought addresses the inner sense exactly as an external reality · resembling it would address the same feelings going in through the ordinary gates of sense-perception. This is the distinctive trait of poetic expression. Verse is an added grace, which is useful in so far as it lends smoothness and musical quality to the discourse, and is a token of the complete control which the creative artist exercises over his material. Verse also serves a purpose in idealizing the style and so setting it apart to nobler uses than those of common every-day life.

The *content* of poetry is spiritual existence and eternal truth, as illustrated in the lives and conduct of men. " The entire circle of the outer world enters poetry only in so far as the spirit finds its activity in ruling over the material ; as the environment of man, also, his outer world, which has its essential value only in reference to the inner of consciousness, but dares not make claim to the honor of being itself the exclusive subject of poetry. Then the word, this most plastic material, which belongs immediately to the spirit, and is the most capable of all of seizing the interests and movements of things in their inner life, must here be applied to the highest meaning of which it is capable.

" Thus it becomes the chief task of poetry to bring to consciousness the power of spiritual life, and especially whatever swells and sinks in human passion and feeling, or passes quietly before the attention; the all-embracing kingdom of human idea, activity, work, fate, the machinery of this world and the divine government. So has it been and still is the most general and broadest teacher of human kind. Its teaching and learning are knowledge and experience of this which is. Star, beast, and plant neither know nor experience their law; but man exists in the suitable law of his actual life only when he knows what he him-self is and what is about him; he must know the power which drives and manages him;—and such a knowledge it is which Poetry gives in its first substantial form." (Hegel.)

The superior power of poetry lies equally in its mode of expression and in its content. In the former because all men comprehend and are moved by picture-building discourse. This mode of expression also lends itself most easily to the artist's way of conceiving truth, which is by direct intuition and not by reason. Hence in the earliest time the deepest eternal truths were perceived, not clearly, but as if through a veil; in epic, ode, psalm, prophecy, and drama they found clearer and clearer expression. And thus long before the philosopher had dis-covered that man had a soul, Poets and seers had shown to the spirit of man the love and providence of his God.

The principal kinds of poetry are three: *The Epic*, which treats of the deeds of heroes, and the fortunes of a people; the *Lyric*, in which the human heart sings its own sorrow, hope, joy, or love; and the *Drama*, in which men live and act before us, and so by collisions and conflicts the lesson of motive and consequence is read.

In its very nature, therefore, the art of Poetry is universal. It belongs to every age, and to every grade of intelligence. And in all it elevates, refines, and educates.

Yet in its very definiteness and the completeness with which the artist may work out his full meaning in it, it leaves less room for the imagination of the reader. And in this respect Music possesses a certain advantage over it. We have thus completed the circle of the arts, and have seen in all, and more and more plainly as we have advanced, that the ideal of them all is the expression of the *True* in sense-forms —in other words, the expression of the beautiful.

Art is a sort of Jacob's ladder on which from the days of Adam until now the angels of God have descended to man, and up which man has gone to seek his God.

PART FIFTH.

STUDIES IN CLASSICAL MUSIC.

LESSON TWENTY-SIXTH.

THE PLAYFUL MOMENT IN THE CLASSIC.

We find the starting point of the playful in the classic in such productions of Bach, as the little fugue in C minor, No. 2 in the "Clavier." (Plays.) Here the playful spirit is unmistakable. It is shown in the rhythm, the quick movement, and especially in the way in which one part catches up another. These, again, are to be referred to the Gigue of Bach, Mozart and other composers of that day, which were an idealized form of an old Italian dance in triplet rhythm.

Observe now the following: (Plays the Scherzo from the Beethoven Sonata in C, op. 2.) This charming little piece deserves to be heard twice. It is one of the most complete little bits of imitative writing to be found in Beethoven. This is in thematic style.

Observe now this: (Plays the Allegro in E flat, ¾ time, third movement of the Sonata in E flat, op. 7.) This is the lyric style at first, but in the second period falls into the imitative forms for a while. The charming feature in this work is its delicacy. Observe that the "trio" refrains from definitely enunciated melody, although a melody is suggested by the progression of its harmonies.

Again, observe this: (Plays the Menuetto from Sonata in D, op. 10.) In point of structure, this little piece very much resembles the Allegro last played. The impressive feature in it as one knows it better, is the peculiarly graceful turn of the melody, in which it is not surpassed by any of the Beethoven short movements.

Observe again this, which is in the form of a Rondo: (Plays Finale of Sonata in G, op. 14.) Here we have a similar spirit, and the agreeable contrast of the singing melody in C which begins in the seventy-third measure.

93

Still more unmistakable in its form, and very beautiful in its way, is the Scherzo from the "Pastoral" sonata of Beethoven, op. 28. This movement goes very fast. It is relieved by a trio which contains a lovely melodic phrase, repeated several times with different harmonies. (Plays.)

Of the same general character are the other playful movements in the Beethoven Sonatas. Those in the sonatas for piano and violin, as well as the trios for violin, 'cello and piano, afford yet more decided humoristic traits. They are full of quirks and catches of time, caprices of motives — in short, they are frolicsome.

Movements of this kind were introduced into the sonata by Beethoven, as a compensation for the greater length and seriousness he imparted to the other movements as compared with those of Haydn and Mozart. Independent movements of this kind are, however, numerous in the Bach, Haydn and Mozart works. See, e. g., the Mozart "Pieces," (Peters' ed.) and similar collections of other composers. All of these movements are idealized dance-forms.

LIST OF ILLUSTRATIONS.

1. Bach Invention in C, No. 1.
2. Scherzo from Beethoven Sonata in C, op. 2.
3. Allegro (3d mov't) of Sonata in E flat, op. 7, Beethoven.
4. Menuetto from Sonata in D, op. 10, Beethoven.
5. Finale of Sonata in G, op. 14, Beethoven.
6. Scherzo from Pastoral Sonata, Beethoven.

LESSON TWENTY-SEVENTH.

THE TENDER AND SOULFUL IN THE CLASSIC.

In order rightly to comprehend the works of the greatest composers we need to give especial attention to their deepest and tenderest moments. These, of course, are to be found in the slow movements of the sonatas and symphonies. These movements are founded upon the people's song; they are in lyric forms, in slow and sustained melodies, which in the longer movements are contrasted with second and third subjects of a different character, as we already saw in our studies in form.

The general type of these movements is the *Cantabile.* They are not to be found in Bach, nor yet in Handel. Haydn gives us the form but not the deep spirit we now look for in a movement of this kind. A pleasing example is found in one of his symphonies. (Plays *Largo Cantabile* from Haydn's symphony in D, No. 5 in Wittman's arrangements for piano solo, Ed. Peters, No. 197.) The second subject is in the principal key of the movement, G, beginning in the thirty-first measure.

The slow movements in the pianoforte works are not so serious or well-sustained, because the pianoforte of that day had not the "singing tone" necessary for properly rendering movements of this kind. For the same reason such movements can not be met with in the Mozart pianoforte sonatas. In these the ideas lack breadth and depth. In Mozart's string quartettes and symphonies, however, we find movements of this kind beautifully sustained, but not characterized by the depth we find in Beethoven. Such a movement is the Andante from the 5th Quintette. (Plays.) Another example is the Larghetto in D from the Clarinet concerts. ("Mozart Album," Ed. Peters, No. 1823, p. 36.)

Beethoven, however, is the great master of this type of composition. We find traces of it even in his earliest works, as in the *Adagio* of the first sonata, op. 2 in F minor. This movement was originally written by him when he was fifteen years old; it formed part of the first quartette for piano, violin, viola and 'cello. The quartettes were not published until after his death. The principal subject is extremely tender and fine. (Plays the entire movement.)

The *Largo appassionata* of the second sonata, op. 2 in A, is a still more notable example. The principal idea of this movement is extremely large, and full of feeling. The second idea, beginning with the last three notes of the eighth measure, is rather insignificant, and indeed is used merely as an interlude. The second subject, proper, begins with the last three notes of the nineteenth measure. The depth and seriousness of this movement are due to its slow pace, the long tones in the melody, and the low staccato notes in the bass, which give an impression of repressed passion.

The beautiful *Adagio grazioso* of the sonata in G, op. 31, No. 1, is perhaps a better example of a purely classical movement of this kind, since it has all the classic peculiarities in a high degree; such as repose, symmetry, moderation, purity, and an exquisite grace such as one may search through many volumes elsewhere without finding. (Plays.) This piece, as indeed the whole sonata, seems a purely classical work. It means absolutely nothing more than it says. It is a beautiful example of Beethoven's most cheerful work when he was at the very prime of his health and powers. Many other works of his mean more than they say and so belong to the romantic. This one is the full expression of its own idea, and for that very reason requires a certain maturity and refinement of taste to properly appreciate it.

A short movement in dance form, but in very much the same serious vein, is found in the Menuetto in E flat, out of the third sonata of this opus 31. (Plays.)

A very long but beautiful movement in similar spirit is furnished by the second part of the sonata in E, op. 90. This is one of the most refined and satisfactory cantabile pieces of Beethoven. It has in it an exquisite air of tenderness and nobility, like that of a refined and noble woman. (Plays.)

Yet another movement of the same kind is found in the *Tempo di Menuetto* of the sonata in G, op. 30, for piano and violin, one of the three great ones dedicated to the Emperor Alexander II. (Let this be heard if convenient.) Nor ought we to overlook the exquisite *Andante* and variations of the *Sonata appassionata*, op. 57, which are also characterized by the same repose and elevated beauty. (Plays.)

In all these movements the predominant impressions are of repose, and depth of soul. As Hegel says of Greek sculpture, "this is the unalterable permanence of the immortal gods."

LIST OF ILLUSTRATIONS.

1. **Largo** Cantabile from Haydn's 5th Symphony, in D, No. 5, in Wittmann's arr. for piano solo, Ed. Peters, No. 197.
2. Andante from Quintette, Mozart.
3. Adagio from Sonata in F, op. 2, No. 1, Beethoven.
4. Largo Appassionata from Sonata in A, op. 2, No. 2, Beethoven.
5. Adagio Grazioso from Sonata in G, op. 31, No. 1, Beethoven.
6. Menuetto from Sonata in C minor, op. 31, No. 3, Beethoven.
7. Tempo di Menuetto from Sonata in G, op. 30, Beethoven.
8. Andante and Variations from Sonata, op. 57, Beethoven.
9. Larghetto in D, from Clarinet Concerto, Mozart (p. 36 in "Mozart Album," No. 1823 Peters.)

LESSON TWENTY-EIGHTH.

THE CONTENTED, THE JOVIAL, THE COMFORTABLE, AS EX-PRESSED IN THE RONDO.

As to its form the rondo consists of a principal subject three or four times repeated, with second and third subjects intervening between these repetitions. As already appeared in the second part of this work, the rondo differs from the sonata-piece in having less thematic work, and less seriousness. The rondo is derived from the people's song, and represents a spirit of cheerfulness, of burgher-like satisfaction; a comfortable contentment in life which is too lively for repose, and too cheerful for work or striving. Thus, e. g., observe the following: (Plays Rondo in E flat from Beethoven's op. 7.)

In the very first idea we have this feeling of rather satisfied comfort, and the secondary matter only serves to bring this spirit out more plainly.

For another example take the rondo out of the little sonata in G, op. 14, No. 2. This is still more playful. (Plays.)

Even in the serious and deeply moved sonatas, the rondo is in a spirit which indicates that conflict has had its victory in happiness or something approaching it. (Plays rondo of sonata *pathetique*.)

One of the most interesting of the Beethoven rondos is the extremely bright and clever Rondo Capriccioso, op. 129, one of his very latest compositions. The theme of this might have been written by Haydn, it is so clear and sunny, but Haydn could never have indulged himself in the endless caprices of the elaboration. (Plays Rondo Capriccioso of Beethoven.)

If further examples are desired, let them be found in the two rondos of Beethoven, op. 51 in C and G, and Mendelssohn's well-known Rondo Capriccioso.

In several of the Beethoven sonatas we find in place of the rondo a movement called "Finale," which is in the same form as the sonata-piece except that a third subject (or middle-piece) takes the place of the Elaboration. An example of this is found in the first sonata in F, op. 2. In other instances the Finale is a sonata-piece, but conceived in

7

a lighter spirit. Such are found in the Sonata op. 10 in C minor, op. 31 No. 2 in D minor, op. 31 No. 3 in E flat, etc.

LESSON TWENTY-NINTH.

THE CYCLE OF THE SONATA.

The form of the sonata-piece and the composition to which it has given its name we have already considered in Lessons XV. and XVI. The emotional characteristics of its component parts have now been considered in detail. We are ready, therefore, to enter upon the study of the work as a whole. This cannot be done profitably otherwise than by repeatedly hearing an entire sonata until one knows it in its separate movements and parts, and again in the unity of the complete work so that one thinks of the different movements as chapters in the same life-history, or as successive and logically-related states of the same person. This unity of the sonata as a whole is one of the peculiar excellencies of Beethoven's works. We do not find the same comprehensive grasp on the part of any other composer in this form of composition.

The first movement represents the earnest and intellectually determined part of the work. The second, the reposeful and deep moments. The third, the out-come into healthful, every-day activity. If there are four movements, a playful moment intervenes between the second and third or the third and fourth, as a sort of interlude. The first movement, therefore, strikes the key-note of the whole work. If its subjects are trivial and scantily handled, no great depth of sentiment in the following part, the slow movement, can reasonably be expected. We already know that the different movements in the same sonata have no motives in common; they are not even in the same key. They are not composed at the same time. Generally we may conceive

of a sonata-piece as having first occurred to the composer merely as a
single motive, with certain dimly-perceived possibilities of elaboration.
Possibly a second motive, that of the lyric digression, was thought of at
the same time. Perhaps the entire Principal was written out immediately; by chance the Second also, though this is not common. The intervening passage work and the elaboration may have occupied the leisure
moments of several days. Thus after considerable delay the composer
is in possession of the entire first movement. It may be a week later
before he composes the slow movement, and a month before the sonata
is finished. Yet this does not go to deny the unity of the sonata as a
whole. For do not novelists write the most absorbing tales in precisely similar piecemeal way? These delays represent the time of meditation, during which the author decides what the natural out-come of
his characters shall be, taking into account all the circumstances of
their history as represented.

In some cases the motives of a work were thought of several years
before they were finally worked up. In Beethoven's "note-books"
(rude memorandum books of music paper, on which he wrote down at
the moment any good idea that struck him) we find the motives of
his symphonies sometimes for several years before the symphony was
composed. Some of these motives undergo remarkable changes before
they come into a form satisfactory to the great master. When the
sonata is done it is not always satisfactory. Thus, the well-known
"*Andante Favoris* in F" of Beethoven was written to go in the Waldstein sonata in C, op. 53. But on trial it did not suit him; perhaps
because of its length. So it was taken out and published separately,
and the short "Introduction" which now stands there, put in its place.
Yet it would be wrong to conclude from this that the association of
pieces in the sonata was a matter of experiment, instead of insight and
logical development. It is rather as if an author had concluded on reflection that in a certain chapter he had allowed an unsuitable weight
to certain tendencies in some one of his principal characters.

A few general traits of these sonatas we may easily observe. Thus,
if the first movement is vigorous and strongly marked, the ensuing
movements partake of the same decision. To take a very strong example, consider Sonata *Pathetique*. Here the Introduction (*Grave*)
opens very broadly and passionately. (Plays.) Then follows an equally
forcible Allegro which goes at an extremely rapid pace, and is strongly
accented and marked by wide transitions of power. (Plays.) The
Elaboration in this is equally forcible, and includes motives from the
Introduction as well as from the Allegro proper. (Plays.) Then after

the completion of this movement, there follows an Adagio of the most
deep and spiritual expression. (Plays.) On this follows a Rondo,
which manifests the habitual carelessness of the rondo, as through a
veil of tears. The third subject in it is perfectly dry and unemotional,
only to give place for an unusual and unprecedented recapitulation of
the principal subject of the rondo. It may be confessed that this rondo, fine as it is, sometimes seems inadequate to the sonata it concludes;
and yet Beethoven put it there, and the world generally accepts this as
one of his most satisfactory.

Again in the sonata in F, op. 2 No. 1, we have an extremely fortunate example of association. The Allegro is founded on one of
Friedmann Bach's. It has no properly developed lyric digression. The
Adagio is one of the loveliest, and as we know, taken out of a youthful
work. The Menuet is pretty, and the Finale charming and impetuous,
and saved from a flavor of the morbid only by the exquisite melody in
A flat (third subject).

It is unnecessary to multiply examples. To properly comprehend
the sonata in all its possibilities is to comprehend everything in instrumental music. All that can here be done to assist the student is to
suggest the unity of the sonata as a whole. More must come by study
and experience. It will be found a profitable experience in every way
to resume this study from time to time, using the four-hand arrangements of the symphonies of Haydn, Mozart and Beethoven. Some
one work is to be taken and each separate movement studied until it
becomes familiar; afterwards the entire symphony, and this, also, several times in succession. It is an excellent thing in a boarding school,
for example, when an eight-hand arrangement of one of these works is
undertaken; we have there immediately four pupils practically interested in one work. The length of time necessary to bring such a performance to a satisfactory state, suffices to thoroughly familiarize the
entire school with the motives and leading features of the work. In this
way very much genuine musical cultivation can be had in places where
orchestral music is never heard. For such a purpose a list is added,
below.

LIST OF ILLUSTRATIONS.

1. Sonata Pathetique, op. 13, Beethoven.
2. Sonata in F minor, op. 2, Beethoven.
3. Four-hand arrangement of Beethoven's Septette, op. 20.
4. Beethoven's 2d, 5th and 7th Symphonies, for four hands. (Peters' ed.)
5. Beethoven Sonatas for Piano and Violin, arranged for four hands. In particular Nos. 5 in F, 7 in C minor, and 8 in G.

LESSON THIRTIETH.

THE BEAUTIFUL IN CLASSIC MUSIC, AND THE TRANSITION TOWARD THE ROMANTIC.

As compared with sensational modern works, classical music seems cold, impassive. Much of this impression depends on one's musical habits of thought. A student who spends a large part of his practice on finger exercises and studies, will find almost any classical sonata musical and grateful to him; but one who idles away his prescribed "hours" on pleasing and capriciously chosen pieces, and never practices exercises or studies, will find a sonata tiresome—at least, until it is heard often enough for its real character to impress itself upon an inattentive player. Still it is by no means necessary for a student to avoid modern works in order to enjoy a sonata. It will be enough if he is willing to decide for himself that he prefers *music* as such, to the strained and forced or empty in expression.

When we take up a piece of Bach's. as, for example, the **first** movement of the Italian Concerto, it at first seems tame. When heard many times, however, a certain fluency and genuine melodiousness appear in it, which betray the touch of genius. (Plays.) The piece seems to our ears somewhat too long. This impression is not due to its absolute length, but to its want of contrast. If we take up a larger piece of Bach's, such as the **Passacaglia** in **C** min. (organ works arranged for four hands), we find in it a certain monotony, yet a decided progress toward a climax. The piece is a set of variations on a "ground bass," or *cantus fermus* which goes through all the variations unchanged. It ends with a splendid **fugue.** When we compare these variations with each other we observe that each is more complex than the preceding. (Plays theme and variations, remarking the commencement of each. Afterwards it would be well to examine the variations in detail, pointing out the motives of each. Then play the whole again.) In all this we have no new disposition or emotional contrasts represented, but only an unfolding of what was already possible in the theme. As the rose in full bloom displays no petals which were not enrolled in the bud, so these latest and most luxuriant blossoms give us nothing that was not already implied in the theme. Nevertheless it was only Aaron's rod that budded, and it is only a theme of such a man as Bach that blossoms out like this.

Here we come upon one o the characteristic moments of classical music. It is that in which music itself is trying its wings for itself. Nothing here seeks expression save only the musical ideas themselves, nay, the single idea of the theme, and its logical implications. In order to appreciate it, therefore, one needs to hear it many times, and especially to have within himself a really musical nature. All the greatest masters since Bach have admired, wondered at, and enjoyed these works of his, the greatness of which lies in the lengths they go as music, and their entire freedom from any thing like *emotional* effort. They are not without emotional expression; they could not be, with a rhythmic pulsation so thoroughly established and so long maintained, for the heart falls in with it and retards or accelerates in sympathy. Add to this the constantly augmenting energy of the motivization, and we have a certain amount of emotional expression in spite of the monotony of the harmonic foundation. Yet with all its energy and strength, and its climax, it remains in some way cold. It is like a wonderful statue in music.

Let us examine it in the light of our studies in the beautiful. Beginning on the lowest plane, we ask what has it for the pleasure of hearing? In answer it must be at once admitted that merely sensuous charm is not here sought. It sounds well; all its dissonances are properly prepared and resolved, and the finest of all harmonic instincts presided over the arrangement of its chord-sequences. Here, therefore, it yields only negative results. We ask again, what has it for satisfaction in contemplation? And in this direction it has much to say for itself. Each period is symmetrical and well concluded. The strictest unity prevails throughout. The work as a whole does not manifest symmetry, since it does not consist of two, three, or any number of sections or members standing over against each other. This element of form is wanting. The Passacaglia is merely the life-history of a single idea from its first simple form through its development to its return again into repose, the *Nirvana* of music. Yet this development itself is traced with such skill, each step follows so naturally on the preceding and the whole is managed without any overdoing or forceful effort, that in the unity and movement of the work we have one of the earliest forms in which the beautiful, as such, found expression in music. Nor is the work without a decided outlook in the direction of the higher perception and spiritual realization of beauty.

Perhaps this is shown in the persistence of the theme; and its final conflict and victory in the fugue. All that goes before is to interest us in the theme. We must not forget that in Bach's day, lovers of music generally were familiar with fugal phraseology and followed with readiness and interest all the vicissitudes of the subject as only musicians now do, so that intricacies of treatment which sound to us somewhat far-fetched and difficult, sounded to them natural and right. On the other hand, the extreme modulations common in modern works, and the brilliancy and comparative looseness of treatment in modern pieces, would have occasioned them a genuine shock of surprise and disapproval.

Again, let us observe the Andante from Mozart's fifth quintette for strings (No. 3 on the list below). It is in the form of a rondo. The principal subject is this. (Plays first subject, 16 measures.) The second subject is in E flat. (Plays.)

Now when we attentively consider the impression this work makes upon us, we immediately perceive that it manifests the elements of formal beauty in a much more complete degree than the Bach works just mentioned. Considered merely as music it is less serious than the Bach pieces. For this reason it bestows less attention upon developing a single subject. The world goes more easily here than there. Life has certain ameliorations. The episode comes not in the form of additional trouble for the theme, but in a complete digression from it, like a visit to a new world. (Plays entire movement again.) Such an introduction of a complete digression within a movement is very rare in Bach. Mozart's appreciation of its restfulness marks his deeper comprehension of the emotional nature of music. Examined with reference to its degree of beauty this piece does not manifest important difference from that of Bach. Thus in the merely well-sounding the Mozart Andante is stronger. It has more symmetry and sweetness; a more evident harmony and proportion of parts; the complete digression into another key relieves the ear. Still this last comparison is hardly fair, for the Passacaglia has its modulatory structure determined by its ground bass. On the other hand the Bach piece is very much more earnest and vigorous. The intellectual element preponderates in it. As already pointed out, it is a monologue, a discussion of a single theme carried out thoroughly in all its parts, with no regard for the hearer. The Mozart Andante, on the contrary, is distinctly lyric. It is a song. And so in all its parts it is simpler, more easily comprehended, more pleasing. Yet both pieces are so masterly in their way that neither can be accredited with a general superiority

over the other. The latter marks a progress in the direction of the
secular, and the softer and less divine sides of beauty.

Or take, again, the Beethoven "Moonlight" sonata. Its first
movement is also a monody on a single theme. (Plays the first strain
of melody of Adagio in sonata.) It is of the most plaintive character.
The same spirit pervades the entire movement. (Plays the entire
movement.) This sonata has always been regarded as a cry of the
heart. The beautiful as such, the symmetrical, reposeful, the well-pro-
portioned and sweet, are not here the objects of expression. But instead
of them we have the very heart of the composer; its sorrow, its grief,
its desire. (Plays again.)

This wonderfully sad movement is followed by a Scherzo which to
some extent relieves the tension. The afflicted mourner takes up again
the sympathies and associations of life; not with undisciplined buoyancy,
but with a sad and tender resignation. Is this all fancy? (Plays Allegretto.) On this, again, follows the Finale, which is in fact a regularly constructed sonata-piece with all its appurtenances. In this we
have the soul in its hours of solitude, when, no longer distracted by the
world about it, all the waves of its grief come over it. At times hope
springs up, but only to be immediately overwhelmed. (Plays the entire Finale.)

Thus in the whole sonata as well as the movements separately, we
have a life history, not of a single musical theme and its implications
(as in the Passacaglia), but a story of the human heart, a voice from
the soul. However fine we may find this sonata in point of construction, we do not listen to it for its music merely. It is distinctly a poem,
carrying a meaning which is not in any sensuous charm of pleasantly
chosen harmonies or agreeable sequences of melody, nor yet in any
formal beauty. Indeed, the beautiful, as such, is not the impression
this work leaves upon us, but its *expression*, its *sorrow*. In this, then,
we come upon the romantic moment of music, when art becomes the
expression of the joys and sorrows of the soul.

Yet another example. Let us take the Beethoven Sonata in E flat,
op. 31 No. 3. This belongs to the more pleasing moments of experience.
The Allegro opens with a motive that sounds like a question, an impression having its source partly in the motive itself but more in the
harmony which supports it. The entire movement is short and not
seriously intended. (Plays entire movement.) This is followed by a
Scherzo which has something song-like in it, although it is in the same
form as the preceding, a sonata-piece. (Plays.) This is followed
by a Menuetto, a genuine *cantabile* movement (one of the loveliest, by

the way), which is a simple binary form. (Plays.) This, again, is followed by the Finale, which also is a sonata-piece, perhaps the only example in the Beethoven sonatas where three of the forms of the same sonata are of this kind. This movement is extremely jolly and pretty. (Plays.) Listen now to the entire sonata. (Plays entire sonata.) Here, as you perceive, we have not a moment of grief or any deep sorrow, nor yet any great moral earnestness. But instead of it the musical, the symmetrical, the pleasing, the beautiful. If now we would be fully conscious of the musical distance we have passed over we should hear again the Bach Passacaglia. (If agreeable the Passacaglia may here be heard again.)

When we thus bring these two extremes, or at least widely separated points, of the musical scale into juxtaposition, we are able to realize that the beautiful itself is not the principal subject of the Bach piece; and that from Bach to Beethoven a great progress has been made in the direction of the lovely and the expressive.

Yet one more example. Let us observe carefully the Air and Variations in B flat by Schubert. (Plays Schubert's air from the Impromptu in B flat, op. 142. Then play the beginning of each variation, calling attention to the motivization of each, and afterward the entire piece.) In this lovely work we have something very different from any thing we find in the Passacaglia, or even in the Mozart Andante. Yet its prevailing expression is one of beauty and grace. A careful examination of it will indicate considerable attention to the well-sounding, a strict but purely unconscious observance of formal beauty, and beyond this a perceptible flavor of more inward and exquisite movement of spirit. Yet this without at all going into the depths of the soul. Like a pleasant sunset, one regards it with delight, but composure. As when the duties of the day are done, its pleasant experiences remembered, all its annoyances and cares forgotten, in peaceful contemplation one awaits the hour of sleep.

In all these examples we have had to do chiefly with formal beauty, save where the "Moonlight" sonata brought us to a still more inward exercise of spirit. The progress thus traced, from the strict musical logic and elevated formal beauty of Bach, through the pleasing and enchanting in Mozart, Beethoven and Schubert, and the deeply heartfelt in Beethoven's latest works, goes yet further in the romantic school, as we shall hereafter see. This same progress is traced from the vocal side in Part VII., on Songs, where new conditions lead to new and important results. The smaller classical composers, such as Clementi and Dussek, display in the main the same general character-

istics as we have observed in Beethoven, yet with less unity and imaginative power.   Indeed we must think of Dussek as an imitator, or
at least follower of Mozart, and as breaking no new paths.   Bach,
Haydn, Mozart and Beethoven comprehend everything that properly
belongs to the classic in music.

LIST OF ILLUSTRATIONS.

1. Allegro from Bach's Italian Concerto.
2. Passacaglia in C minor for the organ. Bach. (Arranged for 4 hands on the
    piano. Peters' Ed. No. 224.)
3. Andante from 5th Quintette, Mozart. (4 hands. Peters' Ed. No. 997.)
4. The "Moonlight" Sonata of Beethoven, op. 27 No. 2.
5. Sonata in E flat, op. 31 No. 3, Beethoven.
6. Impromptu in B flat, op. 142, Schubert.

PART SIXTH.

STUDIES IN THE ROMANTIC.

LESSON THIRTY-FIRST.

THE CHIVALROUS.

"The chief content of Chivalry," says Hegel, "may be expressed as *Honor*, *Love*, and *Fidelity*." The idea of chivalry carries with it the heroic, the tender, the graceful and considerate, and above all the noble and dignified, or, as Southerners say, "the high-toned." This phase of musical expression finds its most congenial expression in the works of Chopin, especially in the Polonaises. Yet the polonaise expresses these graces in many instances with a certain qualification. The Chopin polonaise not only .represents the phases of chivalry, but there runs through it the sad and almost morbid element of Polish character, as if the unfortunate history of this country had imparted a tinge of sadness even to its moments of victory. Of the polonaise in general, Liszt writes :

"While listening to some of the *polonaises* of Chopin, we can almost catch the firm, nay, the more than firm, the heavy, resolute tread of men bravely facing all the bitter injustice which the most cruel and relentless destiny can offer, with the manly pride of unblenching courage.

"The progress of the music suggests to our imagination such magnificent groups as were designed by Paul Veronese, robed in the rich costume of days long past; we see passing at intervals before us, brocades of gold, velvets, damasked satins, silvery, soft and flexible sables, hanging sleeves gracefully thrown back upon the shoulders, embossed sabres, boots yellow as gold or red with trampled blood, sashes with long and undulating fringes, close chemisettes, rustling trains, stomachers embroidered with pearls, head-dresses glittering with rubies or leafy with emeralds, light slippers rich with amber, gloves perfumed with the luxurious attar from the harems.

"From the faded background of times long past these vivid groups start forth; gorgeous carpets from Persia lie at their feet, filagreed furniture from Constantinople stands around; all is marked by the sumptuous prodigality of the magnates who drew, in ruby goblets embossed with medallions, wine from the fountains of Tokay, and shod their fleet Arabian steeds with silver ; who surmounted all their escutcheons with the same crown which the fate of an election might render a royal one, and which, causing them to despise all other titles, was alone worn as *insigne* of their glorious equality."

Thus in the Military Polonaise of Chopin, already heard several times in the course of these studies, we have the martial element strongly brought out. This runs through the whole piece. In form this polonaise is of the simple binary order. The second leading subject beginning:

Ex. 28.

is of the nature of a "trio." Yet in this, where if anywhere we would look for the expression of tenderness, the military ardor glows stil unquenched. After one strain of this we encounter a different spirit. What is it? (Plays the middle strain of trio beginning with the trill on C sharp in the bass.) This is in effect a salute. It is as if we had been witnessing a grand review. Here the general and his staff ride down the line, and we hear the salute of honor, the roll of musketry, the blare of the trumpets, and see the waving of the colors.

On the other hand let us examine a work in which there is much greater diversity of momentary expression, and consequently much less coherence.

Observe, now, the following: (Plays the first twelve measures of Polonaise in C sharp minor, op. 26.) Here the first four measures have the force of a full period; they start off splendidly, with the greatest determination and courage. In the next eight measures this courage still exists, it is true, but with it a vein of weakness becomes apparent. (Plays this phrase; and then repeats the entire period.)

At the twenty-fifth measure a new figure meets us, not referable to any warlike spirit as such. It more reminds one of Liszt's description of the complicated figures and constantly fresh inventions introduced into the Polish dance. (Plays seven measures.) At the tenth measure of this part the chivalrous spirit reappears. (Plays to the end of this part; i. e., to the signature of five flats.)

Here enters an entirely new spirit. Our valiant soldier has become entangled in the snares of love. Yet note how tender his devotion. With what subtle nobility of tenderness he breathes his love. (Plays sixteen measures of this part.) Here at the seventeenth measure a different spirit enters. It seems a conflict, a dialogue. Above we hear the woman's voice, gentle, persistent, tender; below the man's, more importunate, not so reserved and regular. The *denouement* each hearer may imagine for himself. When this little conflict is over we have again the gentle song of love which opened this part. And thus the piece ends. (Plays.)

Observe again the entire piece. (Plays the whole piece.) It consists, as you perceive, of two equal parts or pictures, different sides of the same nature. The first martial and ardent; the second tender and pleading. The work has no unity except in so far as the uniform rhythmic pulsation throughout the piece enables us to recognize, underneath all those moods, the beatings of the same hearts.

Here, again, and in order to study the polonaise from a different stand-point, observe the following: (Plays Polacca Brilliant in E, op. 72, Von Weber.) This, as you perceive, is a melodious and poetic piece, but it lacks the nameless grace and charm of the Chopin works, though to very many, and perhaps to all, there is something extremely pleasing in its freshness, which has nothing in it of a morbid character.

Again, observe this little polonaise of Schumann's: (Plays the polonaise in D, out of the papillons, op. 2.)

In order to understand this phase of music fully we need to examine three more works. The first is the Chopin polonaise in A flat, op. 53. This is in the grand style. Observe the Introduction. (Plays sixteen measures.) See how strong and resistless the impulse! Then enters the theme. (Plays from seventeenth measure to the end of this part, through forty-eighth measure.) Here at the forty-ninth measure there enters one of those capricious figures referred to by Liszt. Evidently it is of a grandiose and somewhat startling character; it is repeated with emphasis (represented by the transposition to a higher degree). At the fifty-seventh measure a grand and dignified melody begins, which presently brings us again to the theme. (Plays four measures and four measures; and then this melody; then the theme and so on through the Principal to the change of signature.)

Here at the change of key a new caprice presents itself. In the treble we have a very quiet melody; under it in the bass a monotonous octave figure repeated over and over many times, at first very softly, then by degrees louder. It expands and expands until it fills the whole field of observation; then it subsides only to mount up once more. (Plays through the passage containing bass running passage in octaves.) At the end of the octaves there enters a gentle figure in G major, afterwards transposed to A flat, and this, after some time, leads again to the principal, and so to the close. (Plays last part of piece.) Observe now the whole work. (Plays the entire polonaise.) This piece, in spite of a considerable degree of contrast between the various strains, is essentially of one spirit, and that of an extremely heroic, dignified, and noble character.

Another work of this class and remarkable for still greater contrasts, though, as a whole pervaded by a more refined (and possibly effeminate) spirit, is the Chopin polonaise in E flat, op. 22. This work is preceded by a charming *Andante Spianato*, which belongs to the tender side of emotion. The polonaise enters thus: (Plays.) In the sixtieth measure of the polonaise proper (not counting the orchestral *tutti* intervening between the andante and the polonaise) a series of strong contrasts begins. Here we have two lines of extremely bold octaves in both hands. (Plays.) In the sixty-seventh measure a soft and delicate melody enters, concluding with some delicate cadencing, in the sixty-ninth, etc. (Plays.) In the seventy-third measure a bold and fiery passage bursts in, closing with an octave passage. (Plays.) In the eighty-third measure a lovely melody in C minor begins. (Plays.) But enough. Suffice it to say that in this piece we have almost every phase of the Chopin nature represented, and it is rightly counted for one of his most exquisite works.

Still another and more sensational work of this school is Liszt's Polonaise in E. This great work (one of the best of Liszt's) contains very few of the refinements we have seen so abundant in the work last considered. Nay, it is even less so than the heroic polonaise in A flat. Yet it is a concert-piece of the same general type, and as such deserves to be carefully heard. The finest work in it is in the Cadenza. (Plays.)

LIST OF ILLUSTRATIONS.

1. Chopin's Polonaise Militaire, op. 40, No. 1.
2. Chopin's Polonaise in C sharp minor, op. 26, No. 1.
3. Polacca Brilliante in E, Weber, op. 72.
4. Schumann's Polonaise in D (out of Papillons, op. 2).
5. Chopin Polonaise in A flat, op. 53.
6. Chopin's Andante and Polonaise in E flat, op. 22.
7. Liszt's Polonaise Heroique in E.

LESSON THIRTY-SECOND.

THE GENTLE AND SENTIMENTAL; THE DEEPLY TENDER

The earliest consistent examples of this kind of spirit worked out in pianoforte music in simple forms, are to be found in some of the Haydn adagios and andantes, and the Field nocturnes, the latter most particularly. Field very probably derived more or less suggestion from the slow movements in Beethoven sonatas, all of which, as far as the "Waldstein" appassionata and "Kreutzer" sonatas, were published before the Field nocturnes. In many of the earlier sonatas of Beethoven we find short passages in the genuine nocturne vein; as, *e. g.*, in the Adagio of sonata pathetique, the Menuet in the sonata in E flat, op. 31, etc. To Field, however, is due the credit of having established the form of the nocturne as an independent piece for piano, in a tender, elegiac vein, and, both in point of difficulty and emotional range, keeping it within the resources of amateurs generally. Here, *e. g.*, is such a piece. (Plays Field's nocturne in B flat.) This piece, like all of Field's, is characterized by an extremely clear and limpid style, and a truly refined and delicate spirit.

Field was not insensible to the advantages of contrast, as we see in the following, where the second subject makes an admirable contrast with the first. (Plays Field's nocturne in D, No. 13.)

Mendelssohn, however, is the magician who first made known to amateurs generally the latent singing powers of the pianoforte. This he did in his famous works, the "Songs Without Words." No doubt the fortunate selection of title had much to do with their immediate popularity, which was very great, and has in fact continued ever since.

The first book of these beautiful works was published in 1829 and contained six pieces, in which the Mendelssohnian spirit is unmistakable. In the first we have a tender melody and a gentle and well-blended accompaniment, which, when well played, is truly charming. (Plays.) In the second we have a vein of sadness or melancholy, as well as the usual tenderness. (Plays.) The third is the well-known "Hunting Song," which may well enough be heard here for the sake of the contrast. (Plays No. 3.) No. 6 is a Venetian *Gondellied* in which one plainly hears the melancholy and passion of a decayed and fading race. (Plays.) Whatever meaning we may be led by their fanciful titles to attach to these pieces, they all speak unmistakably the voice of tenderness and sadness. Whenever we are in any similar mood these pieces chime in with our feelings, and utter the very tones we would ourselves have originated. This is the quality of popularity: to seem to say what every reader would himself have said (if only he had thought to do it). And this quality the Mendelssohn songs possess in the most eminent degree. Another example of the same spirit we have in the lovely Duetto in A flat, No. 18, which may be heard again if desired. (Let it be played if it is not clearly remembered from former citations.)

Chopin took up the nocturne form as Field left it, and imparted to it a greater depth and range of meaning. One of the simplest types of his is the second one, the lovely nocturne in E flat, op. 9, No. 2. This consists of a gentle melody and a delicate accompaniment of chords. It is extremely unpretending, yet it is one of the most perfect gems in this department of composition. (Plays.)

Here, in the 4th nocturne, he avails himself of a stronger contrast. (Plays nocturne in F, op. 15, No. 1.)

Another of the singing nocturnes of Chopin is that in B maj., op. 32, No. 1. (Plays.)

In the 13th nocturne there is a deeper meaning. It tells of greater depths of passion, and has stronger contrasts than those already heard. (Plays the nocturne in C minor, op. 48, No. 1.)

Two of the most admired of these works are those in G, op. 37. No. 1 in G minor is an elegy full of sadness and longing. It is relieved by an episode of pure uninverted triads, like a church piece. In this we have portrayed a deep and spiritual peace. (Plays.)

The second one, in G maj., is of a much more genial and cheerful character, delicate and tender. Owing to the preponderance of thirds and sixths it is extremely difficult to play well. (Plays.)

List of Illustrations.

LESSON THIRTY-THIRD.

THE HUMORISTIC AND THE PASSIONATE.

By the name Humor the Germans denote caprices, whims, moods, change; and not the ludicrous, as in later English usage. There is one side of the modern romantic school which can be appropriately named by no other term than humoristic. This is nearly the same as whimsical, the difference being that the latter term has acquired an objectionable meaning, like the "foolishly humoristic" or the "unreasonably humoristic." This element of musical expression frequently exceeds the bounds of beauty, and is indeed allied to realism, since *realism* in music is in fact nothing but musical expression made subservient to a strictly literal representation of natural sounds or common-place sensations. Humor in music frequently approaches the grotesque. The great exponent of this school is Schumann, whose fancy ran wild in every direction, and only in exceptional cases controlled itself according to the moderate and decorous.

Here, for example, are three little pieces from the Kinderscenen (Plays successively, "From Strange Lands," "A Curious Story," and "Playing Tag," the first three pieces in the "Scenes from Childhood.") These little pieces, as you observe, are entirely unlike each other, and each one is complete in itself. The first a graceful little melody. The second a bright and rather sprightly and forcible little piece in march time. The third a sort of presto with very strong accents. It would be a very superior sort of clairvoyance in any one who should be able to guess the names of these pieces from hearing them played. Yet the names give a very decided assistance toward divining the author's meaning. Observe now the following: (Plays No. 5, "Happy Enough," No. 7, "Traumerei," and "Frightening," No. 11.) Among larger pieces of the humoristic type are to be mentioned the Schumann Phantasiestücke, op. 12. It is of the first of these that Franz Brendel remarks: "It brings us blessed enjoyment, vernal airs, and flowery savors." (Plays "In the Evening.") This dreamy nocturne is followed by a powerfully excited piece called "*Aufschwung*," "Soaring," a name intended to convey the idea of such a mental state as one falls into in

8

wakeful hours of night, especially after taking too strong tea, or a light opiate. Then the brain is preternaturally active, nothing seems impossible; the most brilliant conceptions throng the mind, one visits strange lands, rises into unknown regions, solves impossible problems. The sober light of day dissolves all these visions, but while they last they carry the bewildered visionary captive at their will. Such a piece is this: (Plays "Soaring.") Then follows a sort of musical conundrum, "Warum," "Why." It consists of a single motive many times slowly repeated, accompanied by a restless accompaniment of chords entering on the half-beat. (Plays Warum.) Then follows yet a different strain, called "Whims," of which we need no further explanation than the title. (Plays Grillen.)

In all these pieces we plainly see that the beautiful, as such, is not sought by the composer. They afford neither the sensuous charm of delicately-balanced phrases, sweetly-modulating chords, or any other mere gratification of a love for the well-sounding. Quite as little do they afford satisfaction in contemplation. Formal beauty they do not possess. Their distinctive merits are two: First, their coherence as music. Here comes along a new composer, Schumann, a hundred years later than Bach, and develops musical ideas in ways that are musically right and proper, and yet new. And, second, these humoristic pieces carry us along with them, move us, excite us, as the Bach pieces do not. You may pronounce them unbeautiful if you please, but they are musically right and genuinely expressive.

There is also a darker side of the picture. Observe now this: (Plays Schumann's "In the Night.") It is of this piece that Franz Brendel says: "It is a powerful night-piece, hobgoblin-filled, awful pictures, anxious waking-dreams; a state of soul the opposite of the 'Evening' formerly mentioned." This vein is not uncommon in Schumann, especially in his later years. It also appears in Chopin as the first part of the first movement of the sonata in B flat minor, op. 35, and in many other places. So also many of the Beethoven pieces must have sounded in this vein when they were new, before the listener's ears had become accustomed to the rapid modulations of these pieces and their restlessness. This spirit is also to be met with in Bach, as in the great organ prelude in A minor, and in many other pieces. This prelude, for example, seems to aim at representing a tossed and troubled spirit, like the waves of the sea. Neither the tuneful as such, nor still less the reposeful, could have been intended. They cannot be called beautiful since they are neither pleasing to hear, satisfactory to continually meditate upon, nor inspiring except as they widen the range of musical expression and serve for contrast, thereby heightening the beauty of other movements with which they are associated. This use, however, was not intended either by Bach or Schumann. The former wrote them for the purpose of expressing himself in this direction, which he saw to be legitimate and possible; Schumann, to satisfy his musical instincts in the same way, and also to gratify morbid moods.

LIST OF ILLUSTRATIONS.

1. Schumann's Kinderscenen (Scenes from Childhood) op. 15. Nos 1, 2, 3, 5, 7, 11.
2. Schumann's "In the Evening," No. 1 in op. 12.
3. *Aufschwung*, or "Soaring," No. 2 in the same.
4. *Warum*, "Why?" the same.
5. *Grillen*, "Whims," from the same.
6. "In the Night," No. 5 in the same.
7. First part of Allegro in Chopin Sonata, op. 35.
8. Great Organ Prelude in A minor. (Vol. II. Bach's Organ Works, Peters' Ed.)

LESSON THIRTY-FOURTH.

THE FANCIFUL AND PLEASING.

Pieces of this class represent the lighter sentiments of social life, especially of polite society. We find in them symmetrical and graceful forms, permeated by a bright and pleasing spirit. They are refined and true, but they do not express the heroic or despairing moments of the soul. In consequence of their representing so completely the spirit of social life, they are eminently suitable for parlor performance. Observe this elegant waltz. (Plays Chopin's waltz in A flat, op. 34, No. 1.) This is the very spirit of the world and of society. Another example of the same kind is Rubinstein's Valse Caprice in E flat. (Plays.) Still another, and a famous one, too, is Weber's " Invitation to the Dance." (Plays.) This latter is more perfectly idealized than either of the preceding. The introduction is moderate and meditative, as if undecided whether to dance or not. Fanciful people have imagined that they saw in it the advance of the gentleman and his address to the lady, her acceptance, their quiet and fragmentary talk in the moment before the dance actually begins. Then the dance itself. At the close he re-conducts the lady gracefully to her seat, in the figure of the introduction.

Another example of similar spirit is the elegant Chopin Rondo in E flat, op. 16, which, though long and difficult, is conceived in the spirit of play, and represents the light and worldly side of feeling, yet with true refinement and earnestness. (Plays.) Were we to go further in this field we might bring forward the elegant Scherzo in B flat minor, op. 31, a very beautiful and poetic piece, which contains, perhaps, rather more of meaning than this list properly includes.

This field is practically illimitable. It includes all the lighter works of the greatest composers, except Schumann, who has left nothing properly belonging to it, and almost the entire production of very many smaller writers, such as Schulhoff, Jaell, Hunten, Leybach, Gottschalk, etc., etc.

Pieces of this class should be elegantly written and agreeably sounding. In the nature of the case they are perfectly easy to understand, for which reason we do not dwell upon them, but content ourselves with simply calling attention to them.

LIST OF ILLUSTRATIONS.

1. Chopin's Valse in A flat, op. 34, No. 2.
2. Rubinstein's Valse Caprice in E flat.
3. Weber's Invitation to the Dance.
4. Chopin's Introduction and Rondo in E flat, op. 16.
5. Chopin's Scherzo in B flat minor, op. 31.
6. Mill's 1st Tarantelle.
7. Raff's Valse Impromptu in B flat, op. 94.

LESSON THIRTY - FIFTH.

THE SENSATIONAL AND THE ASTONISHING.

In ordinary English usage, the term Romantic implies something "striking," "characterized by strong contrasts," "sensational," etc. Our studies thus far in this school of music are sufficient to show us the propriety of its name. In the previous lessons we have, indeed, come upon only the more reasonable and justifiable features of the romantic, in which the beautiful in some sense is the supreme object. Recent music, however, and particularly pianoforte music, contains many productions in which the sensational and the astonishing are the ends sought. Of this kind are concert pieces in general, especially the earlier works of Liszt, and most of the productions of other virtuoso players. Such, also, are very many orchestral works, especially some of Berlioz, Saint-Saens, Wagner's "Ride of the Valkyrie," etc.

In making the sensational their object, all of these exceed the bounds of the beautiful, and are of real use in art only in so far as they break new paths of technical accomplishment, and thereby provide means of expression which may afterwards be employed in artistic creation. In this way all great *virtuosi* have illustrated the capacity of their instruments, and in their works have provided useful studies for the mastery of peculiar difficulties. Of this kind, for example, are the Caprices of Paganini, which, while containing many musical and beautiful passages, are in general rather extravagant, and almost entirely wanting in symmetry and repose. They resemble tropical vegetation where in a humid soil and a dank atmosphere the most extravagant and fantastic growths are seen, luxuriant and beautiful in abounding vitality, yet oppressive to the senses.

In all these productions, moreover, there is a certain charm which recommends them to the player. It is not unlike what Ruskin calls "vital beauty, or the appearance of felicitous fulfillment of function in living creatures;" in other words, their remarkable adaptation to the instrument for which they were composed. The study of them has particular value in affording a free and dashing mode of playing.

The sensational in piano music dates from the discovery of the diminished seventh and its chromatic susceptibility. Thus in many of the earlier Liszt pieces there are passages which are neither pretty nor expressive, but which are merely *noise*. This kind we have illustrated in the "Lucia," for instance, and in the Rigoletto chromatic cadenza, described in Lesson XIX.

Another example is found in the cadenza near the close in Raff's Polka de la Reine. (Plays cadenza of diminished sevenths in the bass, and the ascending passages belonging to them; afterwards the entire piece.)

Of this kind are the cadenzas in the Chopin concerto, referred to in Lesson XIX. (Play if convenient.) In the Liszt concerto in E flat, we have many examples of this kind of work, put together much more loosely. (Play, if convenient.)

It cannot be denied that there is something satisfactory in the way in which these effects are planned. Thus in Liszt's "Rigoletto" fantasia we have opening passages which although brilliant and pleasing are not very difficult. Then follows the pretty melody, and, after the striking sequence of chromatic modulations, the cadenza already described comes in. The work then resumes the melody *pianissimo*, with very delicate and pretty runs, rising occasionally to *fortissimo*. Still the general build of these three pages is the *pianissimo*. At the close of this part there is a cadenza which is of extremely simple construction, but when well done is even more showy than that at the end of the first part. This, in turn, is followed by the octave finale, at first softly, but at the close working up to a brilliant and astonishing effect. The success of the piece lies in the care with which the brilliant passages are preceded with those of a soft and pleasing character, and this must be observed by the performer who expects to make a success with it.

This reserve—these long passages of really musical writing leading to astonishing and sensational passages, are the saving elements in *bravoura* pieces. The Liszt concerto is an extremely fragmentary work. It is written on a plan, and very cleverly too; but its primary elements are few, and it entirely lacks the artistic coherence and repose of such work as that in Chopin's concerto in E minor or in F minor. All of the Liszt *bravoura* pieces are written on the same plan, the climaxes being of occasional occurrence and carefully foreseen. Thus the well-known "Tannhauser March" opens brilliantly with the trumpet call, but presently subsides into a very reasonable and agreeably sustained presentation of the chorus. Gradually, however, the movement becomes more and more elaborate, and at last reaches an imposing effect.

All this modern virtuoso *bravoura* rests upon the idea of astonishing by mere sensation, and therein stands upon a lower plane than the cadenza formations of the older musicians. Bach, Handel, Beethoven and Mendelssohn, all were great performers who could entertain the most cultivated audiences by their masterly improvisations. But in their cadenzas they made their effect by the musicianship with which they elaborated and handled their themes, and not with any merely vulgar scrambling about the keyboard in apparently impossible passages.

Nevertheless the ways of Nature are not so crude after all; for every creature has its natural enemy which acts as a check upon its undue multiplication. So here, this sensationalism finally reaches bounds. Such a passage of sevenths as that of Raff's, already referred to, is the limit. This is mere noise, and just as bad and astonishing as any other hideous succession of chords played fortissimo on the bass of the pianoforte. So, also, Liszt in one piece and another covered the possibilities of radically different passages which would at the same time be playable, and therein effective. Hence in the later period of his creative activity he gave over the piano as a *bravoura* instrument, and applied his powers to the reproduction of pieces of every kind upon it, which had hitherto been supposed impossible. And in these, although a great technique and abounding courage are presupposed for the player, the emphasis is put on musical declamation and the imitation of orchestral effects, or at least their substitution by pianoforte equivalents (as in engraving such and such lines represent one color, and such and such another, though all in the engraving are in black and white). In this, while he by no means rises into the plane of original creation, he certainly entitles himself to respect by employing his powers for worthy uses. Three remarkable examples of this kind are afforded by Liszt's transcriptions of the Wagner "Spinnlied," "Isolde's Liebes Tod," and "Lohengrin's Verweis an Elsa." Another fine example is in Bülow's excessively difficult transcription of Wagner's "Faust Overture." These observations hold true of other virtuoso work since Liszt, such as the concert pieces of Tausig, Saint-Saens, etc.

It should be said of these experiments in the sensational that, like most of the prominent features of the romantic school, they have found their inciting cause in poetry, or the effort to represent by means of music something which, properly speaking, is neither in music nor in any strict and proper sense representable by it. This has already been suggested in the lesson on descriptive music, and comes more plainly in review in the next following discussion of Songs.

LIST OF ILLUSTRATIONS.

1. Liszt's "Rigoletto."
2. Raff's "Polka de le Reine.'
3. Chopin Concerto in E minor, op. 11.
4. Liszt's Concerto in E flat.
5. Liszt's "Tannhauser March."

PART SEVENTH.

STUDIES IN SONG.

.

LESSON THIRTY-SIX.

THE INFLUENCE OF POETRY UPON MUSIC.

Modern music owes its development to the co-working of three in-fluences. The first of these is the better comprehension of the nature of music itself; the true relations of tonality, harmonic progressions, melody, and form to each other; and the logical methods of handling musical ideas merely as music, and aside from a definitely chosen emotional content seeking expression through them. The second operative force is the general progress in art conception, and especially the overmastering desire of the Romantic for a natural and valid means of expressing *feeling*, merely as such, and uncolored with conscious thought. The third of these forces is the influence of poetry upon music, and especially of the desire to express, by means of music, ideas not properly belonging to it, but suggested to it by poetry.

These three have operated simultaneously throughout the history of music. Yet it may be truly said that the first of them came soonest to expression; and this very naturally. For in the earliest times, when the development of music began, its relation to the other arts was not understood; indeed the meaning of art in general has only lately begun to be fathomed. So the musician worked by himself as a musician, seeking to comprehend the mysteries of this new form of art, and to reproduce his thoughts in it. Outside influences were not wanting here, particularly that of the church. On the whole, as already suggested in Chapter XXIII, the influence of religion has been of the highest advantage to art by raising and purifying its ideal. But Religion is one thing, and the Church sometimes another. And so while Religion has always performed this service to art, and has further extended her

120

inspiration to music in particular, in the form of sublime hymns and canticles which become truly complete in the liturgy only when music's voice has modulated and shaped the hallowed utterance, the influence of the Church has sometimes tended in the direction of mere conventionality. They have it for a proverb in Germany, that when a composer has written all his original ideas, he can then compose only church music. And so the truly original musicians in every generation have developed and matured their talents in purely secular fields, and only in old age have brought a single wreath (often of flowers how precious! and gathered in fields, how far away!) and laid it with palsied but reverent hand upon the altar. So did Bach in his Passion Music and his one Mass; so also did Handel with his immortal "Messiah," a work in which we hear not the feeble and uncertain accents of age, but the sweet songs of hope and trust, as if the old composer had tasted before time the fountain of eternal youth, or that, like the servant of the prophet, his eyes had been opened so that he saw the mountains full of the chariots of the Lord. So was it with Mozart in his Requiem; and Beethoven with his colossal Mass in D minor. But as a rule, all the composers, who gave coherence and shape to music, arrived at their results by working in purely secular fields, where the swift-coming fancies might all find legitimate utterance. In particular the composers who wrote music, as music merely, were Bach, Haydn, and Beethoven; and, since them, Schumann and Chopin, though the latter is rather to be counted for a worker in one particular province of music, the pianoforte, than in the whole field of absolute and independent music.

The influence of the second of these operative forces has been silent and unconscious, as indeed, inspiration generally is. There has never been an authoritative declaration of the meaning of art, least of all by artists. Each man has builded, moulded, painted, sung or prophesied as the inner force impelled him. His life has gone into his works. When death overtook him he dropped his workman's tools, and sank unconscious into the bosom of mother earth. Sometimes, his very friends have not taken the trouble to count and reckon up his effects, and only the tardy justice of posterity has been able to gather up the precious tokens and place them in the pantheon of art. So was it with Bach, and Schubert; and so almost with Schumann and Berlioz.

Yet in one way this force has operated upon musical development, and that in great power; namely, in the extinction of other forms of art, leaving almost the whole ideality of several generations to seek expression through music. This comes out plainly enough in the dates. Michael Angelo and Raphael were nearly two hundred years before Bach and Handel. Dante was two centuries earlier still. Shakespeare was a hundred years earlier than Bach. Thus Bach, Handel and Beethoven had the stage to themselves for a century, during which there was no absolutely great master in any other form of art. In this way the world gained leisure to attend to music ; and so it has been since, for during the last century there has never been a genius of the highest order outside of music. Thus, what music could do, as music, we must learn for the most part in the works of Bach, Haydn, Mozart, Beethoven, and Schumann. And in the very same works, also, we must measure its value as a form of art and an expression of the ideal. And this has been our labor in these studies hitherto. We now come to the point where we must enter upon the historical and practical study of the relation of music to poetry, and of the manner and extent of the action of poetry upon it. The subject is a very large one, and for full handling takes us over wide lapses of time and a considerable range of topics. In general, however, we shall obtain a fair idea of the course of this development if we attend carefully to the observations following.

In the union of poetry and music, both sides have to make important concessions. These are of so serious and so vital a character that, speaking in a broad sense, we might say that both poetry and music must needs sacrifice their most eminent qualities, as poetry and music respectively, in order to successfully unite themselves in the complex utterance of song. We are already, to some extent, prepared to understand this, by our studies in Chapter XXV. For, as we there saw, the distinctive excellencies of Poetry are its sense-pictures, and its power of awakening emotion by contrasts and collisions of persons, respectively living and acting out the opposing principles between which the collision takes place. The highest poetry, while always in sense-forms, is peculiarly and pre-eminently intensified by thought.

The first and perhaps chief difficulty Poetry has to contend with in uniting with music, is the long time consumed by musical utterance, a time from two to six times greater than speech,—and, it may be added, constantly increasing in the later composers, as we see, for example, in Max Bruch's Lay of the Bell, etc. Almost any poetical picture or scene runs through four lines, and sometimes through ten or twenty, but as all these lines do something towards completing the picture, they must all be retained in the mind at the same time. Ordi-

-ary reading passes so quickly as to permit the mind to do this without difficulty. But when this time is spun out too long, and especially when the unity of the description has been destroyed by the inception and completion of several musical periods to one period of words, the pictorial quality of the poetry is lost in the song. In like manner, the very form of musical utterance is fatal to the intelligible expression of any kind of reasoning, or deduction of conclusions from premises. Not even Beethoven would be able to set to music successfully such a passage as Portia's Plea for Mercy, in "The Merchant of Venice." Music, as we well know, is the expression of *feeling;* when poetry becomes directly expressive of emotion it becomes musical—provided only that its feeling is not outside of or contrary to music. Thus when hate, revenge, or remorse are the feelings seeking expression in the words, music can do nothing to aid them, for they are in their essence contrary to music, and if at all representable in sounds, representable only in harsh and hideous discords. Yet even this range must not be denied the opera; we can only limit its recourse to such extravagant measures, to its moments of brief and insuperable necessity, to be atoned for by many a bar of tuneful penance. Hence we may say in general that, in order to adapt itself to musical expression, Poetry must forego its reason, its long-spun descriptive passages, and, to a certain extent, its coherence. Its pictures must become mere outlines, such as a couple of phrases will compass; its thought sharp, incisive, terse, and never of an abstract character. And it is only when it speaks directly the language of the heart, that musical utterance becomes indispensable to its completeness. A true lyric requires music to fully express it. Of such sort are all true hymns, such as the "Gloria," the "Te Deum," the "Venite," "Jubilate." These without the voice of song are but birds or angels without wings.

On the other hand, Music has much to lose in a direct union with poetry. She, also, must part with her coherence in long forms. Such closely knit and legitimately developed musical creations as the great organ fugues of Bach, and the sonatas or symphonies of Beethoven are entirely foreign to the spirit of song. Here first music has to consider the compass and pitch of the voice, and its effectiveness in different registers. One recalls here the remark of the teacher, himself a distinguished composer, who, when a pupil brought him an anthem in which the tenor had the words "Praise the Lord" on G below middle C, crossed out the passage with the remark, "The tenor *can not* ' praise the Lord' below middle C," alluding, of course, to the non-effectiveness of the tenor voice at so low a pitch. So, also, music

must provide the singer with opportunities for breathing, and inter-
ludes for rest after trying passages. She must not forget to
confine herself within a practicable range of keys, for singers sing on
melodic principles, and no singer sings or thinks a full score. These,
with many other such like restrictions, inhere in the very nature of song,
and hamper the musical composer extremely. The old proverb says
that "necessity is the mother of invention"; so here the necessity of
finding compromises or mutual concessions between music and poetry
has at length led to several well defined types of song, which differ
from each other in the manner and nature of the concessions made.
These are (1) Simple Ballad, (2) The Recitative, (3) The Aria and
Scena, (4) The German Thoroughly Composed Song, (5) The Arioso,
and (6) the union of them all in The Oratorio and Opera.

In all these modes of union there are, however, certain principles that remain constant and must not be violated. These are the
correct accentuation and emphasis of the words, according to the sense,
and the correspondence of the music to the poetry in respect to feeling. All forms of song must observe these conditions. To this extent,
at least, poetry is dominant. Besides, the musical phrasing must be
made to correspond with the grammatical and declamatory necessities
of the text, and this in all forms of vocal pieces. Besides these, there
are important variations in style, resulting from the greater or less attention paid to the convenience of the voice. Thus Italian songs, in
general, are carefully planned so as to suit the voice, and to require effect only at ranges of pitch in which effect is possible. Moreover, this
entire school indulges itself less with chromatic and difficult modulations, and in general is much less elaborate, as music merely, than the
German songs. The Italians consider the *voice* the main thing in
singing; the Germans the *idea*. In thus ranging themselves under
opposite principles, both parties fall short of their goal. The German
ruins his song for actual delivery, by placing it badly for the voice.
This appears continually in Bach, and Schumann, and frequently in
other writers. The Italian's method of work, on the other hand, produces a composition in which the voice makes an agreeable effect; so
that these works are cherished all the world over, as the most convenient show-pieces for singers. Nevertheless he works within so narrow
musical limits as seriously to impair the value of his pieces from the
musical side. And in general it is not too much to say that even the
best Italian music sounds thin and unsatisfactory when compared with
the best German music; while the common run of Italian work is thin
indeed.

Yet, after all, the Italian certainly has the advantage in the matter of taste, and we find in the productions of such writers as Rossini, Bellini, Donizetti and Mercadante, as well as in the simple *canteleni* of less noted composers, a grace and elegance of style which, since Glück and Mozart, is no longer to be found in German song.

LESSON THIRTY-SEVENTH.

THE SIMPLE BALLAD.

The nearest example of the union of poetry and music is afforded by the simple ballad. Musically considered it consists of a symmetrically balanced and pleasing melody, of a quiet character, with words easily enjoyed by the common people. In this form of composition the melody is of the foremost importance, and in very many cases was first composed, and the words afterwards written to fit. As a rule, both words and music are pleasing, quiet, popular, and but a shade removed from the commonplace. Examples of this class are practically innumerable. We may begin with almost any specimen. Let it be Dr. Geo. F. Root's "Brooklet," from the "Curriculum." (Plays and sings.) Another example is "Joys that we've tasted," adapted to an Irish melody. (Plays and sings.) Other examples are the two by Mr. Root so popular many years ago, "The Hazel Dell" and "Rosalie, the Prairie Flower." (Sings "Hazel Dell.") This class also includes many songs of a sad and mournful temperament (as well as many sadly poor ones), such as "Pass Under the Rod," Mr. Root's "Vacant Chair," Miss Linsay's "Resignation," etc.

Of the same kind is Claribel's "O many a time I am sad at heart." (Sings.) The life of this song is mainly in its words. This was not so much the case in the earlier American songs of the same class, as is shown by the continual popularity of the music in cotillons, quadrilles, etc., after the words have been forgotten. This was also the case with Mr. Stephen C. Foster's "Uncle Ned" and "Massa's in the Cold, Cold Ground," "Old Folks at Home," etc. In all of these the distinguishing feature was the agreeable and easily-remembered melody. Another example, depending partly on its words and partly on its music for a deserved popularity is Claribel's "Five o'clock in the Morning." (Sings.) In this the music takes a wider range of harmonies than in any of the American examples referred to. In Claribel's "Come Back to Erin" we have a still more unmistakable example of a purely musical interest and that mainly in the melody. This melody has been sung and played, varied and arranged, all over the English-speaking world. (Sings.)

The apparent depth and meaning of these songs are very much increased when the words are deliberately and clearly spoken, and the melody delivered with artistic emphasis. An example of this was afforded by Nillsen's singing of "Old Folks at Home" in her American concerts, and in the practice of the popular singers in London, as well as Mme. Parepa-Rosa's "Five o'clock in the Morning," etc. Such a delivery would lend dignity and worth to any air, however empty. It is the result of thorough control of the voice and extended experience in the delivery of every kind of song.

LIST OF ILLUSTRATIONS.

1. The Brooklet, by Dr. Geo. F. Root, " Curriculum.
2. Joys that We've Tasted.
3. Hazel Dell. Dr. Geo. F. Root.
4. Pass under the Rod.
5. The Vacant Chair. Root.
6. Resignation. Miss Linsay.
7. O Many a Time I am Sad at Heart. Claribel.
8. Five o'Clock in the Morning. Claribel.
9. Come Back to Erin. Claribel.

LESSON THIRTY-EIGHTH.

RECITATIVE.

Our second type of song is one in which, clearly, the text receives primary consideration. By Recitative is meant a form of song to which the text is set to musical pitch and cadence, but not to a definite speed, rhythm, or in lyrically-adjusted phrases. In this form of song it is the sole task of the music to afford an impressive and suitable delivery of the words. In plain recitative the accompaniment consists only of simple chords. Of all writers, Handel was at times particularly fortunate in his recitatives, and nowhere more so than in the "Messiah." Observe the dignity of the following: (Plays and sings the recitative "Behold a virgin shall conceive," from "Messiah.") And this: (Plays and sings "Then shall the eyes of the blind be opened," also from the "Messiah.")

This form of song admits of great pathos. Handel affords a great example in the tenor recitative "Thy rebuke hath broken his heart." (Sings it.) In this the melodic cadences are extremely clever, and will be the subject of remark presently. Measured recitative differs from the plain, in having a measured accompaniment, and hence in requiring of the voice at least an approximate adherance to the measure. In one instance Handel has contrasted these two methods with fine effect. Thus in the "Messiah" we find the plain recitative "There were shepherds abiding in the field." This is followed by a measured recitative to the words "And lo! the angel of the Lord came upon them." And this, again, by the plain recitative "And the angel said unto them." And this, again, by the measured recitative "And suddenly there was with the angel." (Sings the two measured recitatives first, and afterward the four in succession.) One of the most beautiful examples of measured recitative is found in the opening number of the "Messiah." "Comfort ye, my people." (Sings.)

In all these examples the music is determined in the effort to furnish suitable expression to the words. To recur to an example already given, consider "Thy rebuke hath broken his heart." The very first upward inflection on the word "rebuke," and the downward sweep of the octave in "hath broken his heart," are extremely impressive. So, again, when the words come "but there was no man," the emphasis falls on the last word; but when the same words are repeated the emphasis falls on "was."

In many instances the phrases of recitative are interspersed or intercalated between descriptive phases of the accompaniment. Of this we have many examples in Haydn's "Creation." So we have it in Raphael's "Now furious storms tempestuous rage," which is preceded by the storm in the orchestra. And so successively are set "As chaff by the winds are impelled the clouds," "By heaven's fire the sky is inflamed," "And awful thunders are rolling on high," etc. This plan of structure suggests the Apostolic practice of afterward interpreting the prophecies just delivered in unknown tongues. In the same way is treated "In splendor bright." (Sings.)

Perhaps the most insignificant form of recitative is that where the voice recites on a monotone while the orchestra pursues a measured melody. In this case, of course, the text is little if at all considered. A convenient example of this is afforded by a passage in Ambroise

Thomas's well-known song from "Mignon," "Know'st thou the land," where a difficult and unmusical part of the text is treated in this way. Here, indeed, it is managed with real art, since it but serves to intensify the climax that follows. (Sings Mignon's song.) The musical structure of recitative is necessarily coherent, else it could not be sung. But it does not return upon itself in lyrically-arranged phrases.

LIST OF ILLUSTRATIONS.

1. "Behold a virgin shall conceive." No. 7 of Handel's "Messiah."
2. "Then shall the eyes of the blind be opened." No. 17, the same.
3. "Thy rebuke hath broken his heart." No. 27, the same.
4. "There were shepherds abiding in the field." No. 14.
5. "Comfort ye, my people." No. 1, the same.
6. "And God made the firmament." No. 4, "Creation."
7. "In splendor bright." No. 13, "Creation."
8. Mignon's song from the Opera of "Mignon," by Ambroise Thomas.

LESSON THIRTY-NINE.

THE ARIA AND SCENA.

The aria is a regularly developed musical form. Its text is usually meagre. In the older works it consists of but a single couplet, or at most of but two or three. The music seizes the emotional content of the text, and repeats it over and over, builds out of it, intensifies it in many ways. Examples are innumerable. Let us begin with Bach's "My heart ever faithful." (Sings.) In this we have, first and foremost, good music. And this also is elaborated out of very few motives. The first phrase returns with the persistence of a rondo. In the intermediate couplets, which serve for episodes, the words are broken in two, the syllables separated, and elocutionary proprieties violated with impunity. Yet it is an extremely enjoyable piece of music. In this case we see plainly that music has given up little of its own.

Of the same kind is Handel's "Oh had I Jubal's lyre," except that here there is an evident pleasure in providing agreeable passages for the voice, which, however, are in very good keeping with the emotional stand-point of the song. (Sings.) In other cases the text is treated more seriously, as in Handel's "He shall feed his flock," and "How beautiful are the feet." (Sings.) In both these, as indeed in the previous examples, we have consistently developed musical creations, which in point of form are the same as the gavottes, sarabands, etc. of the ancient binary order. In respect to musical development they partake somewhat of the spirit of the thematic, since the leading motives are often repeated, transformed, presented with various harmonies, modulated into new keys, etc., in a manner very different from what we find in the simple ballad.

The aria is also capable of being applied to descriptive purposes. Of this we have two very pretty examples in Haydn's "Creation," in the well-known soprano songs "With verdure clad," and "On mighty pens." (Sings, both, if convenient.) The descriptive part, it will be observed, is in the accompaniment rather than in the vocal phrases.

Mozart imparted to the aria the simplicity and grace of the people's song, and at the same time contrived for the most part to remain true to the spirit of his text. Some of these songs are of the most exquisite character, as for example, "*Vedrai Carino*" and "*Batti, Batti*," sung by Zerlina in "Don Giovanni." Of the same kind is the tenor aria "*Il mio tesoro*" in that opera. Another one of the same sort is "*Porgi amor*," in Mozart's "Figaro." In "*Dove sono*," of the same opera, we have a more varied treatment. An *adagio*, first part, changes to an *allegro*, closing part. (Let any of these be sung that can be conveniently produced. It does not particularly matter which, since all manifest in general the same traits.)

Another famous example of the aria is Beethoven's well-known song, "Adelaide."* (Sings.) This song is a fully developed piece of instrumental music, in which the voice is treated from a musical standpoint, merely, as if it were a violin or 'cello.

In Italian opera we have various kinds of aria, all, however, having the quality of adaptation to the voice. In these the well-sounding, the effective, the astonishing, the tuneful, are the chief points of concern. Thus in Bellini's "Norma" we have the lovely "*Casta Diva*," an air which is now out of style, and is indeed somewhat wanting in heart when compared with those of Mozart, but which, nevertheless, is tuneful and refined, and, when well done, an extremely pretty piece of singing. (Sings.) In Bellini's "Sonnambula" we have a similar song, "*Ah non Credea*," and, at the close, the famous war-horse of prima donnas, "*Ah non giunge*," where the voice becomes a mere instrument of rejoicing, and the text as such is very little regarded.

Again there is the *scena*, or scene, to be taken into account; a composition in which recitative, arioso, and aria alternate according

*The pronunciation required by the music is ăd-ĕl-ā-ee -dĕ.

9

to the fancy of the composer, in order to meet unusual transitions in the text. Examples of this are found in the great dramatic scene for soprano in Weber's "Oberon," "Ocean, thou mighty monster," and in "Der Freyschutz," where the prayer occurs. In these the fullest resources of the orchestra are unsparingly employed to paint the dramatic situation

Throughout all forms of the aria, the music is consistently developed, as music. The general spirit of the text is seized and represented, but no effort is made to represent merely transitory shades of feeling, except in descriptive arias. When this is done it naturally deprives the aria of its power to absorb and carry along the listener, because such a lingering on separate ideas precludes attention to any single, grand, overmastering impulse of feeling; and *this* is what the aria has for its fundamental design to express. It is to be observed further of the examples here referred to, that they are all from masterworks, by great composers, and are, for the most part, the chief arias in the works in question. They represent, therefore, the highest conception of song in this direction, and for their adequate interpretation demand exceptional voices, thoroughly trained, and musical endowments of high order. Nevertheless, an inferior presentation of them will serve to familiarize one with their phraseology and mode of treatment. Only, if they fail of effect in such presentation, it must be remembered that they are really great works, and require to be heard many times.

LIST OF ILLUSTRATIONS.

1. "My heart ever faithful," Bach.
2. "O, had I Jubal's lyre!" Handel.
3. "He shall feed his flock," Handel.
4. "How beautiful are the feet." Handel.
5. "With verdure clad," from the "Creation," Haydn.
6. "On mighty pens," Haydn.
7. "Vedrai Carino," from "Don Giovanni," Mozart.
8. "Batti, Batti," from "Don Giovanni," Mozart.
9. "Il mio tesoro," from "Don Giovanni," Mozart.
10. "Dove sono," from "Figaro," Mozart.
11. "Porgi amor," from "Figaro," Mozart.
12. "Voi che sapete," from "Figaro," Mozart.
13. "Adelaide," tenor song, Beethoven.
14. "Casta Diva," from "Norma," Bellini.
15. "Ah non Credea," Bellini.
16. "Ah non giunge," "Sonnambula," Bellini.
17. "Ocean, thou mighty monster," from "Oberon," Weber.

LESSON FORTY.

THE THOROUGHLY COMPOSED SONG.

The simple ballad and the aria have this in common, that they both strive first for a symmetrically returning lyric melody. Each ballad or aria represents on the whole a particular phase of emotion, or state of feeling, from which no wide departure is made throughout the song. In the ballad this arises from the necessity of repeating all the stanzas of the words to the same melody; and in the aria it is a natural consequence of the paucity of words. An aria although frequently extended to six or eight or ten periods, rarely has more than two or three couplets of words. Thus, in placing the emphasis upon the *music*, rather than upon the text, both ballad and aria display a decided congeniality of spirit. The aria is a ballad, magnified or exalted to meet more important demands.

We come now to the study of a form of song which we owe chiefly to Schubert and Schumann, in which the text and music receive almost equal consideration, yet in such a way as to afford every part of the text a legitimate musical expression. This necessarily includes the idea of a spontaneous musical activity in the music, for as soon as it ceases to be free in its movement, it ceases to be expressive. The Germans call it the *durchcomponirte Lied*, or "song composed throughout." As there is no English equivalent of this expression in use, the title here employed is "thoroughly composed song;" and the meaning is that every stanza of the song has its own music, different from the others, and suited to the peculiar needs of the words. Unity is subserved by a return of the first stanza, or of something very like it, in the form of a refrain.

We get something of this in the earlier songs of Schubert, as the "Miller" songs. But it is in the grand ballad of the "Erl King" that we have one of the most shining examples. This ballad contains five speakers, the narrator, the boy, the Erl King and Erl King's daughter, and the father. Although the singer represents them all, each one has a particular form of expression. Thus the narrator has a plain figure accompanied by that wonderful figure of repeating octaves. The father speaks in a low voice; the son in a higher one, and with more wildness.

The Erl-King's daughter speaks caressingly, and this, also, the accompaniment intensifies. When the boy is touched by the Erl-King, he cries out with terror, and always a semitone sharp of the accompaniment. This is a touch of realism. Considered merely as music this piece is one of the most remarkable examples of the romantic school; it has been very popular in instrumental arrangements. But it is plain to see that the music has derived its most important suggestions from the words. (Sings.)

Another example, equally fine in its way, though not so diversified, is found in Schubert's "Gretchen at the spinning wheel." In this we have the monotonous whirling of the wheel, the sadness of Marguerite after meeting Faust, her dreams of love, and her fears she will never see him again, and especially the very effective climax at the word "kiss." (Sings.)

Schumann effects a still closer union between the text and the music. Indeed we might say that Schumann's genius consisted in his preternatural quickness in *thinking* music, and his intuitive realization of the true relation between music and emotion. Among the greatest of his songs are the six called "Woman's Love and Life." These are by no means of equal merit. Perhaps the very choicest is " He, the best of all, the noblest," in which the maiden tells the virtues of her love. This song is one of the most remarkable that exist. The interest of it is not in the vocal part alone. The melody is very far from completing itself within the usual lyric limits. The first period closes with a half-cadence into the dominant, and the subject is completed by the piano alone. The harmony is extremely fresh and varied. The principal motive appears in many forms, and modulations are unsparingly employed. Yet the song as a whole has a warmth, a vitality, an onward sweep, such as is hardly anywhere else to be found in a song. And especially the music is remarkably true to the text. (Sings.)

The next one gives us a different phase of the woman's heart.

> " Tis true, I can not believe it,
>   A dream doth my senses enthrall,"

After this follows the charming piece

> " **Thou** ring upon my finger
>   **Thou** dear little golden ring."

a song little if at all inferior to the great one before-mentioned. (Sings.)

The entire Schumann nature is to be found in his songs. One phase of it, although not strictly belonging here, we may characterize as the tender and deep.   It is illustrated by the lovely little piece " Moon-li ht." (Sings.)

Again in " *Waldesgespräch* " (Woodland Dialogue), we have another example of a dual personality expressed by means of a change of style in the music. There are two speakers, the knight and the sorceress " Loreley." The knight speaks in a quick, martial motive; Loreley in more gentle accents and to a harp-like accompaniment. (Sings.)

There is another form of song nearly allied to these, called Arioso. By this is meant an aria-like form, which may be either a small and less intense aria, or a piece in which lyric phrases do not complete themselves by sequences and tonality into regular period forms.   But instead thereof, the melody closely follows the words, and the periods are lengthened, shortened, modulated into other keys, or completed in any way that the feeling of the words seem to require.   Mendelssohn uses the term arioso to denote a small and less complete aria.   In this sense we have in St. Paul the arioso, " But the Lord is mindful of His own." (Sings.) Wagner is the great exponent of this form of writing. He has employed it with the greatest freedom, and, it may be added, with great propriety and beauty. A lovely example is Elsa's balcony song in " Lohengrin." (Sings.)

The thoroughly composed song and the arioso represent the latest advance in the union of music and poetry.   As suggested in the Chap. XXXVI, both music and poetry have something to sacrifice in the union. If we attend closely to the texts of these later songs we shall find that the unmusical elements of poetry have been eliminated, and that the words now express sentiments congenial to music.   On first sight the music seems to have retained its qualities better.   But if we examine these later songs and arioso-pieces we shall find that clearness and definiteness of form have nearly departed from the music.   The period-forms are so vague, and the modulations into so remote keys, and occur so frequently ("near and far," as the song has it) that it requires a special training in the most recent music in order to really enjoy them when heard as instrumental music merely.   If such works are to be enjoyed, it is only when the voice and musical qualities of the singer have been cultivated to an extent adequate to these demands, and are employed in subjection to a strongly conceived and truly dramatic in-terpretation of the text.   They require much more of a singer than the famous "voice, voice, *toujours* Voice."

Of the same general nature as the thoroughly composed song is the *Ensemble,* an important form in opera.   The *ensemble* stands at that

point in the drama where certain opposing principles have been introduced in the personages representing them, and here they are all
brought upon the stage together. The problem for the composer to
solve is to unite these contradictory impulses in the performance (or,
as it seems on the stage, *production*) of a consistent and satisfactory
piece of music, without causing the persons to violate their own individual characters and dispositions. In the nature of the case this problem is impossible of solution. For although a certain amount of individuality in the different parts of an ensemble piece can well enough
be attained by skillful use of counterpoint, it remains certain that no
piece produces a coherent impression, that does not present some leading idea, and therein a dominant emotion, which of course can not be
done without practically extinguishing at least a considerable part of the
opposing element. Many beautiful ensemble pieces are to be found in
opera. In some the librettist has simplified the matter by leaving out
the contradictions. In others the most antagonistic persons alternate
with each other and presently join in as soprano and second, like society
women who kiss in public and back-bite in private, and the music of
the whole goes not as the text goes, but as the composer would have
it. Wagner has attempted to meet this difficulty in other ways, as we
shall see later. Some of the best ensemble pieces are to be found in
Mozart's operas. There is one in "Figaro" which lasts forty minutes
and includes some eight or ten pieces of music. The form is referred
to here merely because it represents an additional phase of vocal writing, the study of which by composers has been of use in ascertaining
how far it is practicable to go in music in the simultaneous representation of opposite determinations.

LIST OF ILLUSTRATIONS.

1. The "Erl King," Schubert.
2. "Gretchen at the Spinning Wheel," Schubert
3. "He the best of all, the noblest," Schumann.
4. "Thou ring upon my finger," Schumann.
5. "Moonlight." Schumann.
6. "Waldesgespräch," Schumann.
7. "But the Lord is mindful of His own," from "St. Paul," Mendelssohn.
8. "Elsa's balcony song," "Ye Wandering Breezes" from "Lohengrin," Wagner.

LESSON FORTY-ONE.

THE OPERA AND ORATORIO.

Oratorio, as is well known, is a musical work for solo voices, chorus, and orchestra, on a sacred subject. It is sung without action, although the text is conceived in a dramatic spirit if not strictly in dramatic form. Of dialogue oratorio has very little if any. The nearest approach to it is in passages where an angel or other speaker delivers a message and a reply is made, but this is rare. The text deals with the large, the heroic or religious interests, and not with those of every day life. Indeed, oratorio was in the beginning an actual part of religious service. This was so with Bach's church cantatas, and the Passion Music.

Handel's oratorios were essentially concert works. As we shall see hereafter (in Chapter XLIII), Handel composed operas for some forty years before he began to write oratorios, and during most of that time had his own singers and theater. So, when actuated by some fortunate instinct, or by the neglect of the public, he began to write oratorio, he changed his style of composition but very little. The use of an English text, the vernacular of his audience, no doubt had a certain tendency to increase his verbal accuracy in adapting his music to it. But such airs as "O had I Jubal's lyre" from "Joshua," and "Rejoice greatly" from the "Messiah" are almost exactly of the same cut as the bravoura arias in his innumerable operas. So, also, very many of the smaller choruses are revamped from some of his former works.

Still, when all this has been said, the difference between Handel's oratorios and his operas is very great; not so much in exceptional moments as in the *average* of the oratorio, which is on a higher and more serious level than the opera. Then, too, between Handel's opera-music and his text there was often a certain contradiction, or at least what seems to be such in our day. The contrapuntal spirit was the habit of Handel's musical thought, and this spirit in its essential nature is suited to grave and elevated discourse. So when Handel fell into the sacred vein, it was not so much a change of style, a conversion, or a rising to a new plane of work, as a choice, fortunate though somewhat late, of a text suitable to the nature of his musical phantasy.

Yet when this change was made and the sacred words applied, and all the best and most elevated of his previous efforts fished up from their waters of oblivion and stood upon honest English feet in marching order, like Ezekiel's dry bones, which, also, the word of the Lord had clothed upon,—even then it is but rarely *sacred* music that comes to utterance, but *concert* music still; music to attract and please, music to elevate and edify;—but not music with which to worship. To demonstrate this position would take us too far. It must suffice here to call over the names of some of these works, leaving the student to confirm or overthrow our position at his leisure. They are "Solomon," "Joshua," "Judas Maccabeus," "Israel in Egypt," "Esther," "Deborah," "Susannah," "Theodora," etc. In some of these he reaches great heights. In particular is this the case in "Israel in Egypt" where those great double choruses must have been inspired by some idea of what his great contemporary Bach had done at Leipsic in his Passions Music.

Oratorio had at least one other decided advantage for Handel, and for the development of music after him. It put the emphasis on the chorus, and not on the solo. The operatic chorus is small at best. It is the peasantry of singers and must on no account usurp a leading interest in the drama. But in music there is a sense in which the Latin proverb is true, *Vox populi vox dei*—the voice of the people is the voice of God.

These Handel choruses have, indeed, a great advantage in their texts, which for the most part are well-known passages of scripture. The familiar word of some Biblical war-cry, such as "Sing to the Lord, for He hath triumphed gloriously," "Worthy is the Lamb," etc., awakens the historical associations that belong to it ; these join in with the inherent majesty and impressiveness of the music, the effectiveness of its instrumentation and especially the deep, thrilling, pervading support of the organ, and all combine in introducing music to the public in a new light, that of the sublime.

Then, for once, it was permitted the almost inspired master to write with headlong haste all through that blessed fortnight, one great work, which stands, and will long stand, as a *ne plus ultra* of musical effort in the direction of the pathetic, the inspiring, and the sublime. The "Messiah" draws a part of its impressiveness, no doubt, from its noble text, which traverses the entire range of the most precious religious associations. And this also helped the composer, who here, at times, rises almost above himself. But to whatever source we may attribute its power over us, it is certain that in Handel's " Messiah " we have a work without which our idea of music would be much lower than it is, and the world would be by much the loser.

In the Bach " Passions Music " we have a different work, and one which is decidedly the expression of worship. But of this subject more is said in chapter XLII. Suffice it to point out here that oratorio is the field in which music has been furnished with the occasion and the means for exercising itself to its farthest bounds in the direction of the elevated, the heroic, and the sublime.

Opera is of the world, worldly. And this for two reasons : As a drama it deals with life, idealized, perhaps, sometimes made ludicrous, but in any case with *life*. Its trinity in unity is " the world, the flesh, and the devil." We have only to run over the librettos, if we have never seen the pieces for ourselves, to find in almost every one of them " the prince of this world" enthroned. Read the books of " Don Giovanni," " Figaro," " Robert le Diable," " Faust," " Il Trovatore," " Il Traviata," and almost all the rest. Then, in the second place, opera stands for an amusement. The opera composer must meet his public. They do not go to the play-house to hear sermons, nor to sing psalms, but to hear, to enjoy, and to be merry.

The opera is the great field in which, sooner or later, all worldly emotion comes to expression. As a form of art it is as blessed in abundant means as the oratorio. For although it lacks the massive chorus, it has a larger number of trained singers, and the advantage of action and spontaneous sympathy with the audience, as helps to inspiration. Librettist, composer, scene-painter, and singers, all combine to place before us a form of art which has in it every possible pleasure of the senses of hearing and sight, and along with this much of a finer and higher character.

From the very nature of the stage and the drama, opera was impossible in Handel's day. The prophet and founder of the modern opera, Glück, wrote his great works more than thirty years after Handel had laid down his operatic pen forever. Counterpoint needed to relax its severity somewhat in favor of the weakness of the flesh in chambermaids and valets upon the stage. Fugue, also, might find artistic justification in a fire, where the first engine company on the ground gave out the theme, the next answered it, etc., but for guests at an evening party it is but a tedious form of utterance. The opera needed the people's song. Glück took a great step in the true direction, and established the canons of operatic work. Mozart went beyond him ; and

Weber beyond him. In "Der Freischütz" we have the very people's song itself.

Besides the people's song, opera needed the neat and pleasing melodic and harmonic forms of Haydn and Mozart. With these it became fully equipped in its department, and went forth under its captains, such as Rossini, Meyerbeer, Weber, Bellini, Donizetti, Auber, Verdi, and last of all, Wagner, to conquer the world of secular music.

In its nature as a form of drama, dealing with men of the present or the immediate past, who in any case are presented on the stage as living before us, and in ranging through all varieties of plays, from roaring farce up through comedy to heroic and elevated phases of life (though these are always given from what, in stage parlance, one might call the "practicable" side as opposed to the "impractical" of oratorio), the opera calls upon music for every form and phase of its pleasant modulation, all its love and its hate, its rejoicing and its sorrow. And what the voice can not do, it offers to complete through the unrivalled riches of the modern orchestra; and in every time of "trouble," where music, as such, fails of power, it produces the "sheep-skin," its diploma of powers yet unexpended.

Thus the opera and oratorio together present us on the whole with every result that has been reached in the effort to clothe words with music, and are to be reckoned among the highest achievements in music. Yet, even in these, all that was said in the beginning concerning the influence of poetry upon music holds true; and all the limitations of vocal music as a form of art are here to be found illustrated. We have on one side Poetry, of which the practicable libretto is but a very small part. And on the other side Music, of which opera and oratorio are, to be sure, a larger part, yet still lacking very much of the elevated sentiment and the epic sweep of pure music, as found in the symphony. Nevertheless, vocal music retains for itself two great points of merit: It is the most understandable form of music, for even the unmusical can follow the words. And, second, through the effort to unite music to poetry, and to extend its range to an equal compass, the true relation of music to emotion has been worked out, and instrumental music itself has gained in freedom of form and range of expression.

PART EIGHTH.

HISTORICAL AND MISCELLANEOUS SKETCHES.

CHAPTER FORTY-TWO.

JOHN SEBASTIAN BACH.

Across this interval of nearly two centuries Bach's life appears to have been very dull and uneventful. He was born at Eisenach, Prussia, March 21, 1685, as Ritter says, "a musician of the fifth generation of one of the most musical families ever produced by any country." His entire life passed in the burgher-like simplicity of the middle class German. His mother died when he was very young; and before he was ten years old he had lost his father also. He then went to his elder brother, John Christopher, organist at Ohrdruff, who gave him his first lessons in piano playing. Bach had scarcely more than made a beginning (which must have been exceedingly easy to so gifted a nature as his) when he cast his covetous eyes on a paper-bound volume containing pieces by Frohberger, Kerl, Pachelbel and others. But such treasures of art were not to be trusted to a boy not yet twelve years old—at least not if the crusty John Christopher could help it—so he locked the book in a corner cupboard, and gave himself no further anxiety on the subject. But the little John Sebastian was of a persevering kind, as we shall see before we have done with him, and his little hand proved able to push through the lattice work door and reach the precious book. But how to make it his own. Why copy it, to be sure. But the awful John Christopher! "Do it at night," said the tempter. "But I've no candles," said the boy. "The full moon." "Sure enough," said plucky John Sebastian, "free to all." So for six long months every bright night found him diligently copying the for-

bidden treasure—copying, we may be sure, with rare patience, and a
singularly fine hand for a boy, for paper was scarce. Alas! just as the
task was done, in an unlucky moment his brother found him out, and
not only confiscated the original but the copy as well, and the poor
John Sebastian had only the comforting recollection that at least he
" had done his best."

After a while the brother died, and the boy was sent to the " gym-
nasium " (or grammar school) at Luneberg, and was soprano singer at
St. Michael's church. While here he lost no opportunity of hearing
good players. On one occasion he went to Hamburg (about forty miles
away) to hear Reinken, who was at that time a famous organist, and
again to Zell to hear the Prince's band there, and especially to become
better versed in the French taste that prevailed. All the while he applied himself so diligently to the study of the organ and piano that at
the age of eighteen (in 1703) we find him widely recognized as an un-
doubted master, and appointed court musician at Weimar. The following year he became organist at the new church of Arnstadt—probably because he could pursue his taste for the organ better there, for
his duties as court musician involved only his services as violinist. In
his new place he manifested the diligence that had all along characterized him. Wherever in all the country around there was a celebrated
organist, there would Bach be sure to go in order to discover the charm
and secret of his power. He went on foot to Lubeck to hear Bux-
tehude, a distinguished master there; and, too poor to take lessons, he
even remained a full quarter of a year a secret hearer of that organist
All this time he diligently exercised himself in organ and piano playing, and in all schools of composition. He studied with the closest
care all the older master works he could lay his hands on. He fervently
desired to make a longer art journey into Italy, but poverty prevented.
By degrees, however, he possessed himself of the chief works of Pal-
estrina, Caldara, Lotti, and the other best writers of the Italian school.
He had already learned the Italian art of singing, from Italian singers
he had known in Hamburg.

With such diligence no wonder his fame spread abroad as that of
a master. Accordingly we find him soon back to Weimar as Court
organist, and later (1717) as chief music director. Here, doubtless, he
composed many of his chief works for the organ and his orchestral
suites.

About this time Marchand, Handel's master, died at Halle, and
Bach was invited to succeed him. He even went to Halle to prove his
qualifications, but for some reason did not take the place. Some time

before this Marchand and Bach had been invited to play in contest before the king at Dresden, but at the last moment Marchand's courage failed him, for he had in some way found out that the young German had an unparalleled fluency of ideas combined with rare skill in treatment; so Bach amused and astonished for hours the great audience gathered by his wonderful performances. Passing over Bach's service as court music director under Prince Leopold of Anhalt-Cothen (extending through six years), and his journey to Hamburg to play the organ, where he excited the greatest wonder in the breast of the veteran Reinken by his masterly improvisations on the chorale, " *An Wasser-flüssen Babylon's*," we come to the year 1733 when Bach was appointed Cantor to the St. Thomas school in Leipsic, where he spent twenty-six fruitful and peaceful years. What good came of this quiet life will appear when we come to speak more particularly of his works. The chief episode of his Leipsic life was his visit to Frederick the Great, at Potsdam, in the year 1747. This visit was paid only after the most pressing invitations from the king, expressed through Bach's second son, Carl Philip Emanuel, who was at that time chapel master to the Princess Amelia. King Frederick was a flute player, and, like the most of the breed, thought himself a fine one. So every night, when not too busy with cares of state, he was accustomed to get his orchestra together and astonish them with his flute virtuosity. In this way he imagined himself greater than a king—a God-endowed artist. One night just as the musical hilarity was about to begin, a servant brought him the list of arrivals. "Gentlemen," said the king, solemnly, " Old Bach is come!" So, all stained with travel and tumbled and torn with the horrible stage-coaching of those days, with never a moment for a hasty bite of something to eat, with scarcely a glass of beer to soothe the inner man, the great king was confronted by a greater, the king of the organ, John Sebastian Bach. Bach, taken from one room to another by the king and assembled musicians, was compelled to inspect and play upon every one of the numerous Silbermann pianos in the palace. After Bach had improvised for a while he asked the king to give him a subject in which to work out a fugue, and the learning displayed in the work was highly admired by all present. He then selected a suitable subject and worked out extempore a fugue in six obligato parts.

The next day they made the tour of all the organs in Potsdam, in in order that the King might hear his organ-playing. On his return to Leipsic, Bach composed the subject he had received from the King in three and six parts, and had it engraved under the title " *Musika isches Opfer*" (musical offering), and dedicated it to the inventor—certainly a neat and proper thing to do, and for which I hope the rather stingy King had the grace to make a fit acknowledgment.

Bach not only used his eyes enormously in reading and writing an immense mass of works in early youth, seriously undermining his sight by the moonlight writing, but in many cases he had engraved his own compositions. In consequence of all this application through more than sixty years, at last his eyes became much inflamed, and finally he lost his sight altogether. This so weighed upon his spirits that he continued to decline for fully half a year, and finally expired July 28th, 1750.

Bach was twice married. The first wife had seven children; the second thirteen, of whom eight were sons. Several of his children were musical, and one of them, Carl Philip Emanuel, was the forerunner of the Haydn and Mozart school of music. His theory was that the instrument must be made to *sing;* accordingly we find him content with shorter forms and less learned musical phraseology than that adopted by his father, whom, on his own ground, he modestly confessed himself totally incapable of rivalling.

As a piano player Bach was one of the greatest of his time. His touch was silvery, distinct and expressive, his legato playing extremely perfect, and his contrasts of power remarkable for that day. He had a short, thick hand, and Prof. Karl Klauser (of the seminary at Farmington, Conn.) says that as near as he can make it out from Forkel's life, Bach's touch must have been much the same as that employed by Dr Wm. Mason—a touch which then, as now, produced the most lovely and varied tones from the piano-forte.

As an organ player Bach has had great injustice done him by those who suppose that every time he sat down to the organ he drew all the stops and " blazed away " by the hour on the full organ. Not he. The organ builders used to complain of his audacity in making combinations. They said he put stops together in the most unheard of and unorthodox manner. And all this is easy enough to understand. Bach was first a violinist, and there is no record of a violinist who could not appreciate melody. He was full of melody. Consider further that he was an orchestral writer of rare power—quite an innovator in his day, coloring his scores to the full scope of the instruments then employed. Besides, his very organ works themselves contradict his notion, for the full organ pieces do not make up more than half the volume of them; but we find trios for two claviers and pedale,

and variations which you may be sure Bach "varied" in combination
no less than in harmony and melody.

While Bach was Cantor of the St. Thomas Church he had two
choirs and an orchestra at his disposal. Music was no small part of
the service. The hearty singing of the German peasants and school
children in the simple chorals, which Bach accompanied with such
wonderful harmonies, and the well-trained choirs, combined to afford
the composer rare facilities for the illustration of the musical ideas
with which his solid-looking old head teemed. So on every feast day
he brought out a new Cantata, a psalm set to music for one or two
choirs, orchestra and organ, now and then a verse of a psalm-tune interspersed, in which everybody took part, and the freest use of solos
that the subject demanded. Of these works about seventy have been
published, ranging from twenty minutes in length to an hour—works
which suggested Mendelssohn's "Hymn of Praise," "As Pants the
Heart," etc.

To be sure but few of the common people knew what wonderful
things they were hearing. Robert Franz tells that he once saw a very old
man who was sexton of the St. Thomas Church while Bach was there.
" And what did they think of his works?" asked the enthusiastic and
reverential Franz. " Mr. Bach's compositions," said the sapient critic,
" were very much alike."

The greatest work of this period was Bach's " Passions Music,"
according to St. Matthew. This consists of about two hours' music,
solos, choruses, interspersed stanzas of hymn tunes descriptive of the
passion of the garden and the cross. It was written for and first given
on Good Friday evening in 1729, and does not seem to have been
given again until Mendelssohn exhumed it a hundred years later, and
gave it on Good Friday 1829. Since then it has been frequently done
in Germany, and always on Good Friday in the St. Thomas Church in
Leipsic. This work has become much admired in London, and was nib-
bled at bravely by the Handel and Haydn Society in Boston at their
Festival in 1871, and finally given entire in 1877, largely, be it said,
through the perseverance of Mr. Dwight and two or three other enthusiastic admirers of Bach.

When given at Leipsic, and as a religious service, the Passion
Music is full of pathos and beauty. Let us imagine a vast, barn-like
church, dimly lighted, with two galleries, one above the other. Far
up in the upper gallery, with never a soul in sight, we hear the voices
of the choirs and organ. The choirs occupy opposite galleries. At the
appointed hour the gentle strain begins, "Come, ye daughters, weep

for anguish," and presently breaks in the penetrating voice of a couple
hundred school children, singing independently the choral, "O Lamb
of God, all blameless," a tone and words as familiar there as the Old
Hundredth here. The effect is totally indescribable. The gentle and
cultivated tones of the choir as they thread the graceful strains of the
counterpoint, the reed-like and lusty tones of the boys' voices, the
coloring of the orchestra, and the sombre majesty of the organ—all this
with never a performer visible; you sit there in the darkness and from
some far-away shore the sounds come to you and overwhelm you
with waves of music. Anon the chorus dies away and a piercing haut-
boy takes up a charming theme which a solo voice interprets, "I'll
watch with my dear Jesus," and softly, yet richly, the chorus responds,
"So slumber shall my sins befall."

And further on the whole congregation, choirs and instruments,
all in tender devotion, take up the strain—

> "O Head, all bruised and wounded.
> Hung up to brutal scorn!
> O Head with shame surrounded
> With crown of cruel thorn!
> O Head, to honor wonted,
> To splendor all divine,
> Now outraged and affronted:
> All hail, dear master mine!"

This indeed is religious art! Not these the utterances of the
bright concert room, for the applause of the unthoughtful crowd; but
here the Christian heart meditates on the mystery of redemption, and
to celebrate that wondrous love tearfully brings every offering that
the musical art affords.

Mr. John Hullah, in his lectures on "The Transition Periods of
Music," holds that Bach's obscurity of expression is such as will forever debar him from wide popularity. This way of putting it does not
seem to me fortunate. "Obscurity of expression" is not properly pre-
dicable of Bach. Nor has he any lack of melody. On the contrary,
he is absolutely the most inexhaustible of all in this direction. It can
not be denied that Bach carried the intellectual in music beyond the
point where technical devices assist the expression of emotion—at least
for our day. But let us not forget that while there are now few musicians who can handle contrapuntal forms well, in Bach's day this was
a common accomplishment, and formulæ of expression which in his
day were clear enough, and dramatic enough, are in the light of this
excitable nineteenth century, too cold.

And however Bach may stand with the public, he has been the great inspiration to all the best and most poetic of later musicians,— as for instance Mendelssohn, Schumann and Chopin—and this, across a century or so, is surely great honor. To the organist and violinist Bach's works are at once the best exercises for developing his art as a player, and the freshest and most characteristic pieces for his instrument. Yet not all Bach's compositions are great. But in the mass (the manuscripts make a pile over two feet high, and, it is computed, would occupy a copyist more than twenty years to copy them— although this, I dare say, is making it rather a fat thing for the copyist) masterworks of the purest conception are to be found, and that in large numbers.

I can not sum up Bach's works better than in the words of Wilhelm Rust, in Mendel's "*Conversations-Lexicon*," article "Bach."

" In all these works, from the greatest and richest in compass clear down to the smallest range of musical formations, Bach maintained his imperishable glory as the lofty representative of the Inner and Spiritual in art, as the boldest and mightiest herald of the ideal in art works. The great contrapuntal skill which holds performer and hearer in the chains of the most perfect polyphony, the mastership of the works in their organic development, and their value and thankfulness for the purposes of study, serve only as means for expressing his ideal. All these are the stuff through which he expresses the spiritual. The purely technical, therefore, can in no way be regarded as Bach's chief greatness, although many still suppose so. His greatness rests not in the ingenious forms of which, to be sure, he is master, so that no one before or since has expressed himself in them so easily and naturally, but rather in the noble, free and lofty spirit, which in its mighty flight is able to rule and control his thoughts and perceptions, and with equal ease strike the strings of a sought-for emotion, or rise into the boundless fields of free music. Deep moral earnestness is the very foundation of his music, and glorifies even his playful creations; æsthetic loveliness adds itself to him, as it were, of its own accord. Only such a strength, eminent in depth of thought, and equally skillful in expression, could possibly have produced such colossal structures and giant forms as Bach has left us in his great church works, which, in all their greatness, are created out of the deepest and most trustful piety."

10

PROGRAMME OF BACH ILLUSTRATIONS.

1. *(Moderately Difficult.)*

1. Prelude and Fugue in C minor, "Clavier" I. No. 2.
2. Loure in G, arranged by Heinze.
3. Sarabande in A, No. 5, Bach "Favorite Pieces," Peters, No. 221.
4. Gavotte in D, No. 3 in the same.
5. Song, " My Heart ever Faithful."
6. Invention in E minor, No. 7 of the 3-part Inventions.
7. Gavotte in D, arranged by Mason.

2. *(Difficult, Employing the Piano, Organ, and Violin.)*

1. Chromatic Fantasia and Fugue.
2. Air for G, string, (As played by Wilhelmj).
3 Courante in E minor, No. 7, from Peters, No. 221.
4. Organ Prelude in B minor, Organ works Vol. II, No. 10.
5. Chaconne for violin Solo.
6. Grand Prelude and Fugue in G minor, Organ works, Vol. II, No 4.
7. Meditation upon Bach's 1st Prelude, by Ch. Gounod, For organ, piano, and violin.

3. *(For Piano and Voice.)*

1. Chromatic Fantasia and Fugue.
2. Song, " My Heart ever Faithful.
3. Invention in F, No. 8, two part.
   Sarabande in A.
   Invention in E minor.
   Gigue in G, (No. 2 in Peters, No. 221).
4. Slumber Song from Christmas Oratorio.
5. Invention in C minor, 3 part.
   Loure in G, Heinze.
   Sarabande in F, No. 6, Peters, No. 221.
   Echo in B minor, No. 8 of the same.
   Gavotte in E major, Arr. by Tours.
6. Echo Aria from the Christmas Oratorio.
7. Grand Organ Fugue in G minor, Arranged for piano by Liszt

CHAPTER FORTY-THREE.

GEORGE FREDERICK HANDEL.

At Halle, in Lower Saxony, Feb. 23, 1685, was born Bach's great contemporary, and, in after times, rival, Geo. Frederick Handel. His father was a physician and surgeon. The little George early showed an immense desire for music, and that to his poor father's discomfiture; "For," said the judicious sire, "music is an elegant art and fine amusement, but as an occupation it hath little dignity, having for its object nothing better than mere entertainment and pleasure." So he kept the boy out of school lest he should learn to sing, and taught him his Latin and humanities at home. But, by connivance of mother or nurse, they say, the boy contrived to get a dumb spinet hid away in the garret, and there, by night, taught himself to play. The "dumb spinet" was a very small piano-forte, of which the strings were wound with cloth so that when struck it gave forth only a mild tinkling sound. They were made for nuns who might want a little music in a quiet way without disturbing the lady superiors.

When still a small boy, scarce eight years old, his father made a trip to Weissenfels, to visit his eldest son, who was in the service of the Duke there. Of course he had no idea of taking the little George Frederick with him, for, at court, the boy would be almost sure to hear some music and so get further strengthened in his pestiferous liking for the shallow art. But as the good old doctor drove away in his chaise the boy ran after him a mile or two, and begged so hard to be taken that the father finally bundled him into the chaise and took him along "to get rid of him." Arrived at court, the boy was left to shift for himself while papa and the big brother were seeing the lions of the place. By a natural attraction the young musician soon found himself in the chapel, and, with the friendly aid of a good natured servant at the bellows, was soon in fine frenzy of harmony at the organ. By a lucky chance the Duke came along, and immediately perceived the real talent of the young player. And here, to his great horror, papa Handel found him a little later. But the Duke assured the old gentleman that the boy had a genuine talent for music which must on no account be hid; that he must put young George Frederick under strict training as a musician, and not try to thwart the plain design of Providence.

So, on his return to Halle, young Handel was put under the instruction of the great organist there, Zachau, who, for about three years, put him through a course of the heroic training those times delighted in. Towards the last of this course Handel wrote a cantata or motette every week—many of them, I dare say, poor stuff; for what else could be expected of a boy of ten, although they must have been technically correct to satisfy the conscientious old pedagogue. At length Zachau had not the heart to keep it up any longer, for a boy who could produce fugues with such facility and of so good an average of merit was already a master, and so Zachau told him. So Handel went next to Berlin, in 1696, and studied the opera school, under the auspices of the Elector. The next year old Dr. Handel died, leaving his family poorly provided for. George Frederick then went to Hamburg, where he hoped to earn a living as violinist in the opera orchestra. Being a rather poor player he got a very subordinate position, that of *ripieno* second violin (a sort of fifth wheel), and was regarded by the other players as a veritable dunce, for he was nineteen, large, awkward, rather shy, and a poor fiddler. But one day the leader was sick and the rehearsal likely to fall through; and Handel took his seat at the harpsichord (or piano) because he could best be spared from his place in the orchestra, and carried the rehearsal through with such spirit that the whole orchestra broke into loud applause.

On the strength of this recognition he appears soon as permanent conductor of the orchestra, and, along with his dear friend Matheson, a chief composer of opera for the Hamburg stage. Here presently he brought out "*Almira*" and "*Nero*," and, probably, "*Florindo and Daphne*," which he had already written while in Berlin. But it was Handel's great desire to visit Italy. So, refusing the liberal offer of Prince Giovanni Gaston de Medici to send him, he saved his money and was straightway able to go at his own expense, and in 1707, at the age of twenty-one, he entered Florence. Here, however, he stayed only long enough to compose the opera "*Roderigo*," for which he received one hundred sequins, when he immediately betook himself to Venice. Here he was received with open arms. The abounding vitality of his music and its sparkling and good natured originality was such as to secure for him the epithet "the dear Saxon" ("*Il Caro Sassone*").

Domenico Scarlatti was the great harpsichordist of all Italy at that time. He was a sort of Chopin of his day, imparting a new grace and scope to piano-forte music, yet not creating in such a masterly way as

to conquer the after-coming generations. Handel, also, excelled as a
harpsichordist, and the relative merits of the two artists were widely
discussed. It was generally thought that Scarlatti played with more
grace; but at the organ Handel was unquestionably the superior.
Scarlatti himself, however, was not satisfied. One night at a masked
ball a disguised player seated himself at the harpsichord and amid
the noise and confusion played away unnoticed. But just then Scarlatti came in and at once his trained ear recognized the masterly touch.
"It is either the Saxon or the Devil," said he. It *was* the Saxon.
Whenever people used to praise his playing he used to pronounce
Handel's name and, with the Italian grimace, cross himself. But Handel
and Scarlatti became fast friends.

Here in Venice, Handel in three weeks composed an opera
"*Agrippina*," which made a furore from Venice to Rome. Here
he secured the patronage of Cardinal Ottoboni, whose band-master
was the celebrated Corelli, a composer and violinist of somewhat refined and gentle nature, but of marked genius. Here Handel wrote
five operas, of which we have no room to speak further.

In 1709 he was back again in Germany, at Hanover, where he was
retained in the service of the Elector George of Brunswick, afterwards
the English George I, at a salary of £300 a year. Here he fell in with
some English noblemen, who invited him over to London. So with
gracious leave of absence from the Elector, he came to London in the
Autumn of 1710, where he found the Italian taste everywhere prev-
alent. To meet this he composed the opera *Rinaldo*, which was
brought out in 1711 with immense success, and was forthwith arranged
for pianos and barrel organs, and was thrummed, whistled and beat
from one end of the kingdom to the other. Walsh, the publisher, is
said to have made £1,500 out of the sale of the pieces of this opera.
Within a few months Handel was back again in Hanover, but the quiet
German Court was not much to his taste after the success in London.
So again he got leave of absence for a visit to London, and in 1712
brought out an ode on the occasion of the Queen's birthday. The following year the peace of Utrecht gave occasion for the *Te Deum* and *Jubilate* (both well known in England), and for these three the composer
received a pension of £200 a year from Queen Anne, and forthwith
Handel (to use a western phrase) "went back" on Hanover and its
rather slow court completely and for good. Now this was all very well
as long as the Queen lived, for the public was ready to hear and pay.
But presently Queen Anne died, and, bad luck for Handel, George I.
in very wrathful mood at the trick played him by his *quondam* chapel

master, came over himself to reign.   Handel was forbidden the court;
but Handel's music was sung and played everywhere, and the new King
not only knew good music when he heard it, but he knew Handel's
music as well as he knew his robust frame and round face.   So one
day as the King went down the river in a state barge, a boat came
after him playing some new and delightful music, which in the turn of
the phrases was Handel's clearly enough.   This was the celebrated
"water music," well enough in its day, but now, in spite of its election
and high calling, rather *passeé*.   But it appeased the ire of the King,
and Händel's pardon was sealed with a new pension of £200 a year.

Mr. Haweis, in "Music and Morals," gives a pleasant picture of
the society in which Handel moved at that time.   "Yonder heavy, rag-
ged looking youth, standing at a corner of Regent street with a slight
and rather refined looking companion, is the obscure Samuel Johnson,
quite unknown to fame. He is walking with Richard Savage. As
Signor Handel, the composer of Italian music, passes by, Savage becomes excited, and nudges his friend, who only takes a languid interest in the foreigner.   Johnson did not care for music ; of many
noises he considered it the least disagreeable.

"Toward Charing Cross comes, in shovel hat and cassock, the
renowned ecclesiastic, Dean Swift.   He has just nodded patronizingly
to Bononcini in the Strand and suddenly meets Handel, who cuts him
dead.   Nothing disconcerted, the Dean moves on muttering his famous
epigram :

'Some say that Signor Bononcini,
Compared to Handel, is a ninny;
While others vow that to him Handel
Is hardly fit to hold a candle.
Strange that such differences should be
'Twixt tweedledum and tweedledee.'

"As Handel enters 'Turk's Head,' at the corner of Regent street,
a noble coach and four drove up; it is the Duke of Chandos, who is
inquiring for Mr. Pope; presently a deformed little man in an iron-
grey suit, and a face as keen as a razor, hobbles out, makes a low bow
to the burly Handel, who, helping him into the chariot, gets in after
him, and they drive off together to Cannons, the Duke's mansion at
Edgeware There they meet Mr. Addison, the poet Gay, and the witty
Arbuthnot, who have been asked to luncheon..   The last number of
the *Spectator* lies on the table, and a brisk discussion soon arises between Pope and Addison concerning the merits of the Italian Opera, in
which the poet would have the better, if he only knew a little more
about music, and could keep his temper."

The Duke had a private chapel, and appointed Handel organist in place of Dr. Pepusch, who retired with very good grace before one so manifestly his superior. The Duke's chapel became a very fashionable Sunday resort of those who wanted to worship God in great company and hear Mr. Handel play the organ. While in this position Handel composed what were called the "Chandos Anthems," numbering over a hundred pieces. These are interesting as marking his transition towards the oratorio; but they are never performed now, except for their historical interest. During his residence at Cannons, which extended to 1721, Handel composed his oratorio of "Esther."

In 1720 Handel was engaged by a society of noblemen to compose operas for the Royal Academy of Music at the Haymarket, of which "*Radamistus*" was one of the first fruits; on this followed "*Floridante*" in 1721 and "*Otto*" in 1733—the latter being considered the flower of his dramatic works. Of the favorite air "Affani del pensier," Dr. Pepusch remarked, "The great bear was certainly inspired when he wrote that song." This career of activity went on with full tide of fashionable favor for four years, including seven more operas. Then the fashion changed. At a rival theatre Dr. Pepusch brought out 'The Beggar's Opera,' composed of all sorts of bits from every source including much from Handel himself, and all the public went to laugh at and enjoy it.

Not disheartened, Handel posted off to Italy to get a supply of the best singers, determined to "fight it out on that line." But fashion is a fickle goddess, and it was many a struggling year before tough old Handel saw her smiling face again. New and better operas were given with new and good clothes; but the public did not respond. Giving operas with Italian singers is apt to try one's temper, as perhaps Messrs. Maretzek, Strakosch and Grau could inform us if they would. It is related that at a rehearsal, after repeated signs of insubordination that had terribly tried the composer's irascible temper, the famous Cuzzoni finally declined to sing "Falsa Immagine." Handel exploded at last. "He flew at the wretched woman and shook her like a rat. 'Ah! I always knew you were a fery tefil,' he cried; and I shall now let you know that I am Beelzebub, the prince of te tefils!' and dragging her to the open window, was just on the point of pitching her into the street, when, in every sense of the word she recanted.*"

The struggle against fate lasted until about 1741. In 1732, we read that "*Hester*, an English oratorio, was performed six times, and very full." Within the next seven years he wrote sixteen operas and

* Music and Morals.

five oratorios. Still, with strange blindness, Handel could not see
that the public had done with his operas. He wrote ballet music
(fancy Handel writing music for "the Black Crook" or "the Field of
the Cloth of Gold") and lavished immense sums in scenery, "new
clothes" and properties. But it was all in vain. In eight years he
lost £10,000 in opera and was obliged to suspend payment and close
the theatre. With failing health he betook himself, sick, discouraged
and mad, to Aix-la-Chapelle. In 1727 he was much amended and returned to England, as Mr. Haweis suggests, "not like Mozart from
Baden, to write his own requiem, but some one's else." It was the
funeral anthem in memory of Queen Caroline that claimed his attention.

Resolute still, he tried the opera again, producing three successively;
but each failed worse than the last. Still many were true to him.
King George II, paid him well for his work, and taught the Prince of
Wales (afterwards George IV) to love his music. "Southey tells us
that Handel asked the boy, then quite a child, who was listening very
earnestly to his playing, if he liked the music, and when the little prince
expressed his delight, 'A good boy! a good boy!' cried Handel. 'You
shall protect my fame when I am dead.'" The best writers, too, stood
up manfully for Handel. Such were Gay, Arbuthnot, Hughes, Colley
Cibber, Pope, Fielding, Hogarth and Smollett. "These were the men
who kept their fingers on the pulse of the age; they gauged Handel
accurately, and they were not wrong. At a time when others jeered
at Handel's oratorios, these men wrote them up; when the tide of fine
society ebbed, and left Handel high and dry on the boards of a deserted
theatre, they occupied the pit; when he gave his benefit concert they
bought the tickets, and when his operas failed, they immediately sub-
scribed and had them engraved."*

The people, also, were true to Handel. His music was played by
bands everywhere throughout the kingdom. He became very popular as a player, and at every oratorio performance performed one or
two "new organ concertos." The year 1739 was a very active one for
Handel; in it he produced the oratorios of "Saul," "Alexander's Feast,"
and "Israel in Egypt." The latter is truly a colossal work, containing
twenty-seven choruses, nearly all of which are double, that is, written
for two choirs. This work has been given by the Boston Handel and
Haydn Society several times, and perhaps elsewhere in this country.
It is very grand, but many regard it as somewhat tedious on account of the
preponderance of choruses. This succession of such mighty choruses

*Music and Morals, p. 167.

has always struck musicians with wonder. Mendelssohn regarded it as something almost superhuman. In the letters from 1833 to 1847, Mendelssohn recounts the use he made of a part of this oratorio in an entertainment of music and *tableaux* given at Dusseldorf, in honor of the Crown Prince. "They took place in the great hall of the Academy where a stage was erected. In front was the double chorus (about ninety voices altogether) standing in two semi-circles around my English piano; and in the room, seats for four hundred spectators. R—— in mediæval costume interpreted the whole affair, and contrived, very cleverly, to combine the different objects in spite of their disparity.

"He exhibited three transparencies: 1st. 'Melancholy,' after Dürer, a motette of Lotti's, being given by men's voices in the far distance; then the Raphael, with the Virgin appearing to him in a vision, to which the 'O Sanctissima' was sung (a well known song, but which always makes people cry); thirdly, St. Jerome in his tent, with a song of Weber's '*Hor' uns, Warheit.*' This was the first part. Now came the best of all. We began from the very beginning of 'Israel in Egypt.' Of course you know the first recitative, and how the chorus gradually swells in tone ; first the voices of the *alti* are heard alone, then more voices join in, till the loud passage comes with single chords, 'They sighed,' etc. (in G minor),when the curtain rose and displayed the first tableau, ' The Children of Israel in Bondage,' designed and arranged by Bendeman. In the foreground was Moses, gazing dreamily into the distance in sorrowful apathy; beside him an old man sinking into the ground under the weight of a beam, while his son makes an effort to release him from it; in the background some beautiful figures with uplifted arms, a few weeping children in the foreground— the whole scene closely crowded together like a mass of fugitives. This remained visible till the close of the first chorus; and when it ended in C minor the curtain at the same moment dropped over the bright picture. A finer effect I scarcely ever saw.

"The chorus then sang ' The Plagues,' 'Hail Darkness' and ' The First-Born,' without any tableaux, but at the chorus 'He Led Them Out Like Sheep,' the curtain rose again, when Moses was seen in the foreground, with raised staff, and behind him, in gay tumult, the same figures who in the first tableaux were mourning, now all pressing onwards ladened with gold and silver vessels; one young girl (also by Bendeman) was especially lovely, who, with her pilgrim's staff, seemed as if advancing from the side scenes and about to cross the stage. Then came the choruses again, without any tableaux, 'But the Waters,' 'He rebuked the Red Sea,' ' Thy Right Hand, O Lord,' and the recitative 'And Miriam, the Prophetess,' at the close of which the solo soprano appeared.   At the same moment the last tableau was uncovered —Miriam with a silver timbrel sounding praises to the Lord, and other maidens with harps and citherns, and in the background four men with trombones pointing in different directions.   The soprano solo was sung behind the scenes, as if proceeding from the picture, and when the chorus came in *forte* real trombones and trumpets and kettle drums were brought on the stage and burst in like a thunderclap.   Handel evidently intended this effect   *   *   *   "

In 1741 Handel composed his master work, "The Messiah," in seventeen days.   For a detailed criticism on this work and the "Judas Maccabeus" I have no place.   It must suffice to say of "The Messiah" that certain numbers of it are masterpieces of the most precious quality. Even the quaint and curious "And He Shall Purify" is one of the most characteristic morceaux to be found in the whole chorus repertory. The "Hallelujah" chorus is now everywhere known.   Still those who have never heard this chorus with hundreds of voices, full orchestra and organ, have not yet heard Handel's "Hallelujah," but only a part hereof.   It is generally known that Mozart added new wind parts to he score of the "Messiah."   These additions in this chorus fill up seven staves, and impart a characteristic splendor to this noble creation, which the orchestra in Handel's time could not attain.*

There is no doubt in my mind that Handel was helped in the "Messiah" very much by the *text*, which contains the most inspiring passages to be found in all literature; besides, in his other works he only rarely rises to the heights he reaches in this one.

"The Messiah" was first produced in Dublin in 1742, for a charitable purpose, and it is interesting to note that this oratorio has contributed more money in charity, first and last, than any other work of art whatever.   The production of these great oratorios was the turning point in Handel's fortunes.   He speedily paid off his debts, and within the next seventeen years accumulated a handsome fortune.   His last oratorio was "Jephtha," written in 1751, about which time he began to be blind, from the affection known as *gutta serena.*   He was couched several times, but he finally lost his sight entirely.   He continued to give oratorio performances, at intervals, until about a week before his death.   He died in London, Good Friday, April 14, 1759, in his seventy-fifth year.   His large property, amounting to something like £50,000 was all bequeathed to charitable institutions.   Handel was

*(Those curious in this matter can obtain the **full orchestral score** of **"The Messiah,"** in the Peters' edition, including Mozart's additions for about three dollars.)

never married, had no vices except an irascible temper, and seems never to have been in love but once.

As an organist, he was of the greatest eminence. The clearness with which he expressed his ideas, the dignity of his musical thought, so well suited to the organ, together with his decision and spirit as a performer, combined to make him immensely successful.

It is difficult to define the relative rank of Handel and Bach as great masters, and to weigh their influence on the course of musical development since. As Brendel well says, they were the culmination of musical progress in their age, but they represented opposite poles. Bach was a quiet home-body, writing always in a highly subjective manner out of the depths of his own feeling. Although the greatest organist of his times, and often listened to by kings and lords, he did not allow himself to change from the ideal of art that was congenial to his nature. Handel on the other hand, a bustling, energetic man, of a truly cosmopolitan taste, had it always for his task to please and attract the masses. Resources were not wanting. He controlled for nearly forty years the best singers and players in the world. His genius had every thing to favor it. To a German honesty and depth of artistic conception he united the Italian art of clear expression; yet all this with no sacrifice of the nobility of his art, and for a genius of such composition, England, the land of common sense, was, of all others, the field of action. Handel has done more to make the musical art respected by the public generally than any other composer. Bach has been the inspiration of musicians. Bach and Handel are the corner stones of Modern Music.

Handel was pre-eminently a composer of vocal music. In his recitatives he attains a dignified and truly musical declamation of the text, as we already saw in Chapter XXXVIII, and occasionally rises to true pathos. In his arias he is frequently diffuse. The leading motive is too many times turned over. Yet this fault is wellnigh universal in the classical aria, which is, as we know, merely a prolongation of a single moment in the dramatic movement. Besides, this prolixity only gave more opportunity to the prima donna. At other times, however, his arias are not too long, even for the rapid age we live in. In very many of them we find a close relation between the text and the music, and always a careful consideration for the voice. His style, although melodious and thus far Italian, was distinguished for its contrapuntal spirit, and its elevation and dignity, and was therefore especially suited to the oratorio. In his choruses he rises to the highest points yet reached in this form of art. Of this one finds very many examples, of which the "Hallelujah," "The Horse and His Rider," "The Hailstone Chorus," "Lift up Your Heads," and "Worthy is the Lamb" are known to all. His instrumental music is not so important. It is melodious, and of course well written, but in general somewhat diffuse. Even his famous organ concertos do not escape the charge of being commonplace.

PROGRAMME OF HANDEL ILLUSTRATIONS.

1. (*Moderately Difficult, Employing the Piano and Soprano.*)

1. Fugue in E minor ("Fire Fugue").
2. "As when the dove laments her love," from "Acis and Galatea." Soprano.
3. Pastoral symphony, from "Messiah."
4. "How beautiful are the Feet" (from "Messiah"). Soprano.
5. Air and Variations in E. "The Harmonious Blacksmith."
6. Aria, "Lascia ch' io Pianga," from "Rinaldo."
7. *a.* Minuet from Samson.
 b. Chaconne in F.
 c. March from occasional Oratorio.
8. "I know that my Redeemer liveth." Soprano.
9. Hallelujah Chorus from the "Messiah."

(2. *Employing Soprano, Alto, Tenor, and Chorus with Piano-forte.*)

1. *a.* "Comfort ye my people."
 b. Every Valley shall be exalted. Tenor Solo.
 c. Chorus "And the Glory of the Lord."
2. *a.* Minuet from Samson.
 b. March from Joshua.
 c. Air Bourée and Double. Arr. by Mason. The Piano-forte.
3. "Hope in the Lord," Arr. by Mason. Soprano.
4. "O thou that tellest," from "Messiah." Alto solo and Chorus.
5. *a.* "Thy rebuke hath broken his heart."
 b. "Behold and see if there be any sorrow." Tenor.
 c. "But Thou didst not leave his soul in hell." From the "Messiah."
6 "How beautiful are the Feet." Soprano.
7 Hallelujah Chorus, or "Worthy is the Lamb."

CHAPTER FORTY-FOUR.

FRANCIS JOSEPH HAYDN.

Up to the time of which I am now about to write, the great creative geniuses, Handel and Bach, had devoted their efforts to vocal
music; instrumental music had received a certain amount of attention,
it is true, and the organ especially was carried no further until the time
of Mendelssohn. But although Bach and Handel were not altogether
above playfulness, it was of a sort essentially masculine and earnest.
The light and easy-going spirit of modern society, which chiefly culti-
vates instrumental music, formed no part of Bach or Handel's nature,
and hence it has no expression in their works. Nevertheless, what they
had done went far to render instrumental music possible, as they imparted to music a degree of emotional coloring entirely unknown before
their time. At the hands of Handel, also, melody had assumed more
definite form. Both these men, also, were able to develop a musical
thought in a purely musical spirit (that is, independently from words,
and influenced simply by conditions of symmetry and contrast, as well
as unity) to a masterly degree, which has never been surpassed. One
of Bach's sons, Carl Philip Emanuel, began the career of instrumental
music. He was wonderfully gifted in the art of improvising, for which
he was amply qualified by the thorough training he had received from
his father. Emanuel Bach was the father of the Sonata.

In March, 1732, in the village of Rohrau (not far from Vienna), a
certain wheelwright, of a musical turn, was blessed with a dark and
perhaps rather scrawny little son, to whom was given the name of
Francis Joseph Haydn. Papa Haydn played a little on the organ and
harp, and sang with a fine tenor voice. Sunday afternoons, when his
official duties as sexton were over, he was accustomed to have a sort of
concert with the aid of his wife. The little Francis Joseph was an
interested assistant at these domestic celebrations, and soon learned to
add his own piping little voice to the family concerts. At an early age
he went to Hamburg with his cousin Frank, who promised to teach
him music and Latin. When yet hardly eight years old the youngster
became celebrated as a choir-boy, and very soon he was captured by

Reuter, the director of the music at St. Stephen's Church in Vienna, who used to make frequent tours in search of promising voices for his choir. Haydn afterwards said that all the time he was with Reuter (over ten years), never a day passed in which he did not practise from sixteen to eighteen hours, although the boys were practically their own masters, only being obliged to practice two hours.

When thirteen years old he composed a mass, which to his great chagrin was mercilessly ridiculed by Reuter. Haydn presently saw that a knowledge of harmony and counterpoint was essential to success in composition. But who would teach a penniless choir boy? For Haydn was absolutely as poor as poverty itself. Bread and cheese and an annual suit of clothes he had to be sure, but the authorities of St. Stephen's Church in Vienna preserved their choir boys as carefully from "the deceitfulness of riches," as many churches do their ministers now-a-days. But genius is indefatigable. Haydn found a copy of a treatise on counterpoint by Fux, in a second-hand bookstore, and by some desperate expedient contrived to get possession of it. Now Fux's book is in Latin, and not in the clearest form. But Haydn knew there were worse things in the world than bad Latin, and one of these was ignorance. So he "pegged away" at it, like the plucky little man he was, lying a-bed in cold days to keep warm, taking his diurnal portion of the sorry old book as conscientiously as he did his daily mass and dinner. About the time he had begun to get easy on the subject of counterpoint, Providence sent him another lesson.

In the *suite* of the Venetian ambassador at Vienna was the great Italian master and singer, Nicolo Porpora. Now Porpora was a crusty old person, and was not a man who at all looked like taking up a *protégé* in the shape of a seedy looking little choir boy. But if Porpora did not know Haydn, Haydn did know Porpora, and that he was the same great master who had been brought over to London to rival the mighty Handel, just now in the very glory of his fame. So Haydn got up early, cleaned the boots, brushed the coat, and curled the wig of the amiable master, whose only recognition of these services was a muttered "*fool*," when Haydn entered the room. But, as Sam Slick discovered, "soft soap" will tell if persevered in, and when to these civilities was added the fact that they were *gratis*, and when the boy had proved himself so useful in accompanying some of Porpora's songs, which the beauteous lady of the ambassador was fond of singing—at last the severity began to relent, and Haydn got many a word of sound advice, and with it the Italian taste in singing. Presently the ambassador recognized the young man's progress by a pension of fifteen dollars a month, and a seat at the secretaries' table. Haydn was now full of activity; as soon as it was light he made haste to the Church of the Father of Mercy, where he played first violin; from thence he hastened to the chapel of Count Haugwitz, where he played the organ; afterwards he sang the tenor at St. Stephen's. He then returned home and finished out the day at his piano. If there is any one lesson that the early lives of these composers teach more plainly than another, it is that laziness is not a sign of genius. Hard work is an indispensable condition of success in any business that is worth following. Haydn's voice broke when he was nineteen years old, and he found himself without employment. A wig-maker named Keller kindly received him as a son, and in this house Haydn gave himself more decidedly to composition. When he was twenty he published six instrumental trios, which attracted general attention. The individuality of his talent was more fully confirmed by his first quartette, which soon followed. Presently he left the house of Keller, and found a boarding place with a Mr. Martinez, on condition of his giving piano and singing lessons to his two daughters. In the same house lived the poet Metastasio, who, being fond of music, took Haydn into his friendship, having him daily to dinner and good converse. In this way Haydn picked up a great deal of general knowledge and some Italian, affording, I dare say, with his simple German nature, fully as much as he gave.

In 1758 he entered the employment of Count Mortzin, as leader of his orchestra. In this capacity some of his works attracted the attention of old Prince Esterhazy, who in 1760 appointed him *kapell-meister*. The old gentleman died a year after, but Haydn continued for thirty years in the service of his son Nicholas, who died in 1790. Within the ten years previous to this appointment, he had composed his opera "The Devil on Two Sticks," a number of quartettes and trios, and just now his first symphony, and here he is twenty-eight years old. Yet this short list of works was by no means all Haydn had written. He had produced an immense mass of pieces of every kind, which had merely served the purpose of giving him that facility of expression, that mastery over the technics of his art, without which a genius, however highly gifted, is curtailed in the most promising flights.

The thirty years that followed were monotonous in the extreme. About two months of every year were spent in Vienna; the other ten at the prince's quiet Hungarian estates. Haydn produced an enormous list of pieces, many of them of great beauty. They comprise 119 symphonies, 83 quartettes, 24 trios, 19 operas, 15 masses, 163 compositions for barytone (Prince Esterhazy's favorite instrument), 44 pianoforte sonatas, etc.

Haydn appears to have been unconscious of the immense reputation he had achieved throughout Europe, and was never more astonished than when, soon after Prince Esterhazy's death, a stranger burst into his room, saying, "I am Salomon of London, and am come to carry you off with me; we will strike a bargain to-morrow." "Oh, papa," said the youthful Mozart, "you have had no education for the wide, wide world, and you speak too few languages." "Oh, my language," replied the papa with a smile, "is understood all over the world." And so at the age of sixty, in the full maturity of his powers, came Haydn to London. Here in little more than a year he wrote six new symphonies, and many other smaller things. These symphonies were brought out as novelties, Haydn conducting in person, seated at the piano.

The bustle of London and the favor with which he was received struck Haydn favorably. "He tells us[*] how he enjoyed himself at the civic feast in company with William Pitt, Lord Chancellor, and the Duke of Lids (Leeds). He says, after dinner the highest nobility— i. e. the Lord Mayor and his wife (!)—were seated on a throne. In another room, the gentlemen, as usual, drank freely all night; and the songs and the crazy uproar and the smashing of glasses were very great. The oil lamps smelt terribly, and the dinner cost £6,000. He went down to stay with the Prince of Wales (George IV.), and Sir Joshua Reynolds painted his portrait. The Prince played the violoncello not badly, and charmed Haydn by his affability. 'He is the handsomest man on God's earth. He has an extraordinary love of music, and a great deal of feeling, but very little money.' From the palace he passed to the laboratory and was introduced to Herschel, in whom he was delighted to find an old oboe player. The big telescope astonished him, so did the astronomer. 'He often sits out of doors in the most intense cold for five or six hours at a time.'"

In 1792 Haydn returned to Vienna, where he brought out his new symphonies. In 1795 he was back again in London, and earned no less than 12,000 florins (five or six thousand dollars). He bought him a little home near Vienna, where he passed the remnant of his days in peace and quiet. In 1795 he began, and in 1798 finished his cantata or oratorio "The Creation," which we commonly speak of as his greatest work. Haydn died at the age of seventy-seven, in 1809, and was buried in the cemetery of Gumpfendorf, Vienna.

*" Music and Morals."

Haydn's works number about eight hundred, many of them of small value, yet all finished with great care. I hardly know whether in strict justice we ought to accord Haydn the greater honor as a vocal or instrumental composer; for, although his works in the line of chamber music and symphony have exercised the greatest influence upon composers, his "Creation" has been very influential (in this country at least) in educating the taste of the public. It is the one oratorio that receives the earliest attention of amateur societies, a pre-eminence it well deserves from the grace and sweetness of its ideas, and the elegance with which they are worked out. And although "The Creation" appears somewhat childlike and bland, for a work in severe style (especially when compared with Handel's "Messiah" or "Israel," Bach's "Passion's Music," or even Mendelssohn's "Elijah"), we can not deny the consummate grace of the lovely airs "With verdure clad," and "On mighty pens," or the almost operatic sweetness of the trio "On thee each living soul awaits," and the concerted duet "By thee with bliss." "The heavens are telling" has been universally a favorite.

Nevertheless the critic turns from this work, which in every trait except grace and sweetness has been far surpassed, to the quartettes; and here, as the conditions have remained substantially the same from his time until now, Haydn has not been so far out-ranked. Mozart had a livelier imagination, Beethoven and Schumann more of Bach's earnestness. Haydn's music, even in its most elaborate moments, is simple in its essential nature—the expression of a child-like, contented soul, so completely well bred as almost to seem never to have required training.

As an orchestral writer Haydn made enormous advances. He gave the symphony the systematic development of the sonata form, introduced many new combinations, and established the type of the *Andante cantabile* movement, which Mozart and Beethoven afterwards carried to so great a perfection.

His pianoforte compositions sound narrow and old fashioned.

In the mere fact of producing so much of a somewhat uniform texture, Haydn did a great deal for the cultivation of instrumental music. He seems always to have had a singularly accurate idea of the practical and the available. We may be sure both that he was a pleasant man to get along with, and an agreeable writer, or he would not have remained so long in one position.

Haydn attached small importance to the actual substance of the germinal ideas in his works. He had such consummate art that he

11

could work up the most commonplace ideas into an attractive and beautiful whole. He said *the treatment* was every thing.

List of Haydn Illustrations.

(*Employing Soprano, Tenor, Bass, and the Pianoforte.*)

1. Sonata in E flat.
2. " My Mother Bids me Bind my Hair," Soprano.
3. Minuet in C (Oxen Minuet).
4. " In Native Worth," Tenor.
5. Variations on " God Save the Emperor" (Haydn Album, p. 38).
6. " Now Heaven in Fullest Glory Shone," Bass.
7. Symphony in D for four hands (No. 5 Peters' Edition).
8. Trio, " On Thee each Living Soul Awaits," Soprano, Tenor, and Bass.

CHAPTER FORTY-FIVE.

MOZART.

Rarely does it fall to the lot of a writer to undertake a more genial task than to sketch the short life of Wolfgang Amadeus Mozart, born at Salzburg, about a hundred miles from Vienna, January 27, 1756—a life of such marvellous richness as to give to a sober account the air of liveliest romance. Bach had died only six years before. Handel was in his old age and blindness, and died three years later ; Haydn was in the very pinch of his hardest fortunes, living in the house with Metastasio, as previously recorded. Yet these proximities of dates look far more significant to us now than they could have looked a hundred years ago; for then there were many other composers of great talents who contested with these giants the claim to immortality. The century that has intervened has been very busy in analyzing and sifting their productions, and this has finally resulted in giving due honor to these great ones, who the more they have been weighed in the balance have proven themselves the more worthy.

Leopold Mozart, the father, was himself a musician of marked talent. He published an instruction book for the violin and held a place as court musician with the Archbishop of Salzburg. When Wolfgang was three years old his talent for music began to manifest itself. When he was four years old he could play a number of minuets and the like, and learned with wonderful facility. He found out for himself thirds and other concords. When yet under six years old his father found him one day writing something which he called a " concerto for the harpsichord." The father of course laughed at such a work by a mere baby, but the little fellow insisted that it was really a concerto, and on examination it proved to be written strictly according to rule, although so overloaded with difficulties as to be impossible. When a little over six years old he performed at the court of Francis I., at Munich, with his eldest sister, where his wonderful gifts excited the greatest astonishment. Still it is but just to say that child-virtuosity was of much easier attainment then than now, for the pianos of that day were very small, the touch light, and the compositions in vogue were of an amiable and unimpassioned character.

Presently young Wolfgang learned the violin, and surprised his father by playing correctly in a quartette. Of anecdotes of this kind the Mozart biographies are full. Suffice it to say, that during his first twelve years his talent shone out brighter and brighter, and on all hands he received the warmest approbation, yet he never became a spoiled child. He was of a gentle, confiding disposition, of a sweet and even temper, fond of play—a queer compound of manly talent and skill with childish tastes and habits. He spent some three years in traveling, visiting France, England and Holland—his public life as a youthful virtuoso being supplemented by regular and daily studies in musical theory, and the regular branches of a polite education. In this way he learned French, Latin and Italian. In 1767 or so he visited Vienna, and composed a small opera, which, however, was never performed. By the command of the Emperor, he wrote a mass for the dedication of the new Waisenhaus church, and conducted with baton in hand. When scarcely twelve years old, he was appointed concertmeister by the Archbishop of Salzburg, and within the next year wrote a number of masses.

But his father was anxious that Wolfgang should become known in Italy, which was at that time the fountain of musical inspiration. So in December, 1769, they set off for Italy, staying some months in Rome, Bologna, Florence Milan, etc. The Pope made him a "knight of the golden spur."

The most significant triumph of this tour was his admission as a member of the Philharmonic Academy of Bologna, at that time the highest musical authority in the world. At its head was the learned contrapuntist, Father Martini, and at his right hand the great singer, Farinelli, also a learned musician. These men and the members of

the Academy generally recognized Mozart's genius as a perfor , but
no one could believe that a boy of twelve could pass triumphantly
through the severe tests in counterpoint required of candidates for admission. Nevertheless, *Padre* Martini rightly judged that the extreme
youth of Mozart made it necessary that his admission to the distinguished honor of membership should be justified to the world by the
severest tests ever assigned. This task was the composition for four
voices of one of the canticles of the Roman *Antiphonarium.* The work
was to be treated according to severe rules, and performed within three
hours in a locked-up room—the Academy waiting as patiently as they
might in order to judge the work as soon as it was accomplished. Men
who regarded themselves great masters had often failed in this task, con-
suming the whole time in the production of a few lines. It was therefore with no small misgivings that Father Martini delivered to the hope-
ful Mozart the task which was to announce his manhood in the most
difficult department of musical theory. But great was his surprise, when
after little more than a half hour the beadle came in saying that the
young Mozart declared himself ready to be let out, having finished the
task.

"Impossible!" said many of the members. "In the hundred
years the Academy had been established such a case had never occurred." Nevertheless, when the committee, proceeded to Mozart's room
they received from him a manuscript, written in his usual neat and
delicate hand; and after careful scrutiny they were compelled to admit
that it contained no faults whatever. I may add that it took the old
doctors about an hour to go through the paper thoroughly enough to
convince themselves that Mozart's rapid work was faultless. The young
composer was then led in, and the whole Academy greeted him with
hearty applause, and recognized in him an accomplished *Maestro,* and
a Knight of Harmony.

Now, the gratifying point of this transaction is, that this highly
gifted boy, traveling from place to place, playing in public almost
daily, found time for such thorough study as to be able at the childish
age of twelve to meet and conquer the most learned theorists on their
own ground. And better than this, he does not seem to have been
puffed up by his success; to him it was not difficult, and while proud of
the commendation of these learned men, and of having proven himself
a master, we find his letters just as simple, and child-like, and modest
as before.

After this Italian tour Mozart returned to Salzburg, which, however, he soon left for Munich. But his future ups and downs we have

not room to follow; for, unlike Bach, Handel and Haydn, whose lives embraced long periods of twenty years and more passed in one place, Mozart was rarely more than a few years in a place, except his last ten years, which he spent in Vienna. It is the more difficult to bring his life into a sketch from the fact that he went much into society, and has left on record a large collection of letters which give a very graphic picture of life at that time. These letters fill two volumes, and are well worth reading. The little book called "Mozart's Early Days," lately published, gives a very lively and entertaining account of his life up to the time of his triumph in the Bologna Academy. Lee & Shepard also publish a book—"Mozart and Mendelssohn"—which not only gives a succinct account of his life, but a great deal of interesting information about his music. To these sources I beg to refer the reader for the details of Mozart's marriage and later life, assuring them that only in the life of Mendelssohn do we find equally rich musical materials.

In 1779 Mozart produced his opera, "Idomeneo," the first upon which his present fame rests. It was followed during the next ten years by "The Marriage of Figaro," "Don Juan," and "The Magic Flute," which comprise his master-pieces in this department of composition. These operas showed a marked advance over similar works of preceding composers, chiefly in their wealth of imagination and fancy, and especially in their geniality. They were in the first place *musical* to a high degree, and this in spite of the unquestionable science displayed in the concerted pieces. What was the state of music as left by Mozart's predecessors? Handel gave a clear form to melody, but we rarely find him successful in avoiding prolixity. His greatest songs are open to this charge. In the line of delicate sentiment he was also out of his element to a degree not always admitted by his admirers. He was fully successful only in a certain rude and genial energy, and in setting passages of such overpowering emotional import as to carry him beyond himself. In such airs as, "Oh, ruddier than the cherry," we find, to be sure, freshness to the last degree gratifying, yet it is not sentimental music.

Haydn, as we have already seen, developed *musical* life as such; for, in his manifold symphonies and quartettes, we find musical motives worked out in a manner at once elegant and musical, and essentially independent of words for their explanation. At the same time, Haydn was simply *genial* and *good natured* and not, in a high degree, *poetic* or imaginative, still less dramatic. His "Creation," indeed, was written after Mozart's death, and here Haydn builds on Mozart, notwithstanding that twelve or fifteen years before Mozart had built his first symphonies on Haydn's foundation.

In Mozart's operas we find the orchestra treated with a fullness greater than in the Haydn symphonies. An equally masterly working out of germinal ideas meets us here, but how changed! Mozart had rich imagination, and no small amount of the dramatic spirit. He had studied singing thoroughly, and well knew what was suitable for the voice. Still better, he knew what would please the public. And those amateurs who hold up their hands in blind worship of Mozart's operas (as some literary men do of every thing bearing the name of Shakespeare), imagining that he evolved them out of a prophetic inner consciousness, a striving after the ideal, with no consideration for the approval of the public of the day, show in this a strange ignorance of the man and his music. What is there in "Figaro," I ask, unappreciable by the Prague public of 1787? Nothing at all! Of this the best proof is that it was played *the whole Winter long* in that theater where first brought out. It is not the fate of prophetic masterpieces (music of the future) to succeed at once with the theater-going public like that.

Let it suffice for the operatic fame of Mozart to say that he first wrote melodies of matchless grace (see "*Vedrai Carino*," in Don Juan) and the most genial and bewitching sentiment. It was the beautiful especially in its lighter aspects that Mozart came to reveal. These bewitching strains of opera, ground on hand organs, sung by amateurs, and strummed on pianos the world over, were exactly the new revelation needed to render music a household word among all enlightened people.

Mozart's indifference to all but music is further shown by his finding himself able to set such objectionable texts as "Figaro" and "Don Juan;" this, as we shall hereafter see, would have been impossible for Beethoven or Mendelssohn, or for any man of sensitive moral earnestness. Nor do I find myself able to attribute to Mozart the dramatic ability many think they find in his works. But to discuss this would take me too far. In the opera, then, we see Mozart reaching the highest triumphs of his age, namely, fascinating and individualized melodies, the loveliest instrumentation, and a high degree of dramatic contrast.

In the symphony his success was almost equally great—although he gives no foreboding of the transition from the purely musical symphony of Haydn to the tone-poem symphony of Beethoven. His great art is in the increased wealth of instrumentation he displayed, more dramatic contrast, and an incomparable elegance and fascination of style.

Mozart left a great many string quartettes, duos, etc., of the most lovely character. In this kind of composition he was eminently successful, as the instruments and the sphere of that kind of music were as well understood then as now.

His pianoforte sonatas, though much talked about in school catalogues and the like, are really old fashioned, narrow and meagre works; possessing, indeed, beautiful ideas, yet, on the whole, so far inferior to more recent productions as to convey but an extremely imperfect idea of Mozart's real powers.

Of his church writing much might be said. He left a large number of masses, nearly all composed before he was twenty, and, therefore, full of a lively spirit of cheerfulness and hope, but not characterized by the deep and reverent devotion of Bach or Handel. Mozart was not distinctively a *religious* writer, but a *worldly*. He was fond of dancing, of society, loved every beautiful woman, liked a glass of wine, and in every thing was the opposite of the ascetic, self-forgetful church composer. Still, these works contain many beautiful movements, and give another side of the richly endowed Mozart nature. The last of the so-called sacred works was the *Requiem*, written shortly before his death, under the circumstances so well known as not to require recounting here. This "Mass for the Dead" is a fitting climax to the life of the great composer.

One of the most useful services of Mozart was the addition of wind and brass parts to the score of Handel's "Messiah"— a helpful act which has undoubtedly done much to prolong the popularity of that sublime masterpiece. Mozart died on December 5, 1792, at the early age of thirty-five, worn out by hard work and too much society.

It deserves to be remembered that while this great master was endowed by God with a wealth of musical inspiration, so that in this respect no one has yet surpassed him, he found time to thoroughly study the works of his predecessors—especially of Bach, Handel, Glück and Haydn; and thought himself not above the drudgery of mastering the theoretical principles of his art; and in this way only did he contrive to leave on record such a brilliant list of beautiful creations.

PROGRAMME OF MOZART ILLUSTRATIONS.

1. (*Employing Soprano and Pianoforte*).

1. Symphony in C, "Jupiter," for 4 hands, The Piano.
2. Air, "Vedrai Carino" from "Don Juan," Soprano.
3. Air, "Voi Che Sapete" from "Figaro," Soprano.
4. *a.* March from the Magic Flute.
   b. Menuet in E flat, arranged by Schulhoff, The Pianoforte.
5. Air, "Dove Sono" from "Figaro," Soprano.
6. The Overture to "Figaro" for four hands, The Piano.

CHAPTER FORTY-SIX.

BEETHOVEN.

All our studies throughout this course have revolved around Beethoven. His works furnished a part of the illustrations of the very first lesson, and there is scarcely one of the thirty-seven practical lessons in the present course where his name does not appear. Not only is this the greatest name in Music, but it is one of the greatest that has appeared in Art. When men think of the grace and refinement and incomparable beauty of his work, they call him the Raphael of music, although such a title by right should belong to Mozart. When they listen to the Heroic Symphony or the Mass in D minor, they call him the Michael Angelo, or the Milton of music. But both these are misnomers. Others call him the Dante of the tone-art, or the Shakespeare. These, also, are unfruitful suggestions. There *is* no Shakespeare in music, nor can be; the arts are too dissimilar. For the same reason there is no Raphael, nor Tintoret, nor Angelo in tones. Mozart had a grace and sweetness equal to that of Raphael's. But besides these qualities there is in Mozart's work a simplicity and unaffected naivete peculiar to him. The grandeur and seriousness of Milton exist in music also, and in greater measure, but without the labored and somewhat pedantic form of Milton's phraseology.

What we do have in Beethoven is a genius of as pure a ray as the world has ever seen. He was not technically the most scientific of great composers. Bach, Handel, Haydn and even the genial and spontaneous Mozart, wrote smoother counterpoint, and traveled more easily within the lines of fugue. Yet Beethoven knew *Music* better than any of these, and left works which out-rank theirs in every direction except that of purely formal phraseology. What was it then, in which Beethoven excelled? And wherein lies the secret of the estimation in which he is held by the whole civilized world?

Beethoven's greatness as a composer, and his influence upon the development of music since his day, lies in one point, namely, his intuition of the *relation of music to emotion.* As already pointed out, Bach wrote more learnedly, Handel, at times, quite as heartily, Haydn as

clearly, and Mozart as sweetly; but what Beethoven does is to avail
himself of all these excellencies of form and substance, *in order to express feeling through them*. The greatest of his predecessors, Bach,
also had feeling and expressed it in his Passion Music with great
power. But his style is not easy, the phraseology is too learned. It
seems to us cold. The composers after him relapsed his severity, as we
have seen. Through Handel, the sons of Bach, Haydn, and Mozart —
the World and Art were drawing nearer each other. In Beethoven
they coalesce. And so it is the proud pre-eminence of this Master to
have expressed his soul in music as fully and as exclusively as Shakespeare expressed his in his plays, or Raphael in his cartoons, and with
such force and range of imagination, and such exquisite propriety of
diction, that all the world immediately listens to him. Like all these
geniuses of the very highest rank, his soul is in his works. His daily
life is nothing. He is never a citizen, magistrate, a teacher, a writer,
a talker, or a man of property; but always and only a creative Artist.
In early life he was, indeed, a virtuoso, not through study and drudgery, but by sheer force of the overmastering inspiration within him.

The world used him, how shall we say? Well, or badly? If we
reflect upon his humble origin, his steady elevation during his life-
time into the highest estimation ever accorded a musician and composer, his comparative immunity from want or the necessity of drudg-
ing toil either in teaching or playing, and this through the ready sale
of the productions of his pen—we must say *well*. On the other hand,
if we think of his lack of education or early training, his solitary life,
his graceless nephew, his deafness and his suspicious and difficult habit
of mind,—in these we recognize the unfavorable side of his relation
to the world; and when we think that all this befell one whose creations
have added delight and beauty to the daily lives, not only of his con-
temporaries and compatriots, but to that of the whole civilized world
in three generations, we can not help perceiving here a certain disso-
nance the resolution of which we are not able to trace.

It is our difficult task, therefore, to outline the life of this man, to
describe his surroundings and personal peculiarities, and to trace his
mode of outward life, so as to bring him before our minds in some resemblance to the form he wore in the eyes of his neighbors and friends;
and yet along with this, to trace, in his works, the transcendently beautiful operations of his mind and inner nature, and to hold them up as
the true expression of the Beethoven soul, which they most certainly
were. If in doing this we might also unite both pictures into one, so
that we could think of Beethoven as a humbly-born, hardworking boy,

of the most determined "grit," yet with a delicacy and sweetness of fancy which is absolutely nobler than even Shakespeare's (for Beethoven nowhere descends to coarseness), and then trace his growth to manhood, his steady pursuit of his one ideal, Music, the blessing that followed him in it, and that has followed us for his being in it; and crown the whole with the still nobler side of his nature in his unselfish and well-meant love and providence for a graceless relative, when he himself was, as we ordinarily say, "a crusty old bachelor" of fifty;—if we could bring all these together into a single consistent idea we should then have performed for the reader a service indeed.

Ludwig van Beethoven was born at Bonn, the *Residenz-Stadt* of the Electors of Cologne, in 1770. His father was tenor singer in the Elector's Chapel, an ill-natured, drunken fellow with a shiftless, easygoing wife. They lived in a very humble way, the annual income of the family being probably less than three hundred dollars. As Mozart was just then at the height of his celebrity, the father of our Beethoven was in no small degree delighted to observe the promising musical talent of the boy—a talent which manifested itself at a very early age. There was music in the family, unquestionably—Beethoven's grandfather having been an organist and a composer of creditable talent. So at the early age of five he was taken in hand by his father and set to work in the laborious German fashion to learn to play the piano and the violin. The crusty father is said to have pulled him out of bed in the middle of the night, to make him finish up the practice he had neglected. Nor was the practice sweetened for him; for the boy was not allowed to play melodies, many of which came to him even then untaught, but only the exercises then most approved for practice.

At that time the works of Bach held high honor for purposes of study, and the boy Beethoven was so thoroughly exercised in them that at the age of twelve he was perfectly familiar with the entire forty-eight preludes and fugues of the "Well Tempered Clavier," and could play them with the utmost facility. All this time he went to the public school, but owing to his father's ambition to bring him out as a musical wonder-child, his studies in letters were seriously neglected. When the boy was about eight years old his father turned him over to the teaching of one Pfeffer, an oboe player and pianist, under whose kindlier direction he got along more rapidly and no doubt much more pleasantly. Presently the organist Neefe took him in hand and taught him the organ and composition, so that when twelve or thirteen years old he appears as author of three sonatas for piano, which are small, but very clever for a boy.

For some time, probably since his tenth year, he had played a viola in the orchestra. About this time he became assistant organist to Neefe, although the formal appointment was not received until he was about fifteen. When he was about thirteen, he began to act as pianist and assistant director in the orchestra during Neefe's absence, which frequently extended over several months. The duties of this position were not small. High Mass was performed in church three times a week besides Sunday, and on at least as many days there were elaborate vesper services. The theater gave a light opera or operetta three times a week, and comedies on other nights, for all of which music had to be prepared. This kind of activity seems to have continued until Beethoven was about twenty, interrupted only by his first visit to Vienna, where he somehow managed to go when he was about sixteen. Beethoven's duties as organist must have been very unthankful, since the old organ had been removed from the chapel, and in his time only a small chamber-organ stood in its place. That he had no special vocation for the organ appears plainly from his never having written anything for it. The particulars of his Vienna journey are rather hypothetical, especially the anecdote of his having played before Mozart and receiving lessons from him.

During all these years he attained no recognition in Bonn as a promising artist. On the several lists of the Elector's musical staff, the name of Beethoven figures as organist and player of clavier concertos, but amid many who are distinguished as of exceptional talent, he stands unnoticed and undistinguished.

The theater at Bonn produced a fine selection of works for that day, among which were the best of Glück's operas. On the whole we can hardly imagine a place better calculated to familiarize a young composer with every slightest peculiarity of the composers before his day, than Beethoven found in his six years' service as assistant director at Bonn. In the work of arranging and adapting the scores to the limitations and weaknesses of his orchestra, he could not fail to acquire rare tact, and a spontaneous comprehension of all effects of instrumentation. He played the piano part from the full orchestra score, and it was thus that he developed that lightning-like comprehension of the fullest scores, which he always manifested. Mendel says that Max Franz (the Elector, brother of Joseph II) when he appointed Beethoven second organist furnished funds for him to go to Vienna to make more extended studies.

During this Bonn life Beethoven early attracted the attention of the von Breunings, a wealthy and refined family of that town, and at their house he was always at home. No doubt it must have required a good deal of faith in the diamond concealed in his rough exterior, for the fine von Breunings to have made so much of so unpromising a customer as the boy Beethoven. He was moody, often irritable. He was the very prince of awkwardness, upsetting and breaking every fragile article he came near. Still there seems to have been a charm about him, for as we shall see later, he was through life a favorite among the best people, especially the ladies, of an elegant and ceremonious court. Here at the Breunings' he became familiar with the books and pictures denied him at home. Count Waldstein, also, was one of the friends he made in this early time, and who always remained true to him. It was Waldstein who recommended him to the notice of the titled relatives of his family when Beethoven came to Vienna to live; and it was to Count Waldstein that in 1803 the brilliant sonata in C, op. 53, was dedicated.

In personal appearance Beethoven must have been rather striking. He was of medium height (or rather under), thick set, a noble forehead, small, brown eyes, deeply set in, very profuse hair, generally " towseled," his dress of rather common texture originally, but now rich with the sedimentary deposits of many brushless months. His hands are well shaped, but the nails are not well kept. In movement he is quick and abrupt, often boorish. This want of politeness adhered to him through life. Still, it was his lot to associate with many eminent men, and from them he doubtless imbibed a great deal of cultivation His manners must have been worse about the time of his departure from Bonn and first entrance into Vienna than afterwards.

As to his self-conceit, all testimony proves it. Nor is it difficult to account for it. It must have been perfectly apparent to Beethoven that he was able to improvise music of such rare power over the feelings that nothing of Haydn's or Mozart's or Handel's could be compared with it. We read remarkable stories of this faculty. As, for instance: "Ignace Pleyel had brought some new quartettes to Vienna, which were performed at the house of Prince Lobkowitz. At the close, Beethoven, who was present, was asked to play. As usual, he had to be pressed again and again, and at last was almost dragged by force to the instrument by the ladies With an impatient gesture he snatched from the violin desk the open second violin part of Pleyel's quartette, threw it on the desk of the pianoforte and began to improvise. His playing had never been more brilliant, original and grand than on that evening. But through the whole improvisation, in the middle parts ran like a thread or *canto fermo* the notes, unimportant in themselves, of the accidentally open page, on which he built the noblest melodies and harmonies in the most brilliant concert style. Old Pleyel could only show his astonishment by kissing his hands. After such improvisation Beethoven would break out into a loud, merry, ringing laugh."

This is the spirit of his first entrance upon the Vienna life in 1792. Here he lived until his death, in 1827. At first he was the pupil of Haydn, who since Mozart's death, was king again. For these lessons his fee was exactly eight groschen, *eighteen cents!* Later he went to Albrechtsberger for lessons in counterpoint, and to Salieri for lessons in dramatic composition.

As early as 1800 he began to be hard of hearing, gradually increasing to almost total deafness as early as 1810. This affliction, as well as the false behavior of his two brothers, his nearest relatives, had the effect to cloud his mind with suspicion of all the people around him. In the period from 1792 to 1810, he produced a constant succession of the noblest works. Before he had got beyond the fifth symphony the critics had begun to talk of his "obscurity," "want of melody," etc., just as they did a few years ago of Schumann, and just as they do now of Wagner. Yet, he seems to have cared very little about it, and said that if it amused them to be constantly writing such things about him they might be freely indulged.

His personal habits were whimsical enough. One lodging was too high; another he left because the landlord was too obsequious. He would walk his room half the night through, " howling and roaring" the melodies that filled his imagination, and flooding the floor and ruining the ceiling and tempers of the occupants of the rooms below with the water he poured over his hands to cool his feverishness. He would hire a boy to pump water over his hands by the hour together. It is related *apropos* to his carelessness in money matters that "the waiters in the *cafés* in Vienna were content to be unpaid sometimes, if they were paid double and treble the next day. It was not worth while to quarrel with a privileged person, who always had the laugh on his side, and had been known to throw a dish of meat at the head of a waiter suspected of cheating. Here, after the close of his day's labor, he appeared at his best, and those who knew him speak of his loud laughter, his richness and originality of conversation, his wit, bold and reckless as his harmonies, his strong opinions, his interest in books and politics. On all hands we see the signs of the broad and wholesome humanity which formed the ground of his strangely mingled character, so much caricatured and so little understood by the retailers of anecdote, who can see in Beethoven nothing but an inspired artist, and a mixture of misanthropy and buffoon."* "To his friends he was a warm hearted, unselfish friend, not to be treated carelessly, much less to be played with or slighted; a friend whose friendship was worth a sacrifice, because it was founded on perfect sincerity, could endure no suspicion of insincerity in others. That Beethoven—great Mogul as he was, and capable of many unmannerly words and actions—was not unacceptable to those who loved good society, we may learn from the fact of his having always been well received by the great ladies of a ceremonious court. It was true that his dress was untidy to dirtiness; that he picked his teeth with the snuffers, upset inkstands into the pianoforte, and broke every thing he touched; and that he had been known to play off ill-bred practical jokes on some of his friends; but in spite of all incongruities, princesses and countesses—nay, personages of still higher rank—received him as an equal or a superior This result could hardly have been brought about by his music alone."†

From 1800 to 1806 Beethoven was in the height of his creative activity. During this time he produced the sonatas opus 22 to 57, the third and fourth symphonies, a number of chamber pieces (quartettes, trios, etc.), and the opera "Fidelio." This creative activity continued, with little falling off in speed, and with a decided progress in the quality of the work produced, down to 1815, by which time he had written all the nine symphonies except the last. These years were especially productive in smaller works—such as songs, bagatelles of various kinds, three sets of Scotch and Irish airs, arranged with ritornellos and accompaniments.

Beethoven was now forty-five years of age. He was in ill health, probably for want of proper care of himself. He was overrun with commissions from publishers, and had the most flattering offers to travel in different countries, of which, however, he was too fond of Vienna and too ignorant of the world to take advantage. At this period misfortune befell him, in the shape of a nephew—the son of his brother Carl—left in his guardianship. As already shown, there were undesirable streaks in the Beethoven family. This had not been mended by Carl's marrying a shiftless woman, of bad repute, and it was the product of this union that was left in the composer's care. He undertook the task in the loftiest spirit. Henceforth for eleven years the boy regulated all the affairs of Beethoven's *menage*, and a most thankless time the old gentleman had of it. The very worst housekeeping bachelor that ever was was a prince of managers compared with Beethoven. He had not the slightest "faculty" for business. It discomposed him to be obliged to transact the most ordinary affairs. We may well imagine what a time he had of it with a reckless, ungrateful youth on his hands. His love was repaid with ingratitude, and, to crown all, the nephew seems to have been responsible for his uncle's death; for, when sent for a doctor, he carelessly gave the message to a billiard marker, who forgot it for a day or two, and when the doctor arrived there was no longer a possibility of cure.

These last years of Beethoven are sad in the extreme. That a man should have had so much greatness, yet so little comfort! That his inner world should have been so full of lovely fancies, which he has left on record for the gratification of aftercoming generations, and yet his own daily life have been so unblessed by woman's tenderness, and the amenities of home, is one of the mysteries of life. Yet we may be glad that Beethoven undertook the care of this boy, and stuck to it so manfully; for his letters and the whole history of this time place his character in a much nobler light of self-sacrifice than would otherwise have been the case. And as to the works we might else have had from this period, our composer has already left the highest monument so far in the world of music. Surely it is better for us to know that he was a noble-hearted, true man, than for us to have had another symphony. Besides, there is no doubt that this discipline, painful as it was, must have wrought a great softening and deepening in Beethoven's disposition.

In 1725 he imagined himself in poverty. Moscheles, who was then in London, wrote to him, and arranged for the London Philharmonic Society to give a concert for his benefit, in return for which he was to write them a tenth symphony. This concert was given and a sum of £100 made up and sent to Beethoven a short time before he died. The whole correspondence may be found in Moscheles' edition of "Schindler's Life of Beethoven," and in Moscheles' "Recent Music and Musicians."

Beethoven died March 29, 1827, at the age of fifty-seven, during a violent thunderstorm. He was buried at Wahring, a small village near Vienna, and was followed to the grave by an immense concourse of people (over twenty thousand, some say).

Beethoven's genius was distinctly that for expressing feeling. Feeling is the source of the all-penetrating unity, which is perhaps one of the most conspicuous marks of his work. We do not mean by this that he is always in a passion, or under the influence of some dark or disturbing mood. Far from it. The genius of his music is characteristically the *peaceful*, the *tranquil*. In these qualities he is hardly surpassed by Mozart. It is the unity and the repose of the great, the lasting, the true. Beethoven was extremely fond of the open air and the country. When the weather was fine he would spend whole days and half the nights wandering about the fields or stretched at ease in the shade of a tree. In these walks his eye was quick to notice every pleasant bit of landscape, every pretty flower, or effect of light, and if he had a companion, he remarked upon these things with warmth and force.

Such beauty and quiet took musical shape within him. Out came the memorandum book of music-paper roughly stitched together, and the walk and discourse gave place to that curious "howling and roaring" with which his labor of composition was always accompanied. His published works are full of ideas which may be traced sometimes for years, through wide and strange changes from the forms in which they at first suggested themselves to him to the shape in which they were at last employed. Those tranquil days under the pleasant sky are all expressed in his music. Of such a spirit are the pianoforte sonatas in E and G, op. 14, the "pastoral," op. 28, that in G, op. 31, and several of those for piano and violin, as well as the pastoral symphony, and the seventh and eighth. In deriving his inspiration from external nature as a source, Beethoven was like Schubert, in whom every movement of soul translates itself into tones. With Beethoven there is, however, this difference, that he selects the more significant for publication, and then shapes and prunes it with more care. Beethoven is never too long; certainly never tedious.

Another of the most remarkable peculiarities of Beethoven's music is the clearness and beauty of his orchestral coloring. No other composer knows better just where to throw in a few notes of the flute, a soft low tone of the horn, a clever bit of the bassoon, or just how to place a subordinate phrase in order to have it express itself without interfering with the blending and harmony of the whole. This delicious reserve is one of the most eminent traits of the symphonies, although no doubt, a part of it is apparent only, and due to the remarkable heightening and strengthening of orchestral coloring since his day.

Were we to attempt to measure up and estimate the place of these works on the scale of beauty, we should be first struck with their elegance, clearness and the agreeable nature of their sound. They have for pleasure of sensation all that they could have and still retain their distinguishing elevation of sentiment. In formal beauty, likewise, they hold an extremely high rank, perhaps as high as any. There is in Mozart a certain sweet and spontaneous grace, an unconscious sweetness, such as we rarely find in Beethoven; but Beethoven compensates for this lack, if lack there be, by a greater coherence and unity, through which he reaches a more serene repose, especially in the classical moments of his art.

And then, finally, we come to the symphonies. These are the thoughts Beethoven had while he lay under the trees out in the country. Far on into the night he would wander, and drink in his fill of the silent teaching of nature. Her in the symphonies we have them all. If in the pastoral symphony we have a moment of pleasantry in the bird song or two, it is thrown in only to bring us still nearer the inscrutable mystery of the growing grass; nearer to the trees, by their subtle chemistry building themselves up out of intangible air and the hidden riches of the ground; nearer to the light and fleecy clouds, and the golden and crimson sunset, fitly emphasizing the finished day, ever more to be numbered with the infinite ages of God; and, above all, nearer to the greater mystery of thoughtful life, the image of the Invisible, the sure witness of the Infinite. No other instrumental music so completely seizes and exalts the hearer.

The inner nature of Beethoven allies him to Bach. They were both *universal* musicians, innovators and experimenters in every direction, according to the light and resources of their respective generations. Both found in a particular style and form, a field which, on the whole, satisfied them and afforded room for the elaboration of their most beautiful ideas. Bach's was the fugue. There was no kind of musical production known to Bach's day which he did not to some extent try, except, perhaps, the opera. The suite, church pieces, organ works, and compositions for violin and almost every instrument, he produced in large quantities. But, after all, the one form which he always adopted, or came back to for a climax, was *fugue*. This great form, the *ne plus ultra* of musical logic, was not original with Bach. On the contrary it had been worked out by three centuries of experimenters and geniuses, until it assumed the form in which Bach found it, and in which it is in effect the valid and final solution of coherent 'onality. Counterpoint, which is the basis of fugue, is the exhaustive solution of melodic invention. Bach's work was to seize this form and appropriate it to the needs of musical revelation. He filled it full of novelty, grandeur, caprice, humor, true musical feeling and beauty.

12

He exhausted it, completely filled up the capacity of the form, so that since Bach there is no longer any thing new to be said in Fugue.

In like manner Beethoven was a composer of sonatas. The *rôle* of his works embraces every kind of production known in his day; but the one form which he made his own, and in which his most beautiful and characteristic ideas are expressed, is the sonata. This form includes his thirty-three for piano solo, which would eternally have established his fame if they alone had constituted his serious works; nineteen sonatas for piano and other instruments; eighteen trios, mainly for piano and other instruments; twenty-three quartettes and quintettes; the sextette and septette, and the nine symphonies. In all, more than three thousand large pages of sonata writing. Beethoven, like Bach, was in every way progressive and an innovator. He experimented in all forms, and in all combinations of means of expression. Yet, on the whole, he was a composer of sonatas.

This form he found ready to his hand in the works of Haydn and Mozart. The form, as such, he accepted with little improvement. But he put into it such a wealth and many-sided possibility of expression as surpassed their efforts in every direction, and amounted finally to completely exhausting the subject. There have been, really, no genuine composers of sonatas since Beethoven. Every great master has tried it out of deference to public opinion, but the chief ideas and distinctive excellencies of all composers since Beethoven are expressed in other forms and not in the sonata. Even in symphony, where they have enjoyed the inestimable advantages of modern wealth in instrumentation, no one has been able to create works at all equal to his, or even such as add any thing essentially new and important to what he has said.

Again, Bach and Beethoven were both of them characteristically instrumental composers. Although both have written works employing the human voice in solo, ensemble and in great masses, and have therein reached the most sublime heights yet attained in musical creation, they have in all cases treated the voice like an instrument, and with almost total disregard of the conditions of its agreeable and pleasing exercise. This limitation, of course, is a detraction from their success, for if they were to use the voice at all, there was no valid reason why its convenience and inherent capacity should not be as much regarded as that of any other instrument. Bach and Beethoven are both of them exponents of the *inner* in music. While they both reach the highest mark of formal beauty, they do so accidentally, so to say; as an incidental result of the spontaneous expression of the inner and spiritual.

Beethoven marks a giant stride in musical progress since Bach, in the direction of the humoristic. Bach himself was full of this spirit, and of playful phantasy, as all his works show. But the new forms developed or perfected by Haydn and Mozart, and the lessons taught by their disregard of scholastic tradition, and especially the vigorous flight of his own all-comprehending and untamed spirit, enabled Beethoven to go vastly farther than Bach in this direction, and to reveal music in its true nature as spontaneous expression of heart, feeling, and imagination. And thus he not only concentrated in himself and fulfilled all the tendencies and prophecies of musical history before him, and enriched the world with some of the most precious and immortal productions of the human spirit, but afforded in turn the most pregnant tokens of possibilities in music yet unrevealed — indications of new paths, which the great masters since have occupied themselves in exploring.

LIST OF BEETHOVEN ILLUSTRATIONS.

1. (*Moderately Difficult, Employing the Pianoforte and Tenor.*)

1. Sonata in G, op. 14, No. 2.
2. Menuet in E flat out of Sonata op. 31, No. 3.
3. Scherzo in C, out of Sonata op. 2, No. 3
4. "Adelaide." Tenor.
5. "Nicht zu Geschwind," out of Sonata in E, op. 90.
6. Rondo in G, op. 51, No. 2.

2. *Difficult.*

1. Sonata Appassionata, op. 57.
2. Air and Variations in A flat, op. 26.
3. "Adelaide." Tenor.
4. Sonata in A flat, op. 110.
5. Rondo Capriccioso, op. 129.

CHAPTER FORTY-SEVEN.

MENDELSSOHN.

Felix Mendelssohn was born in Hamburg, February 3, 1809. He was the son of Abraham Mendelssohn, a banker, a man of very refined tastes, and grandson of Moses Mendelssohn, the eminent Rabbi and philosopher. The name Bartholdy was his mother's, and was taken later in life as a condition of some property inheritance. Felix was the second of four children, of whom Fanny, the eldest, manifested the most remarkable talents in music. When Felix was only three or four years old the family removed to Berlin. At the age of eight he already played the piano well. The theorist Zelter was his teacher in composition, and Berger in piano playing. When only twelve he was pronounced by Zelter his best scholar. In 1824 Zelter wrote to Goethe: " Yesterday evening Felix's fourth opera was brought out here in a little circle of us, with the dialogue. There are three acts, which, with two ballets, occupied about two hours and a half. The work was received with much applause. I can hardly master my own wonder how the boy, who is only about fifteen, has made such progress. Everywhere you find what is new, beautiful and peculiar — wholly peculiar."

In the year 1824 he became the piano pupil of Moscheles, and so began the long and delightful intimacy, which, like a golden thread, runs through the volumes of Mendelssohn's charming letters and Moscheles' "Recent Music and Musicians."

In 1829 Mendelssohn started to visit London. He made a long tour through many places of interest, especially in Italy, before he reached England. Among the new pieces he brought to show Moscheles, were his overture to "Fingal's Cave," "Walpurgis Night," and his G minor concerto for piano-forte and orchestra. In London, Mendelssohn was rapturously received. His organ playing excited the greatest astonishment, and remains to the present day a bright tradition with English musicians. Yet it is but fair to say that the opinion there held of his organ playing was by no means shared by the best authorities in Germany. There is very good reason for believing that his pedal technic was by no means superior, however charming his manipulation and registration may have been. Be this as it may, he undoubtedly gave a decided impetus to English organ playing, especially to the study of Bach.

Mendelssohn came to Leipsic in 1835, and remained there all but one year of the rest of his life. He assumed direction of the Gewandhaus concerts, which, henceforth, reached a delicacy unknown to them before. The oratorio of "St. Paul" was written for the Lower Rhine Musical Festival, held at Düsseldorf in 1836. It excited the highest enthusiasm.

In the Spring of 1837 Mendelssohn was married to Miss Cecilia Jeanrenaud, of Dresden, a daughter of a clergyman, with whom he lived very happily until his death.

"St. Paul" was brought out at the Birmingham festival, in 1838, where it at once took a high place. Three of his psalms, "As the Hart Pants," "O Come let us Sing," and the one hundred and fifteenth were the product of this period.

In 1843 the Leipsic Conservatory was opened with about sixty pupils. The teachers were Mendelssohn, Schumann (piano), David (violin), and Becker (organ). Other teachers were soon added. This renowned institution seems to have been chiefly the creation of Mendelssohn's brain, and to him it owes its character. It has turned out a a vast number of pupils, all more or less well grounded in music. No school has had greater influence in this country. There is one drawback to the association of a man like Mendelssohn with such a school namely: that after he leaves it his charming manner and peculiar ideas become the ideal which places subsequent directors, however talented, at a disadvantage. There is some reason to believe that the Leipsic school has not been entirely free from this failing. One good point about this school must not be overlooked: that there they always hold *content* for the first merit of a work. This, in a town enriched by the labors of Bach, and Mendelssohn, and Schumann, is what we might expect.

Space does not permit to follow closely Mendelssohn's subsequent career. It embraced a year's residence in Berlin, frequent visits to England, where he brought out "Elijah," in 1846, as well as constant appearances throughout Germany, as director, composer and pianist. His life was a ceaseless round of activity, and it is little wonder that the delicate frame wore out. He died in Leipsic, November 4, 1847

In personal appearance Mendelssohn was rather under the medium size, graceful in walk and bearing. His forehead was high and arched, his nose delicate, slightly Roman; his mouth fine and firm, and his head covered with glossy, black, curly hair. His countenance was very expressive, and his whole manner fascinating in the extreme. He was the idol of men and women alike in every circle where he moved. He inherited large means, which he freely dispensed in the most delicate and unostentatious charities. His entire independence of the need of labor for sustenance gave no slackening to his ardor in composition. In my opinion, Mendelssohn's chief characteristics must have been his genial fancy, his exquisite taste and kind heartedness. In his charming letters from Italy and Switzerland we have these qualities fully exhibited. Two more delightful books than those of his letters do not adorn literature. The same qualities shine out in his music. Everywhere we meet a romantic and delicate fancy, a sprightfulness and ever-present sense of the beautiful, which carries us back to Mozart.

As a composer Mendelssohn built on Bach. By this I mean that Bach stood to him as a model of true greatness in music. It was not possible for such a nature as Mendelssohn's to emulate the lofty repose of Bach's greatest things. Still everywhere in his serious moments we find the traces of the influence of the sober old Leipsic cantor.

Mendelssohn's greatness as a composer lies in his oratorios and psalms. Brendel regards these as no longer *religious* works, strictly speaking, but as "concert oratorios," in which he thinks the worldly element comes forth. In this he is right to a certain extent. Handel's "Messiah" does not manifest this worldly spirit, because the subject forbade it. In the first place, this spirit manifests itself in a lingering over details, such as beautiful tone effects of one sort or another (just as the ribbon, the ornament, or other little piquancy of dress, betray a woman's instinct for being admired), and, for this sort of thing, the haste in which Handel wrote the "Messiah" left him no time. Besides, as I have before said, the text of the "Messiah" inspired in him an elevation of sentiment to which he was commonly a stranger. Moreover, the worldly element in music was then in its infancy. The foundation of it was there, namely, the taste of the public. The "Messiah," and all of Handel's oratorios were written for the concert, and not for religious use. In this he differs from Bach, who had nothing to consult but his own ideal. His pieces were written for church and played in church. Religious worship was their inspiration. It is the absence of the influence of the public that permits Bach's unquestionable prolixity, which, in our day, seems tediousness.

It is in "Elijah" that Mendelssohn most fully moves the public. The dramatic story, the picturesque contrasts, the richness and taste of its orchestration, its novel and fascinating choruses, and especially the beauty and graphic appropriateness of his melodies, give this oratorio a wonderful charm. One should read Mr. Dwight's glowing description of it, found at the end of Lampadius' Life of Mendelssohn. I confess that there is hardly a tedious moment to me in this lovely work. From the first recitative, "Thus saith the Lord," through the entire work, I find the rarest appreciation of beauty, and the rarest truth to the words. How overpowering the choruses, "Thanks be to God," and "Be not Afraid;" how sweet and lovely "He, watching over Israel;" how graphic the recitative where fire descends; how mighty the contrast in the quartette and chorus, "Holy, Holy, Holy, is God the Lord!"

In this oratorio Mendelssohn seems to have reached the acme of taste in the compromise he has effected between the religious and the merely beautiful. This same admirable taste manifests itself also in the psalms. Take, for instance, the "Hear my Prayer." Here we have a solo, "Hear my Prayer," the excited chorus, "The Enemy shouteth," and, finally, the altogether unique solo and chorus *obligato*, "Oh, for the Wings of a Dove!" Nothing could be more beautiful.

In his piano forte music, especially the "Songs Without Words" we have the same loveliness of fancy and sentiment. These are works which all tasteful people admire. The larger pieces no longer hold the position in the estimation of musicians they once did, although it would be impossible to find two more lovely pieces for ladies' performance than the "Rondo Capriccioso" and "Capriccio in B minor."

It is further in proof of the ruling quality of Mendelssohn's mind that the *scherzo* is his most perfect triumph. There we have a fairy-like playfulness truly exquisite and altogether *unique*. The "six organ sonatas" were made up for the English market. They have marked beauties and are ecclesiastical in tone; and, in spite of their peculiar "sonata" form, I hold them in high estimation. Besides, there was a justification for this irregularity (which, perhaps, I ought to explain, consists of their having but two movements in place of the usual four), in the congeniality of their spirit to religious service, and especially the benediction like effect of the soft and songful *andantes* forming their conclusions. In quartettes, quintettes and symphonies, Mendelssohn was also extremely successful, but it may be questioned whether he ever surpassed his lovely overture to the "Midsummer Night's Dream," the work of his boyhood.

LIST OF MENDELSSOHN ILLUSTRATIONS.

(Employing a Soprano, Alto, and the Pianoforte.)

1. Overture to the Midsummer Night's Dream (for four hands).
2 "On Wings of Music," Tenor (or Soprano).

3. Rondo Capriccioso.
4. "Jerusalem, Thou that Killest the Prophets," Soprano.
5. *a.* Hunting Song (No. 3).
   b. People's Song (No. 4).
   c. Spring Song (No. 27).
6. "O! Rest in the Lord," Alto.
7. "Duetto" (No. 18 in Songs without Words).
8. Duet, "Would that my Love," Soprano and Alto.
9. Finale from "Italian" Symphony, (four hands) Pianoforte.

CHAPTER FORTY-EIGHT.

CHOPIN.

Frederic Chopin was born at Zela-zola-Wola, near Warsaw, March 1, 1809, and died at Paris, October 17, 1849. Within these forty years were bound up the activities of one of the most remarkable spirits in music. In Chopin we have another example of precocious talent, such as are seen in Mozart, Schubert, and Liszt. At the age of nine he played in public a concerto by Gyrowetz, and improvised. His studies were begun under the direction of Ziwna, a passionate admirer of Sebastian Bach, and carried on later under Joseph Elsner, principal of the Conservatory of Warsaw. The records of Chopin's early life are extremely meagre. We know that he was then a fluent Bach player, to whom through life he remained devoted. We are also sure that even as early as sixteen he must have been a great virtuoso, not only equal to every thing that had been planned for the piano before his time, but already the author of the completely new methods indicated in the excessively difficult variations on *La ci darem la mano*, the first nocturnes, op 9, the early mazurkas and waltzes, and especially the great studies op. 10 and the two concertos. These studies have passed into the standard repertory of advanced piano-playing, and the two concertos, although weak in orchestral handling, are extremely brilliant and poetic for the piano, and have the great merit of complete novelty and freshness of style.

With these great compositions already finished, as well as many others of a character more immediately available, he set out for Vienna, Paris, and London, at the age of nineteen. He reached Paris, and there met Liszt, with whom he formed a devoted friendship. Here

Chopin found a congenial public. He was of a shy and delicate nature, proud, yet somewhat effeminate, and public appearance was distasteful to him. In manners cultivated and refined, and quick of intellect, Chopin immediately became the center of a considerable circle of artistic people, who esteemed him no less for his personal qualities than his remarkable musical gifts. He was overrun with pupils, of whom, however, he would take but a small number. In 1837 the lung disease, with which he had been threatened since childhood, developed itself. In company with his devoted friend, M'me Geo. Sand, to whom he had been introduced by Liszt, he resided at the island of Majorca for several years. Deceived by a show of returning health he came back to Paris, and, as already recorded, died at the age of Raphael and Mozart.

Chopin's music is not the *universal* music of the German composers, nor is it the humoristic music of the romantic school, although with both these it has something in common. It is a contradiction. He is wild, passionate, capricious, yet always graceful, subtle, refined, and delicate. Nothing could be less like Bach's music, yet it has much in common with it. Chopin's genius is especially for the piano. All the grace and elegant manner of modern virtuoso piano-playing come from him. Yet the inner life, the musical feeling which is the determining cause of this grace and refinement, comes rather from Schumann. Chopin was an innovator for piano in his matter and manner. He gave depth to the nocturne; enlarged the poetic range of the piano by his Polonaises, Scherzos, Impromptus, Ballades, and Etudes. His passages are new, ingenious and beautiful. Like Schumann he writes mainly for the pianoforte. Unlike him, he does so in a manner which completely harmonizes with the nature of the instrument, and, indeed, foresaw its latest improvements. Hence we find in Chopin's works the well-sounding always considered. Nevertheless they are not reposeful. Although the themes are fully developed, the harmonic structure and the rhythmic organization of these pieces gives them a character of restlessness and dissatisfaction. By so much they fall short of great art. In all of them it is rather the manner of saying which charms, than the actual idea itself. Psychologically considered they are unhealthy. There runs through them a vein of sadness and morbid feeling which renders them too exciting for the weak and nervous. Their most conspicuous external quality is the subtlety, the evanescence, of their harmonies. It is this which makes Chopin's music so difficult to remember. Its technical novelty was partly in a new and freer use of the pedal, and the effective employment of extended chords, and partly in better sustained and more brilliant passages, especially those constructed on the diminished seventh. As to its metrical structure, Chopin's music is lyric. His period-lengths are remarkably uniform, as compared with those of Beethoven or Schumann. The other qualities of his music appear best in the actual illustrations.

LIST OF CHOPIN ILLUSTRATIONS.

1. *Moderately Difficult.*

1. Polonaise in C sharp min., op. 27.
2. Valse in D flat maj., op. 64.
3. Nocturne in E flat, op. 9.
4. Impromptu in A. flat, op. 29.
5. Prelude in D flat.
6. Valse in E flat, op. 18.
7. Nocturne in G min., op. 37.
8. Polonaise Militaire in A, op. 40.

2. *Difficult.*

1. Etudes out of op. 10, No. 8 in F, No 5 on the black keys, and No 12 for the left hand.
2. Nocturne in C min., op 48, or in G maj , op. 37.
3. Fantasie Impromptu in C sharp, op 66.
4. Andante Spianato and Polonaise in E flat, op 22.
5. Prelude in D flat.
6. Ballade in A flat, op. 47.

CHAPTER FORTY-NINE.

ROBERT SCHUMANN

Robert Schumann was born in Zwickau, in Saxony, June 8, 1810 His father was a bookseller and publisher, a man full of energy and circumspection, and of decided literary tastes and ability The boy was sent to school and began to learn music at an early stage As early as the age of seven or eight he wrote some little dances, although ignorant of the rules of harmony. It is said that even then he was fond of sketching in music the peculiarities of his friends, and did this "so exactly and comically that every one burst into loud laughter at the similitude of the portrait." Schumann was scarcely nine years old when his father took him to hear Ignatz Moscheles, the famous pianist, whose playing made the most profound impression upon him. At the age of ten he entered the academy, and here formed a companionship with a boy about his own age, with whom he played many of the works of Haydn and Mozart, arranged for four hands. His father evidently encouraged his love for music, and gratified him with a fine piano and plenty of new music.

Presently the boys came across the orchestral parts of Righini's overture to "Tigranes," and forthwith mustered their forces for performance. They had two violins, two flutes, a clarionet, and two horns. Robert directed and undertook to supply the missing parts upon the piano. Their success encouraged them to undertake other tasks of a similar kind, which, also, Robert directed. He also set to music the one hundred and fiftieth psalm for chorus and orchestra, and this was given by the same performers, assisted by a chorus of such boys as could sing. In all these and such like exercises, the father recognized the plain indication of Providence that the son was intended for a musician, nor was he disposed to thwart the design. The mother, however, had a poor idea of the musical profession, and thought only of the hardships it carried with it.

As a boy Robert was full of tricks and sports. But at the age of fourteen a change came over him, and he became more reserved and prone to revery. This habit never forsook him through life. It was, perhaps, increased by the death of his appreciative and kind-hearted father, which took place in 1826, when Robert was but sixteen. In deference to his mother's wishes he matriculated at Leipsic as a law student in 1828.

Through his father's example he had already made the acquaintance of Byron's poems. He now became infected with a perfect fever for Jean Paul. Here, also, he made the acquaintance of Friedrich Wieck, and became his pupil in piano-playing. The daughter, Clara, then but nine years old, attracted him very much by her remarkable talent. Schumann left Leipsic for Heidelburg for a while, in order to attend certain lectures there. Now ensued a still more violent contest between law and music, which resulted at last in his return to Leipsic in 1830, for the purpose of devoting himself to music, which he began to do again under Wieck's instruction. But this course was not rapid enough for the impatient student, who imagined himself the discoverer of a secret by which the time of practice could be much shortened. The experiment, whatever it was, worked disastrously, and had the effect of destroying the use of the fourth finger of the right hand, and consequently in disabling him from piano-playing altogether.

He now devoted himself to composition, and produced his op. 1, variations on the name "Abegg," and directly his "Papillons," or scenes at a ball. In these his talent and originality were plain enough, as well as the lack of clearness. Incited by the criticism which these works met on all hands, he took up the study of counterpoint and composition, and little by little acquired smoothness of style. Thus he produced his two sets of studies after Paganini, op. 3 and op. 10, the *Davidsbündlertänze*, op. 6, the Toccata, Allegro, Carnival, op. 9, the sonata in F sharp minor, and the "Phantasie Stücke," op. 12. The latter set of pieces has become universally favorite, and shows Schumann's originality in a favorable light. They have already been analyzed in Chapter XXXIII, and need not here be taken up again.

One of the most remarkable of the works of this first epoch is the *Etudes Symphoniques*, an air, twelve variations, and a finale. These variations are not so much unfoldings of the theme, as associated or congenial ideas and images called up by it, as it is dwelt upon in the mind. It would be impossible to conceive any thing less like an ordinary set of variations. Instead of the usual, somewhat timid progression from one variation to the next, we here effect the boldest transitions. At times we lose the theme completely. Then it re-appears. This work is extremely interesting, because the forms are short, and the musical nature of the whole is of the most precious quality. Of similar excellence is the Kreisleriana, op. 16, and the Humoreske, op. 20.

In 1833 Schumann united with a few others in establishing the *Neue Zeitschrift für Musik* (New Journal of Music), as the advocate of progression, and as opposed to pedantry and (other people's) conceit. Like all journals devoted to art, it was published at a loss, but was kept up for several years, and to it the world is indebted for the preservation of Schumann's opinions and criticisms upon contemporary music. Two volumes of his writings are now available in English, and exhibit him in an altogether favorable light. Meantime his affairs of the heart made haste slowly. After several episodes, he finally settled down to the conviction that Clara Wieck was indispensable to his happiness. Father Wieck objected, for reasons not publicly stated, but probably on account of doubt of the lover's fixity of purpose and stability of talent. At length an engagement was allowed, and in 1840 Schumann burst out in song, composing in a single year one hundred and forty. Among them were those two sets "Woman's Love and Life," and "Poet's Love," which still remain among the most highly prized achievements in this line. In this year he was married to Clara Wieck, on the 12th of September.

He now turned his attention to orchestral instruments and produced his piano quartette and quintette, and his B flat symphony. This was followed by other orchestral works, and in 1851 by the symphony in D minor. In 1841 he became connected with the Conservatory at Leipsic as teacher of piano-playing, composition, and the art of playing from score. This continued until his removal to Dresden, which took place in 1844. He had already in 1840 composed his charming and highly romantic work " Paradise and the Peri." As soon as he arrived in Dresden he set to work on the epilogue to the Faust music. The incessant activity of his mind finally resulted in throwing it completely off its balance, and gave rise to distressing symptoms of melancholy. In 1848 he wrote his opera of "Genoveva," which, although full of beautiful music, is not well adapted for dramatic performance. Here also followed, in an order which we have no room to trace, the later compositions for the piano. In 1850 he removed to Düsseldorf as municipal director, and was received with a banquet and concert. His position here was pleasant, but he had as little talent for directing as teaching. In 1853 he and his wife made a concert tour through the Netherlands, where Schumann was delighted to find his music as well known as at home. "Everywhere," he writes, "there were fine performances of my symphonies, even the most difficult."

Still his malady increased. He imagined he heard a tone, which pursued him incessantly, and from which harmonies, nay whole compositions were gradually developed. He became sleepless, and cast down with melancholy. At length he threw himself into the Rhine, from which he was with difficulty rescued. He was removed to a private asylum at Endenich, where he died two years later, July 31, 1856.

"Robert Schumann was of middling stature, almost tall, and slightly corpulent. His bearing while in health was haughty, distinguished, dignified and calm; his gait slow, soft, and a little slovenly. While at home he generally wore felt shoes. He often paced his room on tiptoe, apparently without cause. His eyes were generally down-cast, half-closed, and only brightened in intercourse with intimate friends, but then most pleasantly. His countenance produced an agreeable, kindly impression; it was without regular beauty, and not particularly intellectual. The fine cut mouth, usually puckered as if to whistle, was, next to the eyes, the most attractive feature of his full, round, ruddy face. Above the heavy nose rose a high, bold, arched brow, which broadened visibly at the temples.   His head, covered with long, thick, dark-brown hair, was firm and intensely powerful, we might say square.*"

As a composer Schumann is one of the most important in the entire history of music.   Liszt acutely remarked, "Schumann *thinks* music better than any other since Beethoven."   We have already seen that Bach established modern tonality by taking it as he found it already developed for him in Fugue, and applying it to the expression of musical feeling, the vital element which had been generally wanting in the music written before his day.   After Bach, nothing new was done for music but to invent clearer forms, and to master its use as the expression of light and deep feeling according to the demands of the classical school.   We have also seen that Beethoven, in some of his works, goes beyond the classical idea, and actually enters upon the province of the romantic.   This he does in the stronger contrasts of his works, especially in the pianoforte sonatas, op. 13, 110 and 111 Yet in these works which are so full of feeling, and expressed with such masterful power, there is after all a certain repose and classical dignity beyond which they do not come.   These elements are still more noticeable in his opera "Fidelio," where there was room for him to have expressed himself in a truly romantic manner.   But no! here, as elsewhere, he is distinctly the instrumental composer, considering the music first and the text afterwards.   That the music is far above that of any Italian opera, comes not from Beethoven's seizure of the text, but from his range of expression as a musician.   It is as *music* that "Fidelio" surpassed other operas, and not as a poetico-musical interpretation of a highly poetic and suggestive text.   The same peculiarities of Beethoven's music are still more perceptible in the symphonies, where he is always moved by musical considerations as such.   Nothing tempts him from the strictly appropriate and suitable development of his theme.   True, he does this with consummate beauty, and sets it off by the most delightful contrasts, but in all he is reposeful, elegant, beautiful.   The very fineness of the work makes it ineffective to common minds.   Yet, how much more effective to those who have the ears to hear.

Schubert is in many respects to be counted a romantic composer. Yet we have but to study his music deeply to perceive that his romanticism is spasmodic and temporary, while the natural range of his thought is according to the methods of the classical.   Thus while in his great romantic songs, like the Erl King, he is distinctly a romantic

*Von Wasielwski.

writer, as soon as the stimulus of poetry is withdrawn he develops his musical ideas at great lengths, strictly in the classic method. This is to be seen everywhere in Schubert's instrumental works, and he is especially the *longest-winded* composer of all. No one else is so unwearied in turning over the same idea; and, it may be added, no one else does so with such elegance and grace.

Schumann, on the contrary, is romantic in the very essence of his musical thought. When he is writing to a text he is graphic and flexible in conforming to the spirit of the words. But when he is writing instrumental music merely, he is equally direct and full of humor. The classical method of developing musical ideas is contrary to his nature and impossible for him. All through his life he made the most strenuous efforts to write elegantly, and according to the canons of form. He disciplined himself in counterpoint and fugue under the best masters of his day, and studied eagerly Bach and Beethoven. Yet he could never develop an idea easily and naturally according to the fashion of the classic. His fugues are forced, his counterpoint spasmodic, and his sonatas his poorest work. His songs are at times badly placed for the voice, and entirely unlike every thing that a song ought to be — if we may believe the critics who wrote upon them in Schumann's life-time. Yet they have made their way and are now accepted as among the most successful efforts yet made to unite poetry and music. So also in the instrumental pieces. These little, fantastic, irregular compositions are now played and enjoyed all the world over, although they do not contain a single element of the "grateful" salon piece for the pianoforte.

Yet the classical moment in music had not passed by in Schumann's day. Beethoven's later sonatas were as yet a sealed book. Mendelssohn, although on the whole to be counted for a romantic composer, handled musical ideas with an ease and classical elegance, limited only by the inherent lightness of the ideas themselves. Chopin, a still more poetic writer, and the inventor of very many entirely new ways of proceeding, yet develops his ideas in his own new ways, somehow not unlike the spirit of the classical model. Chopin is everywhere new and original; but he has also a certain epic breadth. He writes long movements, which are well sustained, and thoroughly satisfactory in point of formal beauty.

Schumann, doubtless, would have agreed with the late Edgar A. Poe, that "a long poem is a contradiction in terms." There is never a long piece of music in Schumann. But instead thereof, short pieces, strongly differentiated and contrasted, and out of them are built up, mosaic-wise, long movements. So it is in his pianoforte concertos, sonatas, his quartettes and symphonies. The distinguishing greatness of Schumann, then, is not in his large pieces, for in all of them he is one way or another hampered. In the pianoforte concerto, for example, there are no effective passages. It is in places difficult enough, but it is very far from a bravoura piece. Even the cadenza is as far as possible from any thing likely to bring down the house. Yet it is one of the most delightful works ever written, and full of the most beautiful ideas, although, to be sure, these are mainly for the piano.

It is another peculiarity of Schumann's genius, that he is on the whole a pianoforte composer. Although he wrote a large amount for other instruments and for the voice, his piano works are the ones on which his fame chiefly rests. And it is curious to observe that while this is the case, he has never written "gratefully" for the pianoforte, but always the new and original. Hence his piano pieces had to wait a long time for their merits to become known. One might almost say that they had to wait for a generation of players able to understand them and do them justice.

Schumann is essentially the music *thinker*. He writes well for no instrument whatever, nor even for the voice. The entire art of piano playing, and especially of early technical practice, has had to be re-modeled in order to provide the technical ability with which to properly render these works of his. His symphonies not only are made up out of bits, like all his long pieces, but are badly written for the strings, the very foundation of the orchestra. Yet the music has in it such force and freshness, that these works hold their position, not only against the more reposeful and elegant works of Beethoven and the classical composers, but against modern works also, even though in some cases much better written. Bach established the musical vocabulary within which the entire classical school expressed itself. In like manner Schumann did this for the romantic school. Nothing essentially new has been added to musical phraseology since Schumann, but only to master the use of his new modes of expression. What these are it would be difficult to point out. If we examine the harmony we can not say that Schumann uses any chord that may not be found in Bach. Nor is the novelty in period formations. But perhaps, if in any single element, in the manner of motive-transformation. In this respect the difference between Schumann and Bach or Beethoven is world-wide. In Bach there is, to be sure, a fresh and thoroughly right thematic development, and so in Beethoven. In the latter his fantasy sometimes carries him to great lengths, as in the Rondo Capriccioso

But in Schumann this fantasy becomes much more fantastic and humoristic. In many cases it is so violent as to forbid his adhering to a single idea and working it out thoroughly. Instead of that he flies restlessly from one idea to another, and to yet another, until the listener wearies of it. So he violates all canons of beauty, and destructive criticism breaks all her vials of wrath upon him. Yet the strongest of these pieces has something true and tender in it. When a Rubinstein produces the key that unlocks the magic door, we enter and find here a world of tenderness and fanciful beauty. So has it been with the apparently most unjustifiable of these works, like, for example, the Carnival, the *Faschingsschwank aus Wien*, and so on.

It is Schumann who has in one effort taught the musical world two lessons: that there is *poetry* in music, and that there is *music* in the pianoforte. His creative activity busied itself along the line where poetry and music join. Although an imaginative and fanciful person, he had a true instinct for valid and logical expression in music. So, even in his most far-fetched passages, the melodic and harmonic sequences, although new, are inherently right, and entirely compatible with those of Bach and Beethoven. Hence whatever ground his music has gained, it has held. On the other hand he had also a fancy in which every fantastic idea found congenial soil. The proper, the conventional, the allowable, meant nothing to him. He gave loose rein to his humor and followed it whithersoever it led. Nor yet in this did he lose his balance. For at the bottom he had the key to the riddle, which we have before several times pointed out: *the relation of music to emotion.* And so while his fancy took him far, and into many new paths, his fine musical sense kept him from passing beyond what was inherently right in music, as such. That he often passes beyond the limits of the symmetrical, the well-sounding, or even the agreeable, we can afford to forgive for the sake of the vigor of his imagination, and the inherent sweetness and soundness of his disposition. And it is these which on the whole have supported and justified his works.

LIST OF SCHUMANN ILLUSTRATIONS.

1. (*Moderately Difficult, Employing the Pianoforte and a Soprano.*)

1. "The Entrance," "Wayside Inn," and "Homeward" from the Forest Scenes, op. 82.
2. "The Hat of Green," Soprano.
3. *a.* Romance in F sharp, op. 28.
   b. Hunting Song.
4. "O Sunshine," Soprano.

13

5. Nachtstücke in C and F, op. 23.
6. " Moonlight," Soprano.
7. " End of the Song," from op. 12.

2. *Difficult.*

1. Etudes Symphoniques, op. 13, Theme, variations 1, 2, 3, 7, 11, 12, and Finale.
2. " Thou Ring upon my Finger," Soprano.
3. " Aufschwung," " Warum," and " Ende vom Lied," from op. 12.
4. " He the Best of all, the Noblest," Soprano.
5. Novellette in F, No. 1, Romance in F sharp, and Novellette in E. No. 7.

3. *Illustrations of the Romantic*

1. SCHUMANN. — *a.* Novellette in E, No. 7.
          b. Prophetic Birds.
          c. Traumeswirren.
          d. Warum.
          e. Ende vom Lied.
2. SCHUBERT. — " The Erl King," Soprano.
3. CHOPIN. — *a.* Scherzo in D flat, op. 31.
          b. Nocturne in F sharp, op. 15.
          c. Ballade in A flat, op. 47.
4. SCHUMANN. — " He the Best of all, the Noblest."
5. CHOPIN. — Polonaise in A flat, op. 53.

CHAPTER FIFTY.

LISZT.

Liszt is one of the most remarkable personages who has yet appeared in music. His life is briefly told by Francis Heuffer, in Grove's " Dictionary," as follows:

" Franz Liszt was born October 22, 1811, at Raiding, in Hungary, the son of Adam Liszt, an official in the imperial service, and a musical amateur of sufficient attainment to instruct his son in the rudiments of pianoforte-playing. At the age of nine young Liszt made his first appearance in public at Oedenburg, with such success that several Hungarian noblemen guaranteed him sufficient means to continue his studies for six years. For that purpose he went to Vienna, and took lessons from Czerny on the pianoforte, and from Salieri and Randhartinger in composition. The latter introduced the lad to his friend Franz Schubert. His first appearance in print was probably in a variation (the 24th) on a waltz of Diabelli's, one of fifty contributed by

the most eminent artists of the day, for which Beethoven, when asked
for a single variation, wrote thirty-three (op. 120). The collection,
entitled Vaterländische Künstler-Verein, was published in June, 1823.
In the same year he proceeded to Paris, where it was hoped that his
rapidly growing reputation would gain him admission at the Conser-
vatoire in spite of his foreign origin. But Cherubini refused to make
an exception in his favor, and he continued his studies under Reicha
and Paër. Shortly afterwards he also made his first serious attempt at
composition, and an operetta in one act, called 'Don Sanche,' was
produced at the Académie Royale, October 17, 1825, and well received.
Artistic tours to Switzerland and England, accompanied by brilliant
success, occupy the period till the year 1827, when Liszt lost his father
and was thrown on his own resources to provide for himself and his
mother. During his stay in Paris, where he settled for some years, he
became acquainted with the leaders of French literature, Victor Hugo.
Lamartine and George Sand, the influence of whose works may be
discovered in his compositions. For a time also he became an adherent
to Saint-Simon, but soon reverted to the Catholic religion, to which,
as an artist and a man, he has since adhered devoutly.

"The interval from 1839 to 1847 Liszt spent in traveling almost incessantly from one country to another, being everywhere received
with an enthusiasm unequaled in the annals of Art. In England he
played at the Philharmonic Concerts of May 21, 1827 (Concerto, Hum-
mel), May 11, 1840 (Concertstück, Weber), and June 8, 1840 (Kreut-
zer-sonata). Here alone his reception seems to have been less warm
than was expected, and Liszt, with his usual generosity, at once undertook to bear the loss that might have fallen on his agent. Of this
generosity numerous instances might be cited. The charitable purposes to which Liszt's genius has been made subservient are legion,
and in this respect as well as in that of technical perfection he is un-
rivaled amongst virtuosi. The disaster caused at Pesth by the inun-
dation of the Danube (1837) was considerably alleviated by the
princely sum — the result of several concerts — contributed by this
artist; and when two years later a considerable sum had been col-
lected for a statue to be erected to him at Pesth, he insisted upon the
money being given to a struggling young sculptor, whom he moreover
assisted from his private means. The poor of Raiding also had cause
to remember the visit paid by Liszt to his native village about the
same time. It is well known that Beethoven's monument at Bonn
owed its existence, or at least its speedy completion, to Liszt's liber-
ality. When the subscriptions for the purpose began to fail, Liszt

offered to pay the balance **required from his own** pocket, provided only that the choice **of the sculptor should be left to** him. From the beginning of the forties dates **Liszt's more intimate** connection with Weimar, where in 1849 he settled for the space **of** twelve years. This stay was to be fruitful in more than one sense. When he closed his career as a virtuoso, and accepted a permanent engagement as conductor of the Court Theater at Weimar, he did so with **the** distinct purpose of becoming the advocate of the rising musical generation, by the performance of such works as were written regardless of immediate success, and therefore had little chance of seeing the light of the stage. At short intervals eleven operas of living composers were either performed for the first time or revived on the Weimar stage. Amongst these may be counted such works as *Lohengrin*, *Tannhäuser*, and *The Flying Dutchman* of Wagner, *Benvenuto Cellini* by Berlioz, Schumann's *Genoveva*, and music to Byron's 'Manfred.' Schubert's *Alfonso and Estrella* was also rescued from oblivion by Liszt's exertions. For a time it seemed as if this **small** provincial **city** was once more to be the artistic center of Germany, **as** it had been **in the** days of Goethe, Schiller and Herder. From all sides musicians **and** amateurs flocked to Weimar, to witness the astonishing feats to which a small but excellent community of singers and instrumentalists were inspired by the genius of their leader. In this way was formed the the nucleus of a group of young and enthusiastic musicians, who, whatever may be thought of their aims and achievements, were and are at any rate inspired by perfect devotion to music and its poetical aims. It was, indeed, at these Weimar gatherings that the musicians who now form the so-called School of the Future, till then unknown to each other and divided locally and mentally, came first to a clear understanding of their powers and aspirations. How much **the personal** fascination of Liszt contributed to this desired effect need not be said. Amongst the numerous pupils on the pianoforte, to whom he at the same period opened the invaluable treasure of his technical experience, may be mentioned Hans von Bülow, the worthy disciple of such a master.

"**The** remaining facts of Liszt's life may be summed up in a few words. In 1859 he left his official position at the Opera in Weimar owing to the captious opposition made to the production of Cornelius' 'Barber of Bagdad,' at the Weimar Theater. Since that time he has been living at intervals at Rome, Pesth, and Weimar, always surrounded by a circle of pupils and admirers, and always working for

music and musicians in the unselfish and truly catholic spirit characteristic of his whole life."

Liszt's position in the **world of art is one that is altogether pecu-**
liar and unexampled. He appeared in **Paris** just at **the time when**
Thalberg had made a profound impression by the **ease of** his playing and
the **remarkable** results attainable from the piano. What Thalberg did
was to carry a melody in the center of the compass of the instrument,
principally with the two thumbs, and to surround it with an elabora-
tion of passage-work entirely unheard of before. The melody so car-
ried was not left to itself, or merely pounded out, but made to sing,
and delivered with the utmost refinement of phrasing, as if, indeed,
the player **had nothing whatever to do** just then but to play that
melody. There was **in all of** Thalberg's pieces a certain similarity of
style, and in his performance **a certain coldness.**

All this, which Thalberg did so beautifully **and** elegantly, yet so
coldly, Liszt did spontaneously, **and** with **an endless caprice of**
color and shading as the mood chanced. **Besides these things,** to
which, indeed, he attached little importance, **Liszt's exuberant fancy**
broke out in every direction, especially towards the **new, the startling,**
the astonishing. For his calmer moments he had his **work ready to**
his hands in the elegant but dramatically suggestive compositions **of**
Chopin, and these Liszt played with a fire and strength far beyond **the**
feeble powers of Chopin himself.

As a player Liszt gathered up and combined within himself all
the excellencies of piano-playing known before him, and added to
this, his inherited capital, a perfectly tropical luxuriance of elaboration
in every direction.

The possibilities latent in the diminished seventh and the chromatic scale, were very plainly suggested in Mozart's wind-parts of
Handel's "The People that Walked in Darkness," but they remained
a sealed book to the pianist until Chopin showed them at their true
value on the pianoforte. This new path attracted Liszt, who has
effected a thousand transformations on these elements, most of them
much simpler and less subtle than Chopin's, but perhaps on that very
account all the more effective in concert. And so we find in Liszt's
transcriptions and paraphrases of songs and orchestral works, not only
very effective solos for virtuoso performance, **but** also **an actual** and
very influential enlargement of the available field **of** the piano, and,
more and more in his later works, a demand upon the player for intelligence and musical discrimination of touch. **In** his earlier transcrip-

tions he is concerned with operatic melodies, and those mainly of Verdi, Rossini and Meyerbeer. In his later works he traverses the whole range of musical literature. Symphonies, quartettes, masses, operas, oratorios, and, last and least promising of all, Wagner's "Art-Work of the Future,"—all these re-attire themselves in habiliments of pianoforte passages, and pose for drawing-room use.

Liszt has been the great music teacher of the last forty years. He has never received a dollar for musical instruction, but has given his services in pure love for the art. All good pianists owe much to him ; not only to the silent but forcible inspiration of his printed works, but also still more to his personal example and criticism. As long ago as 1852 he had a class of seven or eight young men at Weimar, all of whom have since become famous. Among them were Hans von Bülow, Carl Klindworth, Joachim Raff, William Mason, Dionys Prückner, and Joseph Joachim. Later additions were Edouard Remenyi and Carl Tausig. Not only were pianists here, but violinists, singers, painters, sculptors, poets, and literary men of all kinds, all of whom found something inspiring and helpful in this magical and unconventional atmosphere. Since 1853 it is safe to say that every concert pianist in the world has been for a longer or a shorter time with Liszt.

A wrong idea of Liszt as a pianist is held by those who suppose that his playing is characterized by great force and extravagance. Imagine a very tall and slender man, more than six feet, with enormously long arms and fingers. He sits bolt upright, his long legs bent at a sharp angle at the knee. The trowsers are held down by straps. His face bears an ascetic expression. His hair is long, white, and floats upon his shoulders. His eyes are half-closed, and he scarcely ever looks at his hands. He sits perfectly still. Those long fingers go meandering over the key-board like gigantic spiders. You shudder at the sight. He seems to be playing slowly. The touch is everything but *legato*. This he does with the pedal. Yet in this easy, nonchalant fashion he is improvising the most wierd or impressive harmonies, or plays at first sight the most difficult productions of other virtuosi. Nay! he even takes a full score of a pianoforte concerto by some new author, and plays it from the cramped and obscure handwriting as coolly and vigorously as if he had written it himself, and at the very same first sight reads also the orchestral parts, and makes spoken comments on the instrumentation as he goes along! This, which sounds like a rhapsodical description, is literally true of Liszt. A virtuoso pupil brings him a fugue on which he has spent much practice. Liszt thinks it too slow, and plays it at the proper tempo The

youngster takes it home and works at it six weeks before he brings it
up to the rapid tempo. If now he were to bring it again to Liszt, he
would be just as likely to play it again in yet double speed.

Liszt seems to have been expressly designed for a sort of appreciative older brother to all new and original composers. For this use
his temperament exactly suits. The points in their work that criticism
sticks at, are, of course, the new and sometimes the very turning-points
of their lasting value. These points Liszt seizes by intuition. Imperfections of a•trifling character, or even of a serious kind, so they do
not interfere with the main idea of the work, have no power to with-
draw his attention from vital points. It was Liszt who first joined
with Schumann in recognizing the genius of Schubert. It was Liszt
who even went beyond Schumann and every other critic in recognizing the high artistic significance of the works of Berlioz and Wagner.

As a composer Liszt has worked in every field. He is never reposeful. His works are generally fragmentary. They are characterized by intense contrasts and sensational transitions. All available
resources he uses unhesitatingly. His influence in art will be very
great, but as a composer it will probably be limited to his own generation. His power is rather in his personal inspiration to other men of
genius, than in a vocation for a distinctly new artistic utterance, except, indeed, upon the pianoforte.

PROGRAMME OF LISZT ILLUSTRATIONS.

(Employing two Pianists and a Soprano.)

1. Concerto in E flat, with second pianoforte accompaniment.
2. Song, "Thou'rt Like a Lovely Flower."
3. *a.* Waldesrauchen, Concert Study.
   b. Spinning Song from "Flying Dutchman."
4. "Mignon's Song."
5. *a.* Polonaise Heroique in E.
   b. Schubert's "Wanderer."
   c. Second Hungarian Rhapsody. (Rivé-King Edition.)

INDEX.

STANDARD GRADED

COURSE OF STUDIES

FOR THE

PIANOFORTE.

COMPLETE IN TEN GRADES.

COMPILED BY

MR. W. S. B. MATHEWS.

Price, Each Grade, $1.00.

These studies consist of standard études and studies arranged in progressive order, selected from the best composers, for the cultivation of

Technic, Taste, and Sight Reading,

carefully edited, fingered, phrased, and annotated, and supplemented with complete directions for the application of Mason's "System of Touch and Technic" for the production of a modern style of playing.   Mr. Mathews has had the help of other noted musicians and teachers, and they have taken the whole field of piano studies and selected therefrom such as are most useful for meeting every necessity in a teacher's experience. Teachers will be delighted with the sterling musical and useful technical qualities of these études.

There are ten grades, a volume to each grade, each containing about thirty pages.   Every difficulty is prepared by being first introduced in its most simple form

10

TWENTY LESSONS
TO A
BEGINNER ON THE PIANOFORTE
BY W. S. B. MATHEWS

PRICE, $1.50

An Epoch-making Work in the Art of Teaching Music. A Wide Departure from all Previous Methods.

HESE "Twenty Lessons" are built upon the following three principles : (1) The supremacy of the ear or inner musical sense ; (2) developing control of the fingers according to Mason's System of Technic ; (3) reading music by thinking and conceiving its effects in advance of hearing it from the instrument.

These radical ideas have been fully tested and proved. It is the experience of those who have tested this method that pupils taught by it learn from twice to four times more in the same length of time than by the old method.

IT INTERESTS THE PUPIL AND CULTIVATES THE TASTE

THE ART OF PIANOFORTE PLAYING
BY
HUGH A. CLARKE, Mus. Doc.

PRICE, $1.50

This is a work embodying the results of thirty years' experience of a practical teacher, who has held the responsible position of Professor of Music in the Pennsylvania University for the last fifteen years.

The design of the work is to furnish a thoroughly *artistic school for beginners*, embodying all the latest results of the best criticism. The exercises have been constructed with great care, and are graded in such a way that the difficulties that beset beginners are almost insensibly overcome.

There are numerous duets for teacher and pupil, all having a specific object in view ; a number of pleasing pieces of a didactic nature, and exercises for strict and mechanical fingering.

5

STUDIES IN PHRASING,
Memorizing, and Interpretation.
By W. S. B. MATHEWS.

This work, which represents the fruit of many years' experience in teaching and unusual success in securing the finer qualities of artistic playing and musical intelligence from pupils, now consists of three books.

PRICE, EACH, $1.50.

FIRST LESSONS IN PHRASING.
Available in the 2d and 3d Grades.

This work, in part, consists of selections from Behr, Baumfelder, Gurlitt, Reinecke, etc.

The selections represent the cream of lyric and fanciful children's pieces, by the best writers. They have been selected for their pleasing quality and their musical and tuneful spirit. There is an Introduction, consisting of two pages of letter-press, containing the principles of phrasing and a method of study.

BOOK I.
Available in the 3d and 4th Grades.

This is the original set of " Phrasing " upon which the general reputation of the series depends.

The work consists of selections from Haydn, Heller, Schumann, Mozart, and Moszkowski. The pieces are singularly pleasing. Varied in style, and interesting as well as formative for study.

NO BETTER COLLECTION OF POETIC PIECES FOR YOUNG PLAYERS HAS EVER BEEN PUBLISHED.

This book practically supersedes the necessity of Heller's Opus 47 and 46, the best pieces from both being in this collection. The introduction also consists of a theory of Phrasing and Interpretation. There is a brief dictionary of terms, and directions regarding tempo. The work is an invaluable piece of apparatus, especially for young teachers.

BOOK II.
Available in the 4th and 5th Grades.

This volume is larger than the preceding, and the pieces more advanced. It contains selections from Mendelssohn's Songs without Words, two pieces from Chopin, several from Schumann, Rubinstein, and Bach.

The end aimed at is the production of a fine quality of lyric playing,—poetic, refined, but at the same time strong and deep. The collection is indispensable.